Keith Douglas

A BIOGRAPHY

Keith Douglas in Egypt, 1942

Keith Douglas
1920 - 1944

A BIOGRAPHY

BY

DESMOND GRAHAM

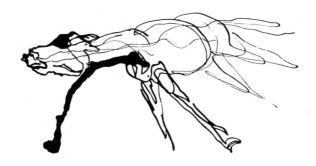

LONDON
OXFORD UNIVERSITY PRESS
NEW YORK   TORONTO
1974

Oxford University Press, Ely House, London, W. I

GLASGOW NEW YORK TORONTO MELBOURNE WELLINGTON
CAPE TOWN IBADAN NAIROBI DAR ES SALAAM LUSAKA ADDIS ABABA
DELHI BOMBAY CALCUTTA MADRAS KARACHI LAHORE DACCA
KUALA LUMPUR SINGAPORE HONG KONG TOKYO

ISBN 0 19 211716 5

© Oxford University Press 1974

Set by Gloucester Typesetting and printed in Great Britain by
W. & J. Mackay Limited, Chatham

For
Jo Douglas
and for
Alison

Contents

Preface

In October 1942 Keith Douglas disobeyed orders that he should remain at Division headquarters and drove his truck to El Alamein to join his regiment in battle. It was not just a poet's desire for experience but a determination to force his will on events which had held him in their control since September 1939. Having seen battle as a tank commander in the desert Douglas wrote the war poems and narrative upon which his reputation firmly rests. But he had no need of war to make him either soldier or poet. From his earliest childhood the military life had attracted him as strongly as, in adolescence, he was to find its brutality repellent. Writing poems against war from the age of fifteen, he had been devoted to the O.T.C. at school, and had joined its Mounted Section as soon as he arrived at Oxford. As a cavalry trooper in 1940 he had been ambitious to do well, and writing as a Yeomanry officer who had seen action he acknowledged the excitement of tank warfare. It was only one part of the truth, but a part which his honesty determined to reveal.

Douglas defied people's expectations of the poet. Horseman, adventurer, soldier, these were the roles in which he wished to be recognized, perhaps because his talents as artist and poet were self-evident. Those who knew him recall that to spend any time with him was to observe the intensity with which for hours on end he redrafted and shaped his work, writing with a passionate calculation proved in page after page of his manuscripts. From the age of fourteen he wanted to be a poet, and with juvenilia which from the start were recognized as astonishingly precocious, he proved that he was one. Auden, Edith Sitwell, the early Yeats, Pound, and Eliot had been imitated and absorbed by the time he left school. At Oxford, Donne, Rimbaud, the later Yeats, and Shakespeare were added, to shape the metaphysical, exploratory style with which he approached the experience of war. By the time his posthumous *Collected Poems* appeared in 1951 his work was already known and admired by those who had seen it in Oxford magazines, a *Selected Poems* (1943), *Personal Landscape* (Cairo), Tambimuttu's *Poetry (London)*, and his own *Alamein to Zem Zem*, the war narrative published with poems in 1946. Re-publication of his work in 1964 and 1966 confirmed his significance for a new generation of poets and readers.

The opposed sides of Douglas's character were so obvious and fitted so naturally that those who met him found difficulty only in placing him in terms of conventional expectations. His personality possessed such clear-cut contours: he was outspoken, fearless, ruthlessly critical, even arrogant, generous, sensitive to the difficulties of others, remorselessly honest, energetic, and passionately, innocently open. That such bold outlines were highlighted by deep shadows was equally evident, but Douglas expected no one to understand his reserve of feeling, for he found difficulty in understanding it himself. He wished to be taken at face value: what more there was to be seen could be found in what he wrote. There, direct

Preface

confessions are insistently covered by his art. As poet he is the virtuoso performer, the explorer, analyst, and recorder, judging with the disquieting detachment or lyric control which remain the individual voices of his work. From the distance of the artist he could look clearly at himself without fear of what he might see. A schoolmaster and friend, David Roberts, once told Douglas that he did not find depth of feeling in his work: Douglas replied that such a view proved one astonishingly insensitive.

In preparing this book my aim was not to close the gap which Douglas used all his craft to make between the man and his work. Its breadth measures his creativity and my task was to chart its proportions, not to fill it with surmise. Starting from an admiration for his writing and still, after seven years, retaining a sense of incredulity at such talent, my intention was to fill in the background, to establish a factual context while memories remained fresh, and letters, manuscripts, and papers were not dispersed. My role was negative: to act at best as a clear glass through which Douglas showed himself, without distortion or obscurity. My main, self-disciplining principle was to avoid at all costs the imposition of my pattern upon a life which was made a fragment by the chance of war. In this last desire, at least, Douglas defeated me. Matching the surface hardness and deeper sensitivity of his character, his poems charted a progress. He capitalized on moments of change and significance, he dramatized himself and his experience to impose on his short life his own symmetry. To allow this pattern to emerge became my final purpose.

Newcastle upon Tyne   DESMOND GRAHAM
1973

Acknowledgements

In expressing my gratitude to those who have helped with recollections of Douglas these acknowledgements cannot hope to convey the impact he had on on those who knew him. Dozens of meetings and hundreds of letters, all so obviously speaking of the same man, have proved his remarkable integrity. He was not always an easy person to know. He allowed few people to know him closely and made few concessions; but to all who knew him he was someone who mattered: a full-bodied character, incapable of anonymity and possessing a capacity for life and a determination to use it well which could not be ignored. From those who knew him best he earned an affection and respect which thirty years have not slackened.

My thanks go first to Mrs. Marie J. Douglas, for her acuteness of memory, her constant searching of cupboards and suitcases, her tireless hospitality and fund of amusing stories which have contributed so much to the pleasure of writing this book. This is not the book she could have written and much of it differs from her view of her son, but her belief in the value of honesty has made my task light. Secondly, and unjustly, I must single out a few from all those who have helped with their recollections. Norman Ilett, who perhaps knew Douglas better than anyone else from school to the Middle East, I thank for his fascinating correction of two drafts of the typescript and for the knowledge he has given me of someone he knew so well. Major John Bethell-Fox, M.C., Douglas's closest friend in the Sherwood Rangers, who first taught me the value of the friends Douglas won, gave me assistance to which I cannot do justice. Betty Jesse I must thank for her understanding of the last few months of Douglas's life, and for conversations which have made thirty years ago very close; Antoinette and Yingcheng, who stepped out of poems to tell me more than I had hoped to know; and Milena, whose sympathetic understanding helped me to follow months of Douglas's life which would otherwise have been blank: these four forced me to recognize Douglas's good judgement. Mrs. David Roberts, Joan Grant and her sister Betty Boyd, Jean Guest and Margaret Stanley-Wrench, I thank for proving what generous friends Douglas could make. John Adams, Joe Ames, David Beaty, Noel Burdett, Alec Hardie, Major Jack Holman, M.C., David Lockie, Raymond Pennock, Tony Rudd, Hamo Sassoon, and Major John Semken, M.C., taught me how friendship could last over many years. I must also thank J. C. Hall, Douglas's first and most recent editor, for six years' considerate help and encouragement; H. R. Hornsby for the astonishing gift of papers he had kept for thirty-five years; and Lt.-Col. Stanley Christopherson, D.S.O., M.C., who not only told me of Douglas and the regiment but lent me a diary and photographs with a courtesy which helped to make real for me the Sherwood Rangers Yeomanry.

Now, hoping that the scale of my task will be understood, I must give only names, behind many of which lie hospitality, hours of patient recollection,

Acknowledgements

repeated letters, and help without which this book could not have been written: David Abercrombie, T. J. Allen, Mrs. John Baber, Mrs. Rosemary Bailey, W. S. Bates, Mary Benson, Edmund Blunden, Colin Bowen, Mrs. Wynyard Brown, A. H. Buck, Sydney Carter, R. W. Chadburn, J. P. Cheevers, Arthur G. Clarke, David Crichton, Christine Cuninghame, Graham C. Cunningham, jr., Mrs. Renée Cutforth, J. G. Davies, Walter Douglas, Julian Drake-Brockman, Jolyon Dromgoole, Graham G. Dunbar, Robin Fedden, G. S. Fraser, Michael Frewen, John Goddard, the late Douglas Grant, Roger Lancelyn Green, R. Gregg, Kenneth Harris, C. T. Hatten, Stephen Hearst, John Heath-Stubbs, David Hicks, C. A. Humphrey, the Revd. Gerard Irvine, Natalia Jimenez, Francis King, Hugh Latimer, Mrs. K. M. Lawson, Lady Linstead, W. R. Macklin, D. S. Macnutt, Lt.-Col. Patrick J. D. McCraith, M.C., T.D., D.L., P. Macnaghten, Edward Malins, Geoffrey Matthews, Bernard Mellor, Michael Meyer, Charles Monteith, G. H. Morgan, J. E. Morpurgo, Iris Murdoch, Mrs. George Murr, Dr. F. W. Nash, Major W. D. Nelson, M.M., T.D., R. Nelthorpe, M.B.E., George Newberry, Lt.-Col. L. W. Parkhouse, D. Payton-Smith, the Revd. J. R. Porter, Lt.-Col. Basil Ringrose, D.S.O., T.D., John Russell, Philip Shapiro, the Revd. Leslie Skinner, R. D. Smith, Mrs. Stephen Spender, Mary Stanley-Smith, Philip Stead, Geoffrey Stockwell, Gordon Swaine, M. J. Tambimuttu, Frank Terry, Mrs. Phyllis Thayer, Lance Thirkell, Terence Tiller, Gavin Townsend, Mrs. Daphne Turner, Mrs. Mary Visick, Sir John Waller, Major F. R. Warwick, M.C., T.D., Denys Wrey, David Wright, and Mrs. Evelyn Young.

Writing close in time to the life of my subject I have endeavoured to respect the personal privacy of all who have helped me. Five names used by Douglas in poems have been retained: Kristin, Yingcheng, Antoinette, Olga, and Milena, as have three names employed by him in *Alamein to Zem Zem*: Andrew, Sweeney Todd, and Evan; Olwen is also a name used by Douglas. Otherwise in both text and notes I have referred to people by the names under which they were known in Douglas's lifetime; their names as they are now are given in the list above.

For permission to quote from Keith Douglas's writings, both published and unpublished, and from his letters, I thank the owner of the copyright, Mrs. Marie J. Douglas, as well as his publishers, Faber and Faber Ltd., for poems from Douglas's *Collected Poems* (1966) and prose from his *Alamein to Zem Zem* (1966); the Trustees of The British Library for material in the Keith Douglas Papers; and all those private holders of unpublished Douglas material listed at p. 262. In addition, I must thank the following for other material, published and unpublished, on which I have drawn; Major T. M. Lindsay, M.B.E., and Burrup Mathieson & Co. Ltd. for quotations from *Sherwood Rangers* (1952); M. J. Tambimuttu and Major John Bethell-Fox, M.C., for a quotation from *Poetry (London)*, no. X; the Clerk to Christ's Hospital for quotations from *The Outlook* and *The Blue*, and the editor of *The Cherwell* for quotations from that weekly; the Ministry of Defence; Mrs. Valerie Eliot, Edmund Blunden, and the owners of the other unpublished source material listed at p. 262. For the illustrations reproduced in the book I thank Mrs. Douglas and the Trustees of the British Library for items from the Keith Douglas Papers, as acknowledged on p. iv; and, for the remaining items, the individuals and sources listed at p. 283.

Acknowledgements

Among the numerous persons who have helped me with information I must offer thanks to M. Burton Brown, Headmaster, Edgeborough School, and Mr. Mitchell, late Headmaster of that school; the Hon. Sec. Christ's Hospital Club, the Clerk to Christ's Hospital, and M. Carrington of Christ's Hospital; the Secretaries of Corpus Christi College, Exeter College, Lady Margaret Hall, St. Hilda's College, and the Slade School of Fine Art; the Principal's Secretary, Somerville College, and the President's Secretary, Magdalen College; the Domestic Bursars of Merton College and Wadham College; Richard Naish, Ruskin Master of Drawing, Ruskin School of Drawing and Fine Art; Major F. J. Dodd, Home Headquarters, The Royal Scots Greys; Major C. B. Allen, The Sherwood Rangers Yeomanry T.A. Centre; Major J. H. Mott, O.B.E., R.H.Q., York and Lancastrian Regiment; Major O. F. B. Burchnall, Leicestershire and Derbyshire Yeomanry (PAO) Squadron; Lt.-Col. G. A. Shepperd, M.B.E. (retd.) of The Library, R.M.A. Sandhurst; Col. Sir Ian Walker-Okeover, Bt., D.S.O.; and Lt.-Col. Douglas Johnson of M.O.D. P.R.

Among others who have offered help on various details and specific queries I must thank Nigel Bell, Northrop Frye, Geoffrey Hill, D. W. Jefferson, the Rt. Hon. Reginald Maudling, A. F. Meredith, John Speirs, Mrs. Jenny Stratford, Maurice Wollman, and K. W. Wood; the Black Horse, Giggleswick, Mr. and Mrs. J. Handoll, Castle Service Station, Wickwar, and those living in the White Horse Inn, Wickwar; and the Editor of the *Times Literary Supplement*. I must thank the Trustees of the Frank Gott Scholarship, Leeds University, and the University of Newcastle upon Tyne for financial assistance; Professor Hermann Fischer, the University of Mannheim, for a splendid office; and Mr. and Mrs. K. W. Wood for ideal conditions in which to write.

Finally I must thank Miss Catharine Carver, whose patience and sensitivity over three years of constant discussion and advice have helped me more than she can imagine; and my wife who, for the ceaseless understanding, critical insights, and commitment she brought to seven years' sharing me with Keith Douglas, now shares with his mother the dedication of this book.

D.G.

1973

If at times my eyes are lenses
through which the mind explores
constellations of feeling
my ears yielding like swinging doors
admit princes to the corridors
into the mind, do not envy me.
I have a beast on my back.

('*Bête Noire*', London 1944)

I

Childhood
January 1920 - September 1931

I

As a child he was a militarist, and like many of his warlike elders, built up heroic opinions upon little information—some scrappy war stories of his father. Most of the time he was down in the field, busy, with an absurdly purposeful look on his round face, about a tent made of an old sheet, and signposted with a board saying 'Sergeants' mess'. He was quite at home there for hours, while he was four and five, telling himself stories as he ran about, and sometimes stopping a moment to contemplate the calf who shared that field, a normally quiet animal, but given to jumping five-barred gates. As you would expect, he played with lead soldiers, and toy artillery, and was most fond of the cavalry and the highlanders. Unlike the other troops who either marched sedately with sloped arms or sat bolt upright on their caracoling steeds, the highlanders were charging, their kilts flying at a swift angle out behind them and the plumes upon their heads also flying out, though often in the wrong direction for the broken heads were fixed back on with matches and swivelled easily.

The writer who defined his childhood thus while still a schoolboy, was born Keith Castellain Douglas on 24 January 1920 at the Garden Road Nursing Home in Tunbridge Wells. His parents had connections with Kent, for his mother had spent most of her childhood near Tunbridge Wells, where her parents still had a house, and his father, who had been for a year to Tonbridge, had passed his earliest years in the county.

Keith's first home was in Cranleigh, Surrey. There his parents had rented, since November 1919, a large Tudor cottage at the end of the village's long green. 'Curfew Cottage' had its own small orchard to one side, herbaceous borders lining a brick path which led to the front gate, and wisteria covering the weathered red brick of the front wall which faced the green and its pond. Keith's parents loved the place. It was their first real home since their marriage at Chatham in 1915, for Keith's father had meanwhile served in the war; but life in Curfew Cottage held little promise of security: since leaving the army in February 1919 Keith's father had been unable to find regular employment. Financial uncertainty was not new to Keith Sholto Douglas, but behind the bitterness of returning from army service to unemployment lay the disappointment of leaving the army itself, which he had not only enjoyed but in which he had wished to make a career.

Trained as an engineer, he had volunteered in the first month of the war, and after two months he was commissioned in the Royal Engineers. In June 1914 he had become engaged, and finding that he was to be sent not to France but to the Near East, in the summer of 1915 he and his fiancée, Marie Josephine Castellain, were married. In July, Lieutenant Douglas embarked for Gallipoli with the 71st Field Company, Royal Engineers, and from there moved to Mesopotamia, landing at Basra in February 1916. In the course of the campaign there, Douglas had malaria and sandfly fever, was wounded in the thigh ('shot by a measly old Turk,' as his son later put it), and earned the M.C. for his part in the bridging of the Diala under fire. When he was discharged at Newark, on 6 February 1919, he had attained the rank of captain, and his credentials testified to his 'initiative', 'resource', and 'quite fearless behaviour' at the front.

Although the civilian world was unable to provide Captain Douglas with a job, his wife Josephine was employed, and it was through her work that the cottage in Cranleigh came to them at a nominal rent. Since the start of the war she had acted as secretary to an artist, Lawson Wood, who was serving at the front. Along with handling his correspondence she pantographed his nursery friezes and coloured in their backgrounds and those of his illustrations for children's books. For one of his commissions, Warne's 'Mr. and Mrs.' series of children's readers, she also composed the stories. It was work she enjoyed but did with no previous training, for she had grown up in a family which held that schooling was something for boys.

Born in 1887, Marie Josephine Castellain was the second of four children, and with a half-brother and two half-sisters from her father's first marriage, she had been brought up in the family's large house a mile or two outside Cranbrook. At sixteen, at the invitation of a half-sister who taught there, she had spent six months at a finishing school in Switzerland—her only academic education and her one glimpse of life abroad before her marriage. At eighteen, however, she had sought independence by going to live with a family in Lincoln to help with the children, and when the parents were away had found herself running the household and its staff. Returning south she had taken similar work in the Lawson Wood household, which had led, on Wood's departure for the front, to the secretarial work which occupied her at Curfew Cottage.

In October 1920 Captain Douglas at last found a post with a building firm in Hemel Hempstead. The job was a temporary one, so his wife

Curfew Cottage, Cranleigh; KD in his pram, with his mother and
grandmother

remained at Cranleigh and her parents moved in with her to help look after
the eight-month-old Keith. With the outbreak of the Irish civil war, Captain Douglas had a chance to return to active duty with the Royal Engineers.
He arrived on the Curragh in January 1921, hoping for five years of service.
But after twelve months spent organizing construction work he was back in
England, and at the end of June 1922, having served a further five months
at Borden, Hampshire, he was in Cranleigh, once more looking for a job.
Keith, by now two and a half, had spent his first active years in an elderly
household, his only male companion an eighty-year-old grandfather who
said little.

Charles Castellain, grandson of a French aristocrat from Lille who had
fled the Revolution, had spent his whole life under the protection of private
means.[1] Educated at Harrow and Balliol, he was first a cotton broker in
Liverpool, then a merchant banker in Egypt before the war of 1882 forced
his return to England. Mr. Castellain had no liking for business, and after
Egypt he retired prematurely to Kent, where he supported his family out
of his capital. He did a little private tutoring in mathematics, more for
pleasure than money, for considering it improper for a gentleman to take

[1] His mother was the daughter of Frederick Huth, the German banking magnate known
as 'the Napoleon of the City'.

3

With his mother, at eighteen months

pay for such work he only accepted the occasional honorarium. He had been happiest during a country childhood in Lancashire, spent largely with stable-boys and gamekeepers, and had returned to a life of country walks, bird-watching, patience, and chess. In his second marriage, to the daughter of John Towse, solicitor to the Fishmongers' Company, his wife remained the dominant partner in the marriage.

Mr. Castellain afforded his grandson good company once Keith was old enough to walk. Taking him on his daily stroll, he told the boy the names of flowers and imitated for him dozens of different bird-calls. In the evenings, sitting in the chimney corner, he told him stories, at first of fairies, but when Keith was old enough to comprehend them, stories of his own childhood. As Mrs. Douglas was busy most of the day and grandmother Castellain had not much liking for the company of small children, Keith spent most of his time on his own. He had an amiable nature and a boisterousness which refused to be quelled by such a pacific household. From a very early age he became adept at entertaining himself. He drew pictures with anything he could find, even scraping them on the ground with a stick, and for hours talked stories to his toys.

His father's return in the summer of 1922 brought a new dimension to this life. Keith was in effect seeing him for the first time, and the impact of this burly, masculine soldier on Curfew Cottage's sedate matriarchal order must have been enormous. Captain Douglas liked children, and in a bustling, roistering way brought Keith the new experience of wrestling and boxing, sing-songs, and instant, impetuous discipline. Grandfather Castellain had been almost unknown to raise his voice, his wife reprimanded through disdain, Mrs. Douglas tried to steer between the two of them: but Captain Douglas acted with simplicity and directness. Now a noisy spanking would be followed by an account of adventures in Mesopotamia or a game of hide-and-seek. Within twelve months Keith's allegiance was proved by his adoption of military dress. With a cap given to him by a man down the road, a row of military buttons, puttees, and a medal made by himself out of a halfpenny, he patrolled the garden, challenging all who passed.

Keith's guard duties were not performed at Curfew Cottage, however, for at the beginning of 1923 the family had moved to another house in Cranleigh, 'Dalkeith', Avenue Road, a plain stuccoed house in strong contrast to the charm of Curfew Cottage. But with it went two and a half acres of land, and in these Captain Douglas saw a chance of gaining security. With his army gratuity and his wife's savings, he bought house and land and set about the creation of a chicken farm. Building a series of two-storey hen houses to accommodate 150 laying birds, Captain Douglas designed his own watering system to provide running water for each house. Then there was the construction of brooder houses for the raising of a thousand day-old chicks, and the installation of incubators. To help Mrs. Douglas with the extra work of running the farm and the house, Olwen, a young girl whose family Mrs. Douglas had known for some years, joined the Dalkeith household.

Aged three, with grandfather Castellain

'Dalkeith', Avenue Road, Cranleigh

Childhood

Although Olwen's arrival brought Keith youthful company, at Dalkeith he still spent much of his time alone. But three was an age at which, he recalled in adolescence, 'Even the rain was interesting. In cold weather every frozen puddle in the road hid the bone of some prehistoric monster, and in the winter evenings, the unlit passages were afang with lurking dragons.' The dragons were those of his grandfather's stories, the monsters mammoths which Mr. Castellain had shown him in Arthur Mee's *Children's Encyclopaedia*, explaining how for centuries they remained frozen in ice. Keith had set off the next frosty morning to find them in the ice-topped puddles. Where adolescence recalls the sense of adventure, at three Keith had been more impressed by the failure: returning home furious, asserting that the encyclopaedia was a liar and refusing to be pacified until his mother had explained the relative sizes of mammoth and man.

For Keith was already impressively rational. When his father told him of a dog which might be blind in one eye Keith suggested that its owners could easily discover the truth by putting a patch over the other eye. By four, he was able to read *The Times* fluently if not accurately. In the evenings his mother had taught him to read by making him trace over the shapes of letters with his finger and then point out words he recognized in a page

of print. Such was her success that on an early occasion he found the 'the' in 'nevertheless'. At four also, he was introduced by his grandfather to the pleasures of words' derivations: for although Mr. Castellain thought poetry an unmanly pursuit, words and their origins possessed for him an attraction similar to that of mathematics.

An early self-portrait

But as the story Keith wrote of his childhood affirms, at four he was more militarist than scholar. He was a 'tough guy', a climber of trees, inhabitant of the 'sergeants' mess' and follower of his martial father, whom he loved to call him 'old bean'. Such admiration, however, was not always immune to superior claims. In his story he is Keir, his friend, Billy:[1]

'My father', said Billy, 'shot a German point blank. He saw him coming out of a pillbox and shot him before the German could shoot Daddy.' Keir was a little annoyed that Billy should tell this story, condensed though it had become, so often. But point blank was admittedly a good thing to say and in return he explained how his own father was shot by a Turk. 'My father wouldn't have let a measly old Turk shoot him,' said Billy and Keir's riposte was squashed. Yet he was very proud of his father and went home to supper sadly. . . .

Keith's story moves on through a full evocation of his family's life in Cranleigh: his father 'ferociously' reciting 'Yukon Jake' for him, raising a chair in one hand and shaking it as he spoke; his grandmother Castellain, preparing supper in the kitchen and telling him to 'go and wash your hands' with a phrase which 'galled' him—'there's a good boy'; his grandfather in the drawing room playing patience and willing to tell him a story once he had finished the game.

Keir waited two minutes before he asked for his story again, and received the same answer, out of the corner of his grandfather's mouth, as the card game, for

[1] In fact Keith had for some time been called Billy by his family, the name taken from the cartoon figure 'Billikin'.

long the most exciting part of the old gentleman's life, drew to its most exciting moment and completion. The minutes continued to drag slowly by, and at last, Keir realised that he would soon be hauled storyless to bed. When he had asked once more and received the same unhurrying answer, he suddenly grew furious, and overturned the old gentleman's precious ricketty table.

Mr. Castellain had never been so near anger in twenty years. But after Keir's simple explanation that he wanted his story, he said kindly, 'You're sorry you turned my table over, aren't you, little man?' And on Keir's admission of penitence (for he saw that would begin his story soonest) the story was begun.

Keith's mother appears in the story, returning from shopping and watching while Keir ate his supper, looking 'pretty but tired out'. The running of the chicken farm was proving a strain.

Once the farm was established it had found good markets. Cranleigh School provided a steady customer for the eggs and any surplus could be sold in Guildford market: Mac Fisheries in Guildford took all the table birds they could offer. For such deliveries and the collection of chicks and foodstuffs the Douglases bought a pony and cart, but supplying their customers still took plenty of time. In addition, Olwen and Mrs. Douglas had to collect, clean, and pack the eggs, pluck and prepare the table birds. Such activities were not the concern of Captain Douglas: new schemes for watering, improved runs and houses, and over-all expansion absorbed him. They also absorbed most of the income. Mrs. Douglas, in charge of accounts, found that despite their good markets a diminishing amount of money was available for the day-to-day expenses of running the farm, paying food bills, and buying new stock.

As the farm moved harassingly towards the end of its second year she found herself suffering severe headaches and a lassitude which was difficult to combat. Such troubles seemed easily explained by the combination of worry and constant work, but when at the end of 1924 she collapsed and was taken to Cranleigh Village Hospital, she was found to be suffering from *encephalitis lethargica*, or 'sleepy sickness': an illness now virtually unknown in Britain but endemic after the Great War. Keith, not quite five years old, had witnessed her departure, and in his story told of what he had seen.

... Keir was woken by the sun and the birds and lay in bed listening to them and thinking to himself, until it occurred to him that people were about in the house and his mother's and father's beds were empty. He went and peered out, and saw through the bannisters a group of people standing in the hall, about his mother, who lay asleep on a stretcher or as it seemed to Keir a funny sort of bed. He realised almost at once that his mother was ill and ran downstairs on his bare feet asking what was the matter with her, as they took her away out of the front door. Someone he had never seen took him back to his bed with some unsatisfactory explanation, and locked the door on him. He began immediately to scream and beat upon it, but they had all gone and he was alone, locked in. He became frantic, fell on the floor and shouted curses he had heard 'Curse damn bother darn bloody' in a string as long as he could put together, until he got up from the floor and hit his head on the door knob. It hurt and with some idea of punishing the door knob he hit his head on it five or six times more, very hard, and then subsided on the bed sobbing.

In a few minutes his grandfather came up and succeeded in calming him, explaining that his mother had an illness called Sleepy Sickness, but she would be well soon, when she had gone to the Hospital and had a rest. With that, for the moment, Keir was content.

Mrs. Douglas remained in hospital for some months but on her release could only look forward to very slow recovery. It was an illness noted for its prolonged after-effects, and in fact a specialist had told Captain Douglas that if his wife did survive the attack she could well remain a mental invalid for the rest of her life. As much as eighteen months after her collapse, she found herself incapable of concentration, subject to bouts of amnesia, and still the victim of lassitude and headaches. While Mrs. Douglas was in hospital Olwen had kept the farm going as best she could, but at the end of 1925 returned to her family. The hospital fees had placed an extra burden on the farm's economy, having to be paid out of money needed for its current expenditure; and with no hope of further expansion, the venture lost its interest for Captain Douglas. His role had been that of architect, builder, plumber, and carpenter: collecting, washing, and delivering eggs made a mockery of the inventive talents which had brought him to the scheme.

Before the war he had led a life as unsettled as it was varied. His father, William Douglas, a Scot educated at Queen's University, Belfast, and at Edinburgh, was a physician whose entire career had been in private practice, and though not wealthy, he had money enough on his retirement to buy a large house in Staines about the time of his grandson's birth. His marriage, however, had not been successful, and for many years his Scots Canadian wife lived apart from him, in Canada. As a result his son Keith Sholto had had little family life, and at twenty-two, with his education at Tonbridge and Dunstable behind him, set out in 1904 to visit his mother. He got as far as New York, where he stayed for a year attending an art school, then moved on to Indiana to work for the Vandalia Railroad Company. In six years with the railway he rose from rodman to chainman to transitman. When he returned to England in 1911, he added a theoretical base to this practical experience by taking a two-year course in civil engineering in Sheffield, and in the war was commended as 'a most able second in command' of a company doing mining, sapping, and other 'valuable work' in the trenches.

Now, after only three years, it was clear that the chicken farm, product of the skills he had earlier brought to engineering, would have to be sold. Already it had lost a lot of money and the proceeds of its sale would be spent mainly on paying outstanding accounts. But now Keith was six, his future was as much at stake as his father's hopes for a stable career. The chances were that Captain Douglas would once more be forced to leave home in search of work, and until he had found something permanent there

Aged six

would be no security for his family. With the help of a loan from a friend, Keith's parents decided to send him to boarding school. This would both protect his future education and remove him from the difficulties and uncertainties at home. So, in September 1926, Keith went off to Edgeborough School in Guildford. On 25 September, two days after his arrival, he wrote home: 'I am very much enjoying myself. The little boy I sleep with is sometimes nice and sometimes boring.'

2

One of four boys in Edgeborough's first form, Keith's new life divided into Latin, Mathematics, French, and English; the English subdivided into History, Scripture, Geography, Literature, and Essay. In the first term there was football, in the second, rugby, in the third, cricket; there was also

Bathing at Dymchurch, 1927

swimming, and Keith made an early mark by entering a competition in his second term without telling anyone that he could not swim. With a furious dog-paddle and great determination to compensate for lack of skill, he won.

Edgeborough, in its large Victorian house attractively set in the wooded outskirts of Guildford, within walking distance of Newlands Corner, prepared boys for the Common Entrance Examination and public schools. With only eighty pupils and a staff of nine, it did so in a relatively personal atmosphere, with only twelve boys to each class after the first. From his arrival, however, the new boy's role was cast. By thirteen he was to have reached the required standard in each of his academic subjects, shown character on the sports field and efficiency in Drill, learnt to mix with his fellows and to understand the workings of authority and the hierarchies of age and prowess. There were walks on Sundays, letters home twice a week, regular class lists, and cups for sports. There were prize-winners, captains and dormitory captains, and First XI or First XV 'characters' defined each term in the school magazine: forwards who 'must learn not to run back with the ball' or who played with 'pluck and dash', three-quarters who knew the value of 'going straight' and would go a long way in 'big Rugger', a half-back who must be careful 'not to use the "cut through" too often, forgetting his insides'. It was the public school in miniature, with its own band of old boys keeping in touch with news of triumphs at Sherborne or Sandhurst, a soccer Blue or a post with Burmah Oil. Keith soon found a place for himself at the bottom of its richly stratified, competitive world.

Already he was outgoing, inquisitive, and able to read and write well. He made friends easily, had neither brothers nor sisters to miss, and was well used to providing his own pleasures. His letters reported his assimilation:

I am above a boy of seven and a half in form order. . . .   (10 October 1926)

I hope to be top of the week's order somewhere around next week or the week after. . . .   (20 February [1927])

Please come one Saturday and watch me play cricket. I generally start by hitting Boundarys. Please send my bat and ball. . . .   [15 May 1927]

I was wacked on Wednesday thank goodness not by Mr. James this time. But by Mr. West. . . .   (27 June [1927])

By Christmas he had made a 'splendid beginning' in Latin and, top of his class of four, had been promoted to Form II, two years below its average age. By July 1927 he had received his first prize, *A Tale of Two Cities*, which he read and enjoyed. His work, despite carelessness and untidiness, had been thoroughly satisfactory, though his behaviour earned a more critical report: 'He is passing through a difficult stage when he does not realize how far he can go with impunity! It will dawn upon him before long, in work as in other ways. I am not anxious about him.'

Earlier in 1927, his grandfather Castellain had died. It was during the school term, and Keith did not come home for the funeral. But four years later he wrote in a letter, without introduction or comment: 'I do miss Grandpa.'

More than two-thirds of Keith's time during the next five years was spent in the simple routine of school, but to its pattern of sports and class lists he brought his unusual energy: an energy which, at nine, he was able to express in letters home:

All the forwards in the Third scored goals except one. Luckily I was not that one. They seemed to slip past me and get out of my way as hard as they could and then

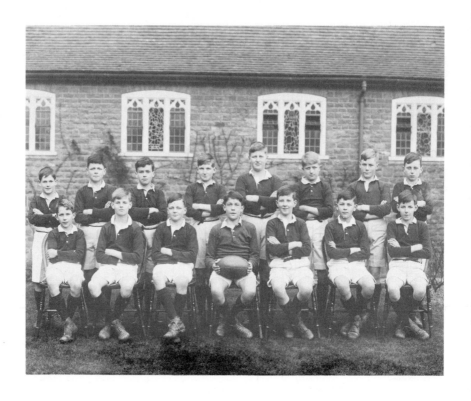

The Third XV at Edgeborough School; KD standing, fourth from left

as you got through to shoot they slobbered up behind you and you had to pass and that is why I only got three goals, because I took it up about ten times but had to pass so much. When I say *I* took it up I mean I and the wing passing like running along the road with a ball while they banged and slid about us.

I've practically never had such a good tea as we had then and I stuffed hard and pressed the boy next to me to eat too much. He was one of their boys and at the end he stuck his fingers in the crumbs and licked them! He kept on looking round to make sure no-one was watching.

The previous autumn, 1928, Keith had gained an English master, Mr. Stokoe, who noticed his literary talent. At Christmas he had reported on 'some very good little essays'; at Easter observed Keith's possession of 'quite an idea of style'; and in the summer of 1929 not only found his work 'very good' but added: 'he has undoubted possibilities here.' This year one of Keith's classroom tasks was to paraphrase *The Rime of the Ancient Mariner*, and in the Lent term of 1930 he was set to write a poem.

Childhood

Dear Mother,

I was second in the Algebra paper and second in the work we did today in Algebra. In English we had to write a poem on any subject in History.

This was mine:

WATERLOO

'Napoleon is charging our squares,
with his cavalry he is attacking;
let the enemy do what he dares,
our soldiers in braveness aren't lacking.'

I forgot bravery for the moment, so I used Poet's Licence and put 'braveness'. This is the second verse:

2

'But naught can his charging avail,
he cannot do anything more;
for not one heart does fail
e'en when 'tis at death's door.'

and this is the third:

3

' "I have you!" Napoleon cries!
but he has a great mistake made;
for every French soldier flies
and is caught by a fierce cannonade.

and this is the last:

4

'Napoleon is charging our squares,
but only in memory now;
we remember his charging mares;
and we always will, I trow.'

If the verse form allowed Keith less freedom of manoeuvre than the description of a football match, his shift from direct narrative to the event as remembered shows subtlety, and his enthusiasm catches the dramatic irony of Napoleon's mistaken shout.

Perhaps everyone in the class chose similarly martial themes, but the subject of war was especially attractive to Keith, whose early reading had included a *History of the Boer War* and who now made the most prized part of his stamp collection those depicting battle scenes. The same year, when he was ten, he collaborated with other boys in his form on a play—a drama of mystery and detection about the invention of a lethal gas, discovered by German spies who paid for their crime by becoming the gas's first victims. At sixteen, it was battles with fir cones, in the woods by St. Martha's church at Guildford, which provided him with a focus for memories of his prep. school pleasures.

Alongside Sapper, Keith at ten and eleven none the less favoured *Puck of Pook's Hill*, *The Good Companions* (in which he cast himself as the pianist), and James Stephens's *The Demi-Gods*: this last book, a whimsical tale of the encounter between Irish peasants and angels come to earth, deeply fascinated him and at one time he designed a full-scale series of illustrations for it. He followed *The Children's Newspaper* and *Autocar*; he most frequently employed the school gramophone to play 'U.S.A. Patrol' and 'The Warblers' Serenade'. He wrote to his mother in 1929, 'The films and things I want to see are "Wings", "The Ghost Train", "Speedy", "Shoulder Arms", "The Gold Rush", "Treasure Island", "Olympia", and any "Scarlet Pimp." films. The one I should like most is Olympia.' He was also a more than competent artist, whose sketches of devils had a market value of sixpence among his friends, and whose range extended from knights on horseback to cartoons of Le Mans. Finally, he was an avid model-maker, designing his own boats, at first crudely, but later well enough to sail them on the Round Pond.

In school holidays, Keith proved capable not only of entertaining himself but of standing up for himself. He was robust and well built, and his successes in the gregarious life of boarding school had given him the knack of making chance friends and finding a place for himself in company of every sort. With Tony Rudd, three years his junior, whom Keith met for the first time in the Easter holidays of 1929, he built a dirt track for racing cars in the front drive of the house at Boarshead, in Sussex, and a mountain railway over the rock garden, and played elaborate and inventive games with toy soldiers. Tony Rudd remembers him as seeming an heroically tough leader whose endless fund of imaginative schemes never disappointed. Whenever possible, their games were outdoors and vigorous: climbing trees, scaling precipices, snowballing passing cars, and continually fighting wars. When the weather or the concern of adults prevented them from putting Keith's plans into effect, they acted them out in their imaginations, and Keith seemed always capable of adding a new twist to a familiar game or extending a fantasy with realism astonishing to Tony. Before Keith's appearance on the scene, Tony had led a sedate life with an elderly great-aunt, and Keith not only opened to him an exciting new world, he revealed to the younger boy an unfamiliar approach to authority. With Mrs. Rudd Keith's behaviour was guarded, but she presented a continual challenge to his powers of revolt, and their encounters were an extended, subtle campaign, both sides gaining local successes but neither achieving a final victory. At ten and eleven, Keith's mother too was finding him difficult to handle, and his father was not there to help.

Keith's holidays from Edgeborough had been spent in a variety of places. In 1927, having eventually been able to sell the farm, his parents had moved into rented accommodation at Shere; his father was working part time for a building firm, and his mother, although still unwell, serving lunches and

School holidays, aged ten

teas in a café during the day and in the evenings doing embroidery for a shop, to keep up with his school fees. Then, at the end of 1927, his father had found a job in Wales with a firm making cold storage chambers. It was a permanent job, with reasonable prospects; at first he was simply to install the machines but later to work on their design. While he was settling into his new post, his wife went to live with her father-in-law in Staines. There she was near Keith's school, and able to act as a buffer between the elderly doctor and the family which looked after him. For Dr. Douglas, now in his eighties, had taken to living with the pattern of the day reversed. During daylight he slept and at night was awake, and although he spent most of the time alone in his study, he needed the normal complement of meals to be served in the night.

In November 1928, having recently bought an annuity with most of his money, Dr. Douglas died. So that Christmas Keith stayed with his mother in London, at the flat of one of her friends in Colville Gardens, Notting Hill. From there he visited the Round Pond to befriend anyone he found and to sail his boats. Rainy days he spent at the Science Museum. By the following spring his mother had moved to a flat with Mrs. Rudd at Boarshead next door to the village post office, whose postmaster was one-legged but none the less rode a bike. Here Keith spent his holidays, with Tony Rudd for playmate, for the next couple of years.

During all this period he had seen nothing of his father. When Captain Douglas had moved to Wales early in 1928, Keith had been told of the importance of his job and his need to save in order to buy them a house— visits, under such circumstances, would obviously waste precious money. Although only eight, Keith had probably gathered from the comparative affluence of his friends at prep. school, that in his family money was a rare commodity. That the lack of it demanded sacrifices was evident enough in his mother's having to work. In the summer holidays of 1930, shortly before going back to school, Keith quite suddenly asked his mother whether his father would ever return. He had shown no open concern before, but the seriousness of his question demanded an honest answer. He was told that his father would not come back. Reminding Keith of her illness, his mother explained how circumstances had produced difficulties which could neither have been foreseen nor avoided but which had made their marriage impossible for her husband. For more than two years she had been only a burden to him and he was someone unable to cope with such problems. He had been happiest in the army, effectively employed and secure in a life without domestic problems. After his struggles to find work, her collapse had proved too much for him. On moving to Wales he had found a simpler life, but he had also found a need for someone to look after him. He had visited Olwen and realized that he loved her; soon now they were to marry.

It had been at Dr. Douglas's death that Josephine Douglas had learned of her husband's wish to separate. When he came to Staines for the funeral, he had told her of his love for Olwen and asked her to divorce him. She agreed. She still loved him, but whether through shock, her illness, or both, felt only the helpless inevitability of the situation. In London that Christmas, the symptoms of her illness had powerfully returned. Along with the headaches and lassitude, she suffered spells of amnesia, on one occasion wandering the streets for hours unable to recall where she was staying. By 1930, however, she had recovered sufficiently to give Tony Rudd tuition in reading and writing.

In September 1930, Keith returned for what was now to be his last year at Edgeborough. Instead of remaining for two more years of captaincies and colours, and the Common Entrance exam to public school, he was to try for a place at Christ's Hospital, where not only were there no fees but where a recognized system of assistance would cover all the other expenses of uniform, equipment, even occasional holidays. At Boarshead Mrs. Douglas lived with her mother on Mrs. Castellain's small pension; there was nothing left over for school fees. Captain Douglas, having sent Mrs. Douglas a small sum from his father's legacy, as a token of his intended support, had little enough money to keep himself and Olwen. It was in fact only through the kindness of Edgeborough's headmaster, Mr. James, that Keith was able to return for this last year. He had assured Mrs. Douglas that Keith would win a place at Christ's Hospital after one more year with him, and she could pay the fees if ever she felt well enough off to do so.

In the summer term of 1930 Keith had been top of Form V, earning the report that 'all goes well with him'. That autumn, however, he showed a less co-operative attitude. At Christmas Mr. James reported:

An improvement lately in his general attitude. It is a pity he assumes such a defiant, almost truculent air at times. It does not help him and often creates a false impression. Again, if he looked nearer home for criticism, instead of criticising others, he would be doing himself much more good.

Next term, Keith gained his place in the First XV, and was found to be 'less bumptious and argumentative—in short much pleasanter to deal with'. His divergence from orthodoxy, however, remained for the next two terms. His Arithmetic master suggested that he should try to work 'on more normal lines instead of trying fantastic methods which lead him astray'; and although he 'worked well' in Latin, his master thought he would do better if he stopped trying to be too clever: 'As it is, he spoils much of his work by never doing anything the normal or obvious way.' Mr. Stokoe's encouragement in English had gone, as another master took Keith's form, but none of the teachers doubted his ability, when he bothered to co-operate.

In the summer term of 1931 Keith went up to London to be examined for entrance to Christ's Hospital. Having passed the normal entry age of nine, he was entitled to sit the examination only as a nominee of an Almoner. This had been achieved by placing his name with Sir Andrew Taylor, along with the recommendation of Mr. James. His mother was apprehensive when he reported that the examination was so easy that he had finished before everyone else, but she was a little reassured when he said he had written on *The Demi-Gods*. During the holidays, they learnt that he had passed.

That summer, Keith went with Mrs. Rudd and Tony on a holiday to Ambleteuse, near Boulogne. Pages surviving from a small black sketchbook reveal that he was fascinated by the new shapes and scenes of France. He sketched the Mairie and the post office, a ship in the harbour, and various very French faces, cigarette in corner of mouth and beret pulled down to one side. He also walked right round the perimeter wall of the Cap Gris Nez lighthouse, chiding Tony for his unwillingness to participate in the feat. On 22 September, having proudly displayed his new uniform to Mrs. Rudd and his mother, Keith departed for Christ's Hospital.

2

Christ's Hospital

September 1931 - September 1938

Now my mind's off again. No tears
Of Catullus move me. Though I know, in turn
We too will praise these years
Of watching clouds through windows, flutter-
  ing pages . . .

('Distraction From Classics')

I

The main quadrangle of Christ's Hospital forms a massive parade ground. Each lunchtime, to the accompaniment of their band, the seven hundred pupils march in ranks from their houses to the dining hall, looking more like priests than schoolboys. Keith Douglas had known Drill at Edgeborough—a couple of dozen boys learning left from right and playing soldiers. This was different. He was now one of a multitude in which each member was dressed in long Tudor coat of blue kersey, knee-breeches, yellow stockings, and white bands pinned to the shirt collar. Thus, their membership of 'the brotherhood' was proclaimed, their separation from the world outside and their possession by a strange new order. In this Spartan realm of bare, high-ceilinged rooms, endless corridors, and dormitories with row on row of plank beds, it is hardly surprising that Douglas wrote in his first letter to his mother, 'I have not nearly settled down yet. I wonder how soon you will come to see me. . . . I do get rather teased, and have made no friends yet, but still, I can't hope to on the second day.' Incompetent with the intricacies of his dress, bewildered by the conventions of precedence and ritual established by the pupils, and ignorant of the geography of the new world in which he seemed continually on the move, Douglas spent much of his first few days wandering from room to room carrying out inexplicable commands, only to arrive late at whatever place he was supposed to be present. His experience was not unique, and his five years away from home gave him more chance of coping than many of his fellows; but he was in a situation which encouraged one desire: to conform. To live in this world he must rapidly learn its rules and conventions, and understand the routines of an institution far greater than himself.

20

Christ's Hospital

Even to an adult, the buildings of Christ's Hospital, a couple of miles from Horsham, are impressive, almost intimidating. To pass down the long drive is to enter an enclave, in which the three hundred acres of domesticated Sussex countryside which form the school's estate are dominated by the urban scale and dignity of the Tudor-style architecture erected in 1902

In his Christ's Hospital uniform, 1931

when the school was translated from London. Established in the City in 1552 as a royal charitable foundation, Christ's Hospital had re-created in Sussex the unique character of an institution neither wholly ecclesiastic, civic, nor academic; and if the newcomer glimpses its benevolence he is in little doubt of its power. In 1931 the school remained a charitable foundation, adapted through centuries and its increasing wealth to a new society: it was a public school—but one for those without money. Each year a large proportion of boys were taken from elementary schools in selected, generally poor, districts of London. To these were added entrants in specific categories, including the sons of naval officers and of 'persons distinguished in literature, science, or art or in the service of the Crown'. Others, like Douglas, entered through an Almoner's nomination; and to complete the social mixture there were boys from certain schools in Berkshire, adding a bucolic flavour. Among the boys snobberies could remain, but the school, having dressed them in identical uniforms, resolutely defied the class distinctions of the world outside. By virtue of being a Housey boy, each of them was superior.

None the less, the school possessed its own élite, offered to the small boys as heroic models or tyrannical overlords. These were neither bloods nor hearties but 'Grecians': boys who at seventeen were destined for University. For while Christ's Hospital cultivated the usual games, the scout troop, and the Corps, only academic prowess could gain a place at the top of its hierarchy. Not only had it shown its affinities by naming Houses after Coleridge and Lamb, former pupils;[1] boys whose academic performance did not justify a longer stay at the school left at sixteen, no matter how the First XV suffered. As a consequence, the intellectuals at the top of the school were responsible for its sporting reputation. In this way Christ's Hospital denied the characteristic public school division between aesthetes and games players as thoroughly as it overruled their dependence upon family wealth.

Placed in 'Lamb A' House, Douglas took less than two weeks to adapt to his new environment, writing home on 2 October that he was happily settled. His height of well over five feet, his large-boned build, and his toughness of outlook ensured his survival in the physical struggles of the first weeks. With successful boarding-school experience behind him he was well able to conform once he understood what was required of him, and conforming meant the establishment of a place for himself in a sharply competitive world. Five days after his miserable start, Douglas had been able to write of his first success:

Everybody here makes an awful fuss about my drawing. The art master says I draw well, and everyone says I shall be an art grecian.

I have managed not to swank about it yet, I think, except, I suppose, in this letter. . . .

Soon Douglas had discovered the House library's gramophone and its 'jolly good books', and proved his strength in rugby. His skill at making models brought him admiration and a group of friends with whom he formed a 'model-making firm'. (Such was his concern for detail in this craft that one holiday he made a miniature replica of the *Trafalgar* and rigged it

---

[1] Another Old Blue, Leigh Hunt, was not to be honoured with a House until the 1960s.

with his mother's hair.) In the classroom, apart from German which was new to him, he found the work simple enough to be boring after the rigours of his final year at Edgeborough. He was now safely set in a 'simple and unchanging' routine which five years later, at sixteen, he described in pseudo-archaic terms:

Rising early in the morning, the boys proceed to a frugal breakfast. Thence they return to their living-houses for a little learning and from them, in a trice to the chapel. . . .

After Chapel the boys go to their classrooms for work, which continues all morning, pausing but a short time for physical exercise. Then to the strains of martial music they march into the Great Hall to their mid-day meal. In the afternoon games are played, rugger, football, cricket and fives.

Douglas's artistic talents were acknowledged with a mention in *The Blue* for the summer term of 1933. Earlier that term he had his first work in the school's literary magazine, *The Outlook*: a linocut of a racehorse and jockey. In the autumn his success at rugby had brought him a place in the scrum of the Under 14 XV, and his achievements in class had led him to the School Certificate form, Great Erasmus. Next summer, 1934, he swam for the school and in a House production of scenes from *A Midsummer Night's Dream* he proved his acting ability in the role of Theseus. With many pupils leaving at sixteen, younger boys at Christ's Hospital generally took a more important part in extra-curricular activities than at other schools, if they had the talent, and Douglas was well equipped for such an opportunity. 'Even in his early teens he was a distinctive figure', recalled Noel Burdett, a contemporary at Housey, and his distinction lay not only in his many talents but in 'a certain charisma which ensured him a following'.

In December 1934 Douglas made his first appearance as a published poet: 'Pan' and '*Ave Atque Vale*' heralded a succession of poems in *The Outlook*, the quality of which was to make Burdett tear up some of his own efforts in shame.

PAN

Tall trees are standing in the twilit hollow:
Leaves on the bushes hanging silent as the night;
Only the rustle of a hurrying rabbit
Scuttling in the bushes in and out of sight.

Softly on the silence breaks a thin shrill piping
Animals are hurrying, scurrying to hear
Following the music, maddening, magical
Falling soft and sweet upon the evening air.

Keith Douglas

In the fireside Arcadianism of the anthologies popular in schools at this time, such as *Poems of Today* and Sir Algernon Methuen's *An Anthology of Modern Verse*, Douglas found a vehicle for his delight in language and his sprightly observation. Pan is not an excuse for cliché but the ruler of a real countryside where 'mist and dew' come at a specific time, 'before the sun is up / As the stars grow pale and few', and the dew actually wets your feet:

> Open your lips: awhile forget
> Old Time's sand-dropping glass.
> Put off your shoes: your toes are wet,
> The dew is on the grass.
> Behind each rough-barked trunk you'll see
> The old Arcadians pass.
>
> ('Song')

At fourteen Douglas wrote poems for his own pleasure: for the fun of alliteration and internal rhyme, the extrovert confidence of bouncing rhythms and the *coup* of a well-chosen word or vivid metaphor. He wrote of a legendary or fairy past, where Pan and Fingal consorted gaily with elves, dryads, or leprechauns. Generally he announced their return but even when he lamented the passing of heroes he did so as a privileged witness, in touch with former glories. Happy or sad, however, it was a world full of sensory life, where 'half-forgotten songs and old brave deeds' moved through the memory 'like shadows slipping through a sunlit hedge' ('*Xaipe*'), where 'Mummers' drawn from the land of 'The Eve of St. Agnes' knocked on doors 'with hands snow-red'.

But Douglas's first Arcadia not only reflected his alert observations of the countryside. The fascination with language, which had led him at six to purchase a sixpenny dictionary of synonyms at Woolworths 'so as not to use the same word too often', made it also a reflection of the wit and humour of the schoolboy:

> Dryads, who make the poets glad,
> Dance on the forest floor,
> Swing to the wild asclepiad,
> Sweet Orpheus sings once more.
> Old Pan, brown-horned and bushy legged
> Watches a skylark soar.
>
> ('Song')

Without loss of face these dryads can 'swing' like dancers in a 1930s jazz cellar, while Douglas relishes the effect of transforming the learned 'asclepiad' into a 'wild' instrument. In this, the age of the Mills Brothers and Fred Astaire, he enjoyed close-harmony singing and was shortly to fancy himself as a tap dancer.

Douglas's varied talents and interests, the increasing confidence that came with experience of a tough, sizeable school, and his skill at making casual acquaintances carried him through the holidays of three years in which his mother's circumstances had again deteriorated. In 1932, the Rudds had moved to a fine double-fronted house in the centre of Painswick, in the Cotswolds, and this provided a new location for holiday visits. There Douglas cycled the surrounding countryside with Tony, talked of school, accompanied records with brushes, and took art lessons from Mr. Kennedy, a man who had been wounded in the Flying Corps during the Great War. The Rudds' move meant, none the less, that Douglas lost Tony's familiar company for most of the time spent free from school. For less than a year, Mrs. Douglas rented a flat above the Boarshead post office, next door to the Rudds' former house. But in September 1932, a day or two before Douglas returned for his second year at Housey, grandmother Castellain died, and her death meant an end to the small pension which had been Mrs. Douglas's only secure income.

While Douglas was away at school that term, his mother's ability to find a way out of her difficulties diminished as her mental lassitude returned. By Christmas she was near to breakdown, when a woman she knew only through meetings on Tunbridge Wells station at the beginning and end of school terms, came to her aid. Mrs. Miles, who had two sons at Christ's Hospital, was the wife of the rector at Little Common near Bexhill. Learning of Mrs. Douglas's plight at the start of that Christmas vacation she asked her to stay at the Rectory until she was better. For six months Mrs. Douglas remained with the Mileses, until, reasonably recovered, she found an unfurnished bungalow to rent in Bexhill. There she put her only asset, her furniture, planning to live in the bungalow in winter and in summer let it furnished while she found cheap rooms for herself and her son. In fact, as she continued in this way for several years, Mrs. Douglas found it possible to let the bungalow at other seasons. Douglas therefore rarely had any home to return to in the holidays, and sometimes he arrived before his mother had been able to find rooms for them.

Sometimes, however, he could stay with the Mileses or a school friend, and at least once a year he was able to stay with Sir Reginald Spence at his house at Blackboys, Sussex. Himself an Old Blue, Sir Reginald remained devotedly attached to the school, and having comfortably retired after a career as wine merchant, he regularly invited Housey boys to stay, and took a fatherly interest in their progress at school.

When Douglas did stay with his mother at Bexhill, after 1933, he saw little of her, for she was out from seven-thirty in the morning till nine at night, as daily companion to an exacting old lady. Even when they were together, he rarely spoke about serious subjects and never about his father.

At first his mother had tried to talk with Douglas about him, stressing Captain Douglas's military record for fear that her son would see him as wholly bad; but Douglas, she remembers, showed no interest and never brought up the subject himself. Now it was not just the fact of his father's departure that hurt, but his silence, for Douglas had not heard from him since 1928.[1]

So Douglas made his own life during school holidays, cycling, playing football, bathing and sketching and making friends with various girls and boys as he came and went. There was never any pocket-money for him and mostly he made his own meals; and yet, writing of the mood of 'November', in an essay at sixteen, it was to these Bexhill holidays that Douglas turned for an image of summer contentment:

Drying in the sun on summer beaches, my mind achieves that almost impossible state, 'thinking of nothing'. I watch the far-off smoke trails, or the precise curveting of seagulls, finding in these things a contentment that is above analysis. Always among familiar companions and continual occupations my summer days pass too quickly, for boredom may be washed off like dirt in the warm sea; and who may think dismally, watching the form of downland take shape under a lucky brush?

2

A change overcame the Arcadia of Douglas's poetry in 1935. Instead of sprightly elves and rabbits there is a strange young man imprisoned in a garden by a vicious spirit, and a sword-bearing youth offered the consolation of dreams for the price of growing old. Neatly observed details remain, but they are woven into a heavier texture with the subdued shades of tapestry in place of the fresh light of spring:

> Your sword is brilliant; through the auburn leaves
> The sun patches your tunic of smooth-woven green,
> Each fold a thousand aery shimmers cleaves
> Dazzling as leaping fish a moment seen.
>
> ('Youth')

The clarity of the picture is that of Rossetti or Burne-Jones, conjuring a scene in which the vitality of the final simile can be absorbed by the formality and stillness of the whole. The innocent energy has gone, replaced by a poetry of self-conscious artistry which offers a more languid Arcadia.

In less than twelve months, the mood of Douglas's poetry had thus moved from the child-like to the adolescent, and in the process, had opened itself to a variety of new impulses.

[1]Captain Douglas wrote to his son when he left school in 1938; Douglas did not take up his suggestion that they should meet.

Christ's Hospital

> Over the meadow,
> framed in the quiet osiers, dreams the pond;
> region of summer gnat-busyness
> and, in the afternoon's blue drowsiness,
> plops among the water-shadows:
> and the cool trees wait beyond.
>
> A young man dwelt there
> with a swift, sad face, and full of phantasy,
> repeating, as he heard it,
> the alliterative speech of the water-spirit;
> smoothing his pale hair
> with automatic ecstasy . . .
>
> ('Strange Gardener')

The landscape of the first stanza appears to be upstream from Millais's Ophelia, and the doomed young man of the second stanza a figure out of Beardsley, in whose own face a year later Douglas discerned an 'intensity and swiftness in the lines and expression'. But the 'automatic' gesture of the last two lines is a transformation of the post-coital behaviour of the typist in *The Waste Land* who 'smooths her hair with automatic hand'. (Douglas unconsciously admitted this last debt by first writing 'hand' for 'ecstasy' when he made a fair copy of the poem in 1936.)

Elsewhere, he fused the styles of two other poets, in an imitation of Pound's 'The Alchemist':

> These are my simples . . .
> toad's blood in tall beakers
> and, in the darkness at the cave's end
> rows of skulls, like after dinner speakers
> grinning their dead fixed laughter
> and the mice
> scrape on each rafter.
> Four days I fasted
> si quis mala vident
> pabula terrae—and my prayers lasted
> from midnight till midnight.
> Now I am ready, now
> Asmoday is coming,
> he is planing, he is swinging,
> breathing foulness he is winging
> swift and wrathful. At my calling
> he is falling
> mighty-winged through cloud and vapours,
> till he capers
> bound in my circle.

27

His wrath is obscene
livid green
his three heads glitter
(bull man ram)
bound in my circle
on his anguineal tail
pale, each scale
glares . . .   ('The Alchymist')

The syncopation and surprises in a rhythm packed with jingling rhymes, macabre imagery, exotic names, arcane and foreign words, and the eccentric extravagance of the whole, all echo the idiosyncrasies of Edith Sitwell's *Façade*, published in 1933.

Douglas may first have been attracted to his Pre-Raphaelite texturing through the murals in the school chapel by Frank Brangwyn; in these crowded biblical scenes Brangwyn, who had at one time worked with William Morris, offered perfect relief from tedious sermons. Beardsley Douglas could have come across in the set of *The Yellow Book* in the school's English department. H. R. Hornsby used the set in his English classes, along with passages from Holbrook Jackson's *The Eighteen-Nineties*, and he was Douglas's English master in 1934–5. Eliot, Pound, and Edith Sitwell Douglas may have discovered for himself; his Housey contemporary C. T. Hatten later wrote that he could not remember the names of such poets as Eliot, Auden, Spender, or Day-Lewis being mentioned in the classroom.

The real world and the modern world entered obliquely into Douglas's poems, if they entered at all; but this same year, 1935, he for the first time stepped out of his fanciful landscape, to encounter a view of experience antithetical to that on which his poems had been based.

·303

I have looked through the pine-trees
Cooling their sun-warmed needles in the night,
I saw the moon's face white
   Beautiful as the breeze.

Yet you have seen the boughs sway with the night's breath,
Wave like dead arms, repudiating the stars
And the moon, circular and useless, pass
   Pock-marked with death.

Through a machine-gun's sights
I saw men curse, weep, cough, sprawl in their entrails;
You did not know the gardener in the vales,
   Only efficiency delights you.

The cold brutality of the weapon directly repudiates Douglas's sensitivity. Its cynicism can be exposed and judged but it cannot be dismissed, for Douglas has discovered something outside the rule of his feelings.

Elsewhere, however, Douglas had adopted something of the weapon's tone as his own voice. Returning to the child-like Arcadia of his first poems, he simplified rhythms, diction, and theme to the point where they showed conscious triviality and carelessness, in a kind of parody of his earlier fancies:

> RABBITS
>
> The rabbits came out of
> the deep cool woodland,
> white tails bobbing in
> the noon heat-haze.
>
> But some great lout of
> a flower-picking housemaid
> sent them back scuttling
> through shadow-spattered ways.
>
> And she went on, just
> treading on beauty.
> Primroses rooty
> she ripped from the ground.
> And she hummed a little song just
> under her breath but
> Death
> was waiting for
> Pan had
> heard her.

In such a world there would be no serious room for Pan unless he were to become a grotesque.

It was the tone of 'Rabbits' which was increasingly encountered by Douglas's teachers during 1935. D. S. Macnutt, who had taught him Latin the previous year, later commented that Douglas held a position always near the top of his set, 'with no great effort on his part'. A. H. Buck, who first took Douglas for Latin in 1935, recalled that 'you could sense his boredom with you and the grammar you were trying to pump into him: in some cases it amounted to a (doubtless deserved) contempt.' Teaching him English, W. R. Macklin remembered someone 'antagonistic' and 'intolerant', giving the impression of cantankerousness and bloody-mindedness.

Douglas still did well academically, in the summer of 1935 winning James Stephens's *Etched in Moonlight* for a prize; but his success was achieved with what appeared to be little effort and less co-operation. His mother recalls that when he was fifteen they spoke less than ever before, and he so often replied, 'I don't agree', that she suggested he should make a record of the expression to save his breath. With her he seemed to have a sizeable chip on his shoulder and she found no way of getting him to talk.

Talk was not a commodity of which Douglas was short at school, but it was increasingly supercilious, critical, or downright aggressive. In a story written the following year, 'The Siren', he left a picture of his own behaviour in the classroom. As the character Chadburn, at first he is merely distracted, looking at a bee buzzing against the window, the dust on a pile of Roman readers, and surveying his fellow-pupils. His one positive desire is that the class should end. When the bell sounds, Mr. Dandy addresses Chadburn in 'his rather pickled voice', using tones that were well known to Douglas, though the content of the attack is probably as fictional as the reply.

'You, Chadburn,' he whispered 'might be supposed to have even less excuse for idleness than your loafing friend in the corner. At least he is wasting only his father's good money. But *your* father, Chadburn, does not pay for your lordly existence here. Yet—here—you—sit, leading a serene and workless life under-myverynose! You have the insolence, the intolerable effrontery to insult me, and the other people who are unfortunate enough to have to work with you, by lounging in your seat and performing your toilet' (John had been unconsciously playing with a comb) 'while you gaze out of the window. Your supreme and quite unfounded self-satisfaction, I must confess, quite staggers me. Forgive my presumption Chadburn if I call you a *conceited puppy*'—Pause—'You may go gentlemen.'

Before the form had recovered from that stupor into which schoolboys can be shocked by any display of calculated ill will by a master, John got up slowly to address Mr. Dandy. His face was so white that the scarlet spots on his cheeks looked painted. 'You' he said 'are a slimy little drunkard.' It was a great moment —anyone acquainted with Mr. Dandy's terrifying presence will agree.

During the summer holidays of 1935, however, Douglas had a brief spell in a world far from that of his struggles with authority. His mother's half-sister, who thirty years earlier had invited her to the Swiss finishing school where she taught, now lived in Gorizia, on the border between Italy and Yugoslavia, as companion to Keith's great-aunt, Countess Calice, in her nineties. For two weeks Douglas stayed with her, free to roam as he liked and explore the pleasures of a new southern world, and for the next five years its powerful sensory impressions were recreated in his poetry. The brown monks with umbrellas against the sun; the shuttered wine-shops with the sound of flutes coming from them to make audible the lethargy of noon; the chatter of barbers and the men who painted your portrait for ten lire, 'Out of proportion, yet interpreting / Your hectic

KD's watercolour of Gorizia, done after his visit in 1935

colours'; the green, long-necked wine bottles, in woven straw jackets, the 'new tang' of their contents and its benign effect on the senses; and above all, the sunlight, shortening the shadows of the avenues, and blackening the doorways:

> Over and over the street is repeated with sunlight,
> the oxen tire even of the leaves,
> the flutes sound in the wineshop out of sight.
>
> The sky is apathetic like a kite
> that cares not how the string below it weaves
> over and over. The street is repeated with sunlight
>
> till only doors are dark among the white
> walls that outstare the sun. And noon achieves
> the flutes' sound in the wineshop, out of sight.
>
> ('Villanelle of Gorizia', 1937)

About fifty kilometres to the north-west was Monte Nero where, Douglas recalled in 1938,

> Some peasant girl fashioned for love and work
> Taught me a smile that I had forgotten . . .
>> ('Forgotten the Red Leaves')

To the south-east, on the coast of the Gulf of Venice, the agricultural village of Aquileia lay alongside the ruins of the Roman port and town which had once ruled the whole region. Douglas visited Aquileia, where the ring-bolts, piers, and approaches of the port, the foundations of shops, walls, and towers offered evidence of what had been the fourth city of Italy. Here, however, Roman and Renaissance remains mingled with the signs of a more recent past. Behind the basilica of Aquileia, with its marine mosaics recalled by Douglas in 'Forgotten the Red Leaves', a war cemetery, a garden of roses and olive, held beauty enough to be a place of pilgrimage. Gorizia itself had a Museo della Guerra, and to the south-west of the town and Monte San Michele, was the Ossario di Redipuglia, with the remains of a hundred thousand soldiers killed in the mountain fighting of 1917.

> Turn away from Monte Nero, that mountain
> to the west. Turn your back on the white town
> of Gorizia, plastered with notices and swarming
> with soldiers. Cross the green Isonzo: go down
>
> by the ruined palace of the archbishop, the machine-gun schools,
> and a company of the Alpini with their mules.
> Now uphill to the woods where hundreds of saplings hide
> where a generation of men and trees died.
>> ('Search for a God', 1939)

This was the country of Hemingway's *A Farewell to Arms*, which two summers later Douglas chose among his prizes.

It was four years before Douglas wrote thus of the marks of war which were everywhere in the landscape of this holiday, but within twelve months of his return from Italy he celebrated its summer pleasures in 'Creed for Lovers' and 'Love and Gorizia': pleasures not only of taste and sound but above all the pleasures of the eye, and the eye of the artist:

> And now in the South, the swallows
> swirling precisely among the dazzled trees
> are not known, not at this season, among these
> small streets and posters which the lamp-light shews:
> but are among the white-dusted avenues,
> and where the ruined palace faces the green
> river, and barbers chatter, the sky is clean.

> Mr. Kennedy, speaking in Painswick among slate,
> insisted on shadows' value, thought
> colour of merely secondary import;
> characteristically, being himself incomplete,
> wound-drained, among these places, where thus late
> the unsatisfied put out their heads, take pleasure
> in reproducing rooftops on rough paper. . . .
>
> ('Love and Gorizia')

To return from the freedom of his holiday, first to the difficult world of his mother at Bexhill and then to the authoritarian society of Christ's Hospital, must have been doubly painful. Although he had a kind of freedom at Bexhill and enjoyed the downs and the sea, he was old enough to be well aware of his mother's hardships and to see his old environment with a new sense of worldliness. At school he had not yet gained the freedoms of seniority but had long passed the innocent subservience of the junior. He looked more like seventeen than fifteen and in Gorizia had been able to drink wine until the street seemed 'Over and over . . . repeated with sunlight'; at Housey, he was not allowed 'beyond the ring fence' outside the school estate without permission from his housemaster. There were rules for his conduct in Horsham when he went there with his mother on her three visits each term, and to ensure that he did not break them he was supposed to remain in school uniform. (Once outside the gates, however, he would change from his kersey coat so that he could accompany his mother to the cinema with less fear of being identified—cinemas were out of bounds.)

Douglas returned for the autumn term of 1935 as an established rebel. His unco-operative behaviour in the classroom extended to every activity involving the school's authority. As a childhood 'militarist' he had taken naturally to the school's O.T.C. when he joined, like everyone else, at the age of fourteen. Yet his keenness at Drill, his imaginative enthusiasm for playing at patrols and ambushes, and his fascination with weaponry had led only to conflict with the major in charge. Though he spent many extra-curricular hours in the art school, he was not noted for his co-operation with the art master, H. A. Rigby; and success at rugby and swimming failed to bring him closer to those who trained these teams. Despite his participation in House activities, it was above all his housemaster, A. C. W. Edwards, who faced his rebellion. Edwards, directly responsible for most of Douglas's day-to-day behaviour, was the person most obviously embodying authority for him. 'Teddie' Edwards was one of the most liked and admired of the school's masters at this time, and a succession of Old Blues from his House returned to visit him. Elderly and bearing a strong resemblance to Mr. Chips, he had great charm: his manner a little patronizing perhaps, but seeming to care and quickly to draw affection. Douglas distrusted him.

While most of his fifteen-year-old contemporaries accepted the strict discipline imposed on their lives and attended to the voices of authority, albeit grudgingly, Douglas fought back, and with an articulateness that was already discomfiting. F. W. Nash, a monitor in Lamb A at this time, recalls that he seemed 'more mature and able to "cope" with authority (when he believed himself to be in the right)' than most of his House mates. Authority did not like being 'coped' with.

The first of Douglas's troubles during this term was his being suspected of homosexuality. This was no more uncommon at Christ's Hospital in 1935 than at other boarding schools, but while some masters, seeing it as inevitable, turned a blind eye, officially it led to expulsion. Nothing was proved against Douglas and to his friends the suspicion seemed ridiculous. This autumn, however, his defiant behaviour did not encourage those in authority to give him the benefit of any doubt.

The second of his troubles lay in his careless view of property, his own and other people's. Noel Burdett recalls a characteristic incident of a couple of years later. The art master kept an immense hoard of his own landscapes and was known never to sell or give away any of them. Burdett suggested to Douglas that they might ask for a couple of water-colours. Douglas shook his head; but the next day he removed two from the art school. 'It's not theft,' he explained. 'Theft is when you deprive a person of something he values, and old Rigby didn't even know he possessed these.'

At the end of the term Douglas asked permission from the major in charge of the Corps to take home an old and useless rifle from the armoury, to clean and restore it and return it in January. Permission was refused. Whereupon Douglas broke into the armoury, removed the weapon, and took it home. Unknown to Douglas, the War Office made a check every four years on the school armoury. A few days after the vacation began, Mrs. Douglas found two policemen at her front door, inquiring about the theft of a weapon. Douglas appeared, and showed them to his room where the rifle was laid out on his table, each part newly cleaned and oiled. He was summoned back to school, interviewed by his housemaster and then by both the War Office major and the headmaster.

In the process all the previous misdemeanours, real and suspected, were brought up—including, with Mr. Edwards, some trivial incident about a food locker. Douglas, sent home to cool off and to await sentence, wrote at once[1] to the headmaster, H. L. O. Flecker:[2]

---

[1] The only surviving fragment of this letter is in Douglas's copy and begins in mid-sentence; it is quoted in full.

[2] Brother of James Elroy Flecker.

hunger first made Preese trades-monitor, and then broke open the cupboard. Someone told Mr. Edwards that I had kept the key in order to have the biscuits to myself. He believed it joyfully.

He then had me in, and, with tears in his eyes (this is no sarcasm, but truth) told me how rottenly I had treated him ever since I had been in the House, adding that he would accept no apology, as he knew I should not mean it. I did apologise, whereupon he growled that he preferred deeds to words.

So I am a thief—driven out of all self-control by what I fancied to be injustice: a liar—to a man who could believe anything untrue against me. But you have behaved squarely to me in all things save one, and I have told you no lies. I have nothing against Major S——, who sets spies and expects lies. But to Mr. Edwards who expects loyalty and gives none, I cannot be loyal. If I were a monitor I would be loyal to the house—and tell fewer lies than any other monitor, bar Nash.

But that would not be hard.

Now (if you have read this far). You have my own point of view. Everything I have set down is true, I shall expect punishment. But you cannot give anything worse than insults you heaped on me before Major S——. If you could have refrained from laughing, when you were discussing whether to make or break a boy's career, I would not mind so much—as it is you cannot punish me more. This letter is for you, and I ask you not to show it to anyone but Mr. Edwards. He shall see that it is the truth, though scilicet he will say he knew nothing of some of it.

Perhaps he could have guessed, if he were not so ready to believe things against me. If you remember that in addition to these things I have had boils, work, extra work, games and extra Certificate A Parades to think of perhaps you will think less hardly of me.

Yours sincerely,
KEITH DOUGLAS

P.S. If I have been rude I must apologise. It is hard to write coolly of something about which I feel so strongly.

Mr. Flecker responded by informing Douglas that he would not be expelled, if on being placed in a different House he would give his word to have nothing to do with former friends in Lamb A. Perhaps the suspicion of homosexuality lingered; perhaps Flecker simply wished to protect Mr. Edwards from possible effects upon Lamb A if Douglas told of the incident or tried to avenge himself by stirring up trouble. Whatever the reason, Douglas refused such an assurance, explaining that it would be impossible to carry out. He was not expelled, but in January returned to a place in a new House, Middleton B.

3

The crisis of December 1935 which had faced Douglas with the prospect of expulsion left him in no doubt of the vulnerability of his position. Even after twelve comparatively peaceful months in Middleton B he wrote to his mother of his conviction that Mr. Flecker would get rid of him 'at the slightest excuse'; for this reason alone he would behave himself. The headmaster became an object of suspicion:

He put Sir Reginald off when he asked about my returning to Lamb A by saying that he wanted me to make good in Mid. B.

I now find that he has taken careful precaution that I shall not be house captain and probably not get a study. He never told me as I suppose he imagines I will go on behaving myself better if I think I may be house-captain.

Mr. Flecker now provided a target for his abuse, recalled by Noel Burdett in an adaptation of the Bing Crosby song, 'I'm an Old Cow-Hand' that began: 'I'm the oily Fleck . . .' Flecker's rule through orders posted on notice boards and signed 'H.L.O.F.', with never an explanation, infuriated Douglas. But without money or family connections he was dependent upon the school, and thus at the mercy of the authority Flecker wielded; so he tempered his rebellion with wry resignation. Commenting in his December 1936 letter to his mother that a headmaster 'with such a sense of justice' was not fit to be a House monitor, he added: 'However I still smile politely at him and laugh at his jokes.' His smile had a notoriously cynical twist but having been shown the unequal terms of full-scale conflict with school authority, he adapted himself to his new role. His most frequent and uncompromising clashes in Lamb A had been with its housemaster, Mr. Edwards; in March 1936 his new housemaster, D. S. Macnutt, was able to assure Mrs. Douglas that her son had settled 'uncommonly well' into his House and had given no trouble. In her anxiety she had also written to C. A. Humphrey, an assistant master in Lamb A, and his reply was similarly reassuring. Douglas was popular with his fellows and should 'go far'. His conflicts with those in charge had been as much their fault as his, Humphrey felt; with experience of being in authority himself Douglas would come to understand its problems.

Douglas's whole conflict had in fact been doubly painful because he desired to do well. He wanted to be a house captain, to have his own study and to live as a Grecian, and he knew that his talents ought naturally to earn him such privileges. It was an additional source of frustration when, as sometimes happened in the classroom, his own rancour impeded his success. When he came to Middleton B, therefore, Douglas tried all the harder to prove himself in every activity: if the school authorities remained unappreciative of his character, then his rugby and swimming, his artistic and literary talents, and his commitment to the O.T.C. would prove his value.

Changing Houses at sixteen was rare, and with each House forming a separate domestic and social unit, could have been a painful process, particularly if one had the reputation of being an awkward character. But within weeks of his arrival in Middleton B Douglas was accepted. While his new companions soon found that the rumoured homosexuality 'was just not him at all', they learnt that his capacity for making trouble could be a source of attraction and amusement. Douglas, standing up in the dining hall, his plate held out and a spoonful of mince pointed towards the distant back of the Lady Superintendent, was a figure whose boldness had to be admired. His scurrilous songs about the staff gave words to the others' discontent, and his excellent mimicry provided frequent entertainment.

Douglas's opposition to authority and his outspokenness gave an edge to his company, but it was his range of interests which brought him companions. These had already given him an unusually wide acquaintance outside Lamb A. Now his contribution to the Middleton B production of *Rookery Nook*, in which he played the German bully during his first term there, helped establish new friendships. His liking for jazz which led him to accompany records, among them Nat Gonella's 'Moon Country', by playing with brushes on newspaper, made him a familiar figure in the House; and his success as runner-up in the school's Lamb Essay competition for the summer of 1936 reinforced his literary prestige. Douglas had a capacity for accepting differences in those he met. Among his friends in his new house John Adams, for example, loathed the Corps and could not take it seriously; Norman Ilett spent most of the summer term at cricket, which Douglas hated. If, as Ilett wrote later, the terms of his friendship were exacting as well as generous, it was loyalty which he demanded, not likeness; in turn, Douglas offered his own individuality.

By the autumn term, established in Middleton B and, by due seniority, a monitor, Douglas gained a 'swab'. There were monitors who took little notice of their swabs and others who bullied them; the majority followed a middle course. Douglas did none of these things. His swab, called Sykes, had not settled well into Housey and Douglas approached their relationship with a sense of responsibility which impressed and amused his fellows. Sykes was made to work quite hard—running errands, preparing Douglas's Corps equipment, even cleaning his razor. All this the boy did without any sense of oppression but as a matter of course. For his part Douglas not only took a keen interest in his swab's academic progress, helping him when necessary with work he found difficult, but seriously cared for his well-being at school, advising and defending him whenever the occasion arose. It was not so much the seriousness of Douglas's concern which impressed his friends, as the naturalness with which he carried it out, without a trace of paternalism.

A similar straightforwardness of approach made Douglas's commitment to the Corps a puzzle to friends and masters alike. To see Douglas as a clumsy but tough second-row forward in the First XV of 1936, who cursed his poor eyesight (and the doctor who had treated his measles),[1] surprised no one at Christ's Hospital, with its footballing intellectuals. But for practically everyone the Corps was at best a burden to be endured, and Douglas, a well-known rebel, was 'fanatically keen' on it, remembered by John Adams as devoting at least half his week to preparations for parade. His unmilitary friends questioned his behaviour but Douglas responded with quiet assurance: as the school had a Corps, he explained, it ought to be an efficient fighting force. Far from being deflected from his own commitment, Douglas was concerned about his pacific friends' disaffection, and with tact and good humour would offer to help them manage better at Drill and give them any extra training they should require. They remained disenchanted: he remained a devotee.

Drilling was the activity which Douglas enjoyed most. Weaponry interested him, as was clear from his 'borrowing' of the rifle, and as his poem '·303', of two years earlier, suggests. Racing around the fields playing at ambushes and patrols with the added reality of uniform and gun, naturally appealed to a childhood militarist. But it was Drill, a ritual which demanded skill, precision, and training and excluded thought, which absorbed individual identity into the discipline of communal order, which most attracted him. For however incredible it may have seemed to some of those who taught him, Douglas believed in discipline. Even after the outbreak of war at the end of 1939 it was as an image of disciplined order that he celebrated the 'Stars', 'still marching in extended order':

> nothing but discipline
> Has mobilized and still maintains them. Thus
> Time and his ancestors have seen them. Thus
> Always to fight disorder is their business
> And victory continues in their hand. . . .

Writing a 'five minute poem' on the boys' lunchtime procession in the autumn of 1936 Douglas lamented their lack of 'spangle'. He responded to the 'pleasantly accidental / medley of blues and browns' which the wind made in stirring their kersey coats and the autumn leaves: but they did not regard the 'spattered' statue of 'Pious sixth Edward, so far removed' which presided over the quadrangle:

> Even their respect for Tradition is tattered,
> Lacking its previous spangle.

[1] Since a bad attack of measles at school in 1933 Douglas had worn spectacles.

> But what possible difference
> Does all this make? Visitors are still
> Impressed, and the tables well laid
> Even though we understand the preference
> Of the prodigal for swine-swill.
>
>   ('Autumn Reflection')

Similarly, the Armistice Day rituals of the same term led him to attack the survival of militarism, the boys 'stupid with drum-daze', and the adults, 'still, still in houses where I have been . . . forgetful of poppies nodding': but the ceremonies themselves commanded his respect. Each boy, though ignorant of the real meaning:

> . . . having pride, each in a member
> Of his own family, pins in his clothing
>
> The symbol, finds his own adjective
> For the slender notes, notes of the Last Post,
> Notes of organs in countless churches
> Chapels, town-halls. I say that you must strive
> Always to think, though tall Time lurches
> Twenty years back at these times. . . .
>
>   ('Armistice Day')

However complicated Douglas's attraction to military activities and appurtenances (he was always impeccable in his Corps uniform despite notorious untidiness in everything else), at sixteen he remained unambiguous about the reality of war and the evil of militarism. In a translation from the French, 'Aftermath', he offered a sensitive response to the peace of nature and the peasant's labours to restore his land after war. The prize of 'the stronger' is blood, the cannon rests 'with the torpor of appetite sated / As a beast's':

> Peasants, strown with war's
>   Bones see your sowing:
> But Spring veils these scars
>   With violets growing
> Flowers mingle, and the grape
>   Hangs on the vine. Your nest
> Poor hierophant, shape,
>   While the guns take their rest.

In an outburst of venom, in the essay he wrote in the back of an exercise book for 1936, he described his school as inculcator of bullying, fascism, anti-Semitism, the love of Hitler, and militarism. Yet this essay also allowed a positive celebration of the school's traditions to seep through the deliberately mannered account which had preceded his vilification.

Douglas was beginning to shape a view of the world, and the ambivalence of his response to soldiering lay at the heart of it. Tradition, order, ceremony he loved—though not religious ceremony, it seems: that produced 'Small bald idolaters incense drunk' who gabble 'polysyllabic parodies' and take the 'bubbling' of their minds as 'the hum of eternity' ('*Te Deum*'). For him, traditions today were only poor reflections of an earlier glory and their exponents foolish or authoritarian. An exception, it seems, he found in the Regular Army N.C.O.s and Privates who visited the Corps: these, Noel Burdett recalls, could at times enjoy Douglas's 'keenest reverence'—unlike Regular officers of whom he was generally critical. Captain Douglas in fact, despite his commission and middle-class family, was far more the Kiplingesque soldier than the gentleman officer, and in 1926 had joined the Territorial section of the Royal Engineers as a private, his captaincy held in abeyance.

In soldiering in the Corps, Douglas could not only prove his efficiency, discipline, and skill at proper command, he could make contact with both an ordered, traditional world, and a world of undeniable importance. For behind the army lay the war, the brutal reality which his sensitive Arcadia had been unable to defeat in '·303'. Being a soldier was to live in contact with this reality: handling weapons which killed, planning strategies to surround and destroy. The aesthetic attractions of marching and drilling and guns, the opportunities for imaginative games of defence and attack were based on the utterly serious, adult world of war, and above all the Great War of his father. If Douglas at sixteen did not directly attempt to explore that connection, his poems of war, his outstanding devotion to Corps activities, and his many sketches of soldiers in uniform make clear the two sides' existence.

It was with this outlook that Douglas now made increasing contact with the poetry of recent writers. Already acquainted at fifteen with Edith Sitwell, Eliot, Pound, and Auden, this summer of 1936 he chose among his prizes Michael Roberts's *Poems* and Ian Parsons's *The Progress of Poetry*, a modern anthology which stressed in its selection and its introduction the work of the Great War's poets. By the autumn term of 1936 Douglas was not merely reading *New Verse* but offering contributions to it: poems which showed something of his response to his contemporaries and their world.

Norman Ilett recalls coming upon him one day in the House day room, tap-dancing alongside the billiard table, a copy of *New Verse* beside him. 'Anyone can write like the stuff in here,' said Douglas. 'Go on then, try: and I bet you can't!' Ilett replied. In October 1936 Douglas heard from Geoffrey Grigson that the two poems he had submitted were unsuitable for publication in *New Verse*: a response which was hardly surprising, for the two poems, 'Poem' and 'Menippus in Sussex', were hardly calculated to endear themselves to an editor whose ruling policy was modernity. Writing of the modern world Douglas, despite the appearance of being reconciled to it, exposed its essential banality:

> Cranes swing heaven on a girder
> and the parasite,
> curling in the blue at the
> end of it.
>
> Centaurs move in threes
> and the perpetual charabancs
> threading the down in single file.
> Surely there is equation
> in cabbages and the alliterative speech
> of spirits.
>
> ('Poem')

41

The cabbages give away Douglas's lack of sympathy with cranes and chara-
bancs; in the next stanza he turns to 'the old lecher / undressing the waitress
with his eyes', making a Rupert Brookeish equation between modernity and
crude realism.

'Menippus in Sussex' more seriously brings the present into collision
with his own Arcadian idealism, but his sympathies are still clearly with
the rejected past:

> Bean-fed Menippus spurns lean hills, loves slum
> Where may some immanent quality become
> Apparent afterwards: perhaps
> Dumb hedge-geometry, bird maps
> Are fare for idealist, a poet's crumb?
>
> And tracheotomy of Time lets out
> At the fouled throat of cul de sac new art
> A faster quality . . .

At the end, the cynic philosopher suggests that the poet should look in
'drains' for 'pearls' and leave Arcadia:

>   '. . . make search
> Apace, leave goatfoot in the lurch'
> Youth shrugs his shining shoulder, turns from trace.

Aware of the consequences for his Arcadia of the intrusion of the modern
world, in these two poems Douglas turns to slum and charabanc with the
relish of someone trying the effect of a Nissen hut in a Capability Brown
landscape. Yet the 'faster quality' released from the blocked throat of 'new
art' elsewhere appealed to him. A poem drafted in the back of an exercise
book used when he was fifteen proved the attraction of bathos, fashionable
reference, and slick vignette. In the poets of his decade and particularly in
Auden and Spender, he had found a criticism of his time parallel to his
own, and even a species of hero-worship more commanding than that of
Fingal and men with spears.

> Here on their seas and tombs and passionate islands
> the greatest, the merciful men rest beautifully
> not stared at. Their remains, minds sayings not interesting
> to jews and hustlers, living where news is valuable
> and where the mass-lord magnate, removing cigar,
> condemned history in the voice which advertises
> up in Olympus the charabanc will be visiting
> They have packed their traps, no propaganda will save them
> those with the beautiful names, from the scholarly columns
> of the Sussex County Mag.

Christ's Hospital

> The old free poets who talked to lustful kings
> of life have only survived for assimilation
> those who were honoured in the generation.

The theme of past heroic poets retained its appeal for Douglas, who in 1936 wrote of the 'unacknowledged rulers' who passed from earth to their 'rarer climate' ('The Eagle in Praise of Poets'). Three times the dead had drawn Douglas's attention: in 'Unfinished—The Dead' they live in a 'looking-glass land', and in 'Fragment—The Dead' they are immune to 'hand-circles', following 'the cycle of life . . . among the swallows'. In the third fragment, which he tried unsuccessfully to shape into a poem, he celebrated their attraction:

> I love the dead, whose skulls are the sharks baubles
> who lie in long rows, catalogued, or stare
> through soft flung feet of sand. Blind eyes
> are satiate and splendid

But when Douglas made a poem from his Audenesque draft, it was not thematic development which concerned him: authority was what he sought, and an authority of pure technique. The mannerism of the draft becomes rigour, its superiority made trenchant, and the free display of wit is replaced by an austere, aloof virtuosity:

> FAMOUS MEN[1]
> And now no longer sung,
> not mourning, not remembered
> more under the sun,
>
> not enough their deserved
> praise. The quick movement of dactyls
> does not compensate them.
>
> The air is advertised of seas
> they smote, from green to copper.
> They were merciful men.
>
> And think, like plates lie deep
> licked clean their skulls,
> rest beautifully, staring.

Varying the pace of his diction, withholding sensory detail until the third stanza's celebration, and forcing home the grim image of his final stanza, Douglas displays his supreme indifference to everything but the poet's power.

[1] First called 'Epitaph'.

It was this very power which he satirized in another display of virtuosity, published in the July 1936 issue of *The Outlook*, which has the humour and warmth he had drained from 'Famous Men'. For his theme he chose the interplay of dream and reality: the opposed forces whose conflict had defeated him in the poems sent to *New Verse*. Now irony doubled on irony surmounts their struggle.

ENCOUNTER WITH A GOD[1]
Ono-no-komache the poetess
sat on the ground among her flowers,
sat in her delicate-patterned dress
thinking of the rowers,
thinking of the god Daikoku.

Thinking of the rock pool
and carp in the waterfall at night.
Daikoku in accordance with the rule
is beautiful, she said, with a slight
tendency to angles.

But Daikoku came
who had been drinking all night
with the greenish gods of chance and fame.

[1] Published in *The Outlook*, with Douglas's linocut, under the title 'Japanese Song'.

He was rotund standing in the moonlight,
with a round, white paunch.

Who said
I am not beautiful,
I do not wish to be wonderfully made,
I am not intoxicated, dutiful daughter,
and I will not be in a poem.

But the poetess sat still
holding her head and making verses:
'How intricate and peculiarly well-
arranged the symmetrical belly-purses
of Lord Daikoku.'

In the autumn term of 1936, however, it was his own, immediate world
which more frequently concerned Douglas in his poems. As creator, wit,
satirist, or realist he had written powerfully enough earlier in the year, but
now he speaks directly, in his own person. Occasionally gesture obtrudes,
or obscurity blurs the impression; but it is himself, in 'Distraction From
Classics', watching a bee on the window-pane at Catullus' expense, or
observing the 'slow / shifting of dancers in the schoolroom' of 'Petition';
and it is his end-of-summer mood which he expresses in 'Draft for Poem:
Affaire':

Autumn not yet over, the negative
Of summer not scratched, I see
As Abelard in his youth, speculative
And unemotional, facing me,

The experiences facing me, without fear
Or favour, of the past six months:
Able to criticise here, and there
Praise them—impartially though. On plinths

The faces stare still, eyes not set
On me, their straight nostrils unaware
Of the smoke-ring from my cigarette,
Constant these last weeks, now not there.

Perhaps you too have forgotten,
Or merely recorded an added letter
To the word, whorl in a pattern;
To help you choose Gods better.

Elsewhere he returns to memories of Gorizia, and with them thoughts of a
girl he had met there:

You small with your red-brown hair how could I mould,
So inconsistent, how could I take you?

('Love and Gorizia')

Thinking of her again, in 'Creed for Lovers', he moves from a day-dream
to a general confession of disappointment:

Consider the cold mosaic, know how valuable
These grow with ageing. Read the unbelieved
Quaint characters, and think here comes
You walking up to me among the angular
Bare shadows of September downs: the things I have wanted
Never coming out of the shadow . . .

If Douglas is using emotions he knew in order to sustain a lyrical voice,
an essay published in *The Outlook* in December leaves no doubt that at
sixteen he was increasingly aware of the course of his own experiences.
Once again the details are accurate, but Douglas's memory reverses their
chronological order, in a pattern which conveys his new understanding:

Drowsing pleasantly through mathematics, grown meaningless by repetition, I
stumble suddenly into the woods by the old church of St. Martha at Guildford,
whose Sunday afternoon peace is disturbed by treble battle-cries.
    Fircones hurtle among the tall tree-trunks, and I, an ammunition-carrier, make
my way down a side-path, hotly pursued by enemies whose supply is exhausted.
So swiftly that I cannot follow the connection, prep.-school days fade, and I am in
a field on a colder afternoon. Ringed about with my breath, I am led forward to
meet my new pony, who is too tall for me. I am given a sugar-lump, which I hold
out to him with friendly directness. He knocks me down.

('November')

He was three when this happened.
    Douglas remains in command here, as in his draft for the poem 'Affaire'
and his statement of disappointment. Once in this year, however, he wrote
a poem which passed beyond this control. It starts with a strange fantasy
and moves into disturbingly crude adolescent feeling. By the end one is left
in no doubt of the pitch of emotion on which the poise of his other writing
was built.

INTERIOR

I have arranged the scene: the doll is you
Wearing your green dress, and the sixpenny beads
That broke so soon. And there the curtains hide
That painting of the downs; 'I always say, it needs
Youth to admire this' you said and chuckled, prancing
Your false teeth sideways in your mouth. . . .
I look uncomfortably through the dirty pane the view.

At the wind-bent trees in the school garden
And glancing
Sideways I know she is behind, amused at me
At that I must turn, bow, beg her pardon
Say that I did not hear, and see her plain
Warm cheek flush suddenly
Lord how I wish you were here
Lord how I wish
You were in the kitchen.

In December Douglas copied his poems into an exercise book, tracing his development through the headings 'Earlier Efforts', 'Transitional Stage', 'Translations', and 'Later Style'. He started a second book for poems from January 1937, but after a piece on the death of a rich cripple, and a couple of attempts at a love poem, he filled the pages with sketches

of horses and soldiers. That January, however, his poetry was published for the first time outside the school. With a double irony which would have appealed to his Menippus, a poem appeared in the journal he had satirized in the draft of 'Famous Men', *The Sussex County Magazine*: it was the Arcadian 'Song' he had written at fourteen, renamed 'Pan in Sussex'.

4

On 24 January 1937, his seventeenth birthday, Douglas 'received his buttons', becoming a History Grecian. In 1935–6 he had been a Deputy Grecian in classics, but as a Probationary Grecian in the autumn of 1936 he had transferred to history: a choice which the classicists thought proved a boy's distaste for the rigours of learning. But as there was no English Sixth at the school at that time, history was the obvious choice for someone of Douglas's talents, and a choice which brought him as tutor one of the most liked and admired of the masters, the Hon. David Roberts. Roberts, second son (of twins) of Baron Clwyd, saw his role in the school as extending well beyond the teaching of history. Recently married to a young wife and living outside the school estate, on the Worthing Road, Roberts tried to give his History Grecians access to the more civilized and domestic pleasures absent from boarding-school life. Classes were sometimes held in his home, in a study lined with books and a collection of paintings which often provided the focus for discussion. When he taught in school he often held classes in the art section of the library, using an art book as a point of departure for the historical and critical discussion of a painting. Roberts not only tried to introduce his pupils to the cultural components of history—it was a joke at the school that his boys gained their University places through their general essays rather than their history—he emphasized the value of articulate criticism. Douglas was well suited to such an approach. For although, as Noel Burdett recalls, he tended to turn discussion into argument and replace logic with acerbic wit and 'verbal brilliance', he was incessantly and articulately critical. Roberts was quietly spoken and wry, with a genuinely liberal tolerance, but he found in Douglas an antithetical quality which he later described as 'that magnificent prejudice, which was one of his greatest attractions!' To him Douglas's poetry lacked 'depth of feeling' and he thought he would be a novelist: Douglas responded with the vigorous assertion that such a view proved one 'astonishingly insensitive'. He became a regular visitor to the Robertses' house, for Roberts encouraged his Grecians to visit at odd times outside the school day, and as a bringer and sustainer of conversations Douglas was always welcome.

In the autumn of 1936 the marriage of D. S. Macnutt had brought to Middleton B a new housemaster, H. R. Hornsby. He knew Douglas through classes in English, Latin, and Roman history and although he recognized his cleverness and had seen him work hard at Roman history, he had observed his ability to behave in a conceited and, on occasions, insufferable manner. In the house he soon discovered Douglas's capacity for impressive untidiness. Beside most of the other housemasters, Hornsby, in his early thirties, was a young man, but he carried an air of established and rigorous authority. His nickname 'Troops' he had earned through the cry of 'Come on, troops!' with which he urged on rugby teams from the touchline; he often referred to 'the troops' in conversation, meaning the members of the House. His tall, somewhat military appearance, and manner which was matter-of-fact to the point of at times appearing brusque, gave added point to the name, and in fact Hornsby, who was an O.T.C. officer, was to become a lieutenant-colonel in a Gurkha regiment during the war. Hornsby ran the First XV and coached its forwards, so Douglas, joining the scrum this autumn term, saw plenty of him.

With this closer acquaintance Hornsby found that Douglas's rebellion was based on principles which he himself valued: a hatred of sham and pretence and a strong sense of justice. Hornsby shared none of the boy's rebelliousness but he did share his independence. He himself possessed an unusual capacity for openness towards people whose ways were different from his own. Douglas knew precisely where he stood with Hornsby and found a directness in the master's personality which he knew he could absolutely trust. Increasingly, through 1937, long after the rest of Middleton B was asleep, Douglas would come downstairs to talk to Hornsby about the injustice of life and the injustice of people, particularly Mr. Flecker. Recognizing that this was rather 'against the government', Hornsby did nothing to discourage it, for he felt that without this safety valve, Douglas would blow up. Douglas also spoke occasionally of the personal subjects which he rarely discussed with others: his mother's hardships and lack of money and his father's prolonged silence. Hornsby listened, sometimes gave an opinion, and Douglas returned to bed. Hornsby's clearly defined character had few pretensions and it was typical of him to write thirty years later that, apart from the friendship between them, he did not think he had taught Douglas 'anything worth tuppence. He taught me far more.'

As another 'safety-valve', in the better weather Hornsby allowed Douglas to visit a farm at Southwater where Captain and Mrs. Brodie entertained a number of Christ's Hospital boys, especially ones from Middleton B. 'They had a few horses and took us to Pony Club dances, hunter trials etc. A laugh, really. Not our scene at all,' Norman Ilett recalled; but the Brodies were genial and hospitable and their household possessed the added attraction of a fifteen-year-old daughter, Liz, whom Douglas particularly befriended.[1] Another family called Jones, who farmed just across Donkey Bridge, about a mile from the school, offered a similar welcome. Douglas also rode there— the daughter in this case was called Brenda. Noel Burdett, who took up an offer from Douglas to teach him to ride during the summer term, remembers pints of tea in a stone-flagged kitchen, and a drink made in an old cider press which the boys found stronger than sherry.

[1]C. T. Hatten has suggested that the poem, 'For E.B.', signed 'Flip', in *The Outlook* for July 1938 is Douglas's, and addressed to Liz Brodie. It is a farewell to love.

KD taking a fence, at the Brodies' farm; (*below*) with Liz Brodie,
grooming their horses

Douglas gave a lively performance in a House production of *Laburnum Grove*, in March 1937, and in his second summer term with Middleton B proved his talent for soldiering by leading his No. 5 Platoon to victory in the school's Somers Clark Trophy competition in drill, turnout, map-reading, weapons training, and tactics. As a result of this Corps success, Sergeant Douglas was asked to choose a squad for the August camp's Inter-Schools guard-mounting competition. Among those he selected were Noel Burdett and Joe Arsenault, and they both remember the enthusiasm with which he trained them. Probably through one of the Regular N.C.O.s whom he befriended, Douglas managed to fit out his squad in new tight-fitting uniforms, and he brought them to a peak of smartness with all the tricks he had learned from Regulars. It was to no avail. Burdett recalls a long night at camp with Douglas, trying to persuade him that he was not solely responsible for their failure. In the course of the conversation Burdett learnt to his surprise how many of his activities Douglas, who had always seemed the embodiment of confidence, pursued with little expectation of success. While writing was excluded from this area of uncertainty, Douglas's appearance was not: 'I have the face of a parrot,' he told Burdett, 'and a Jewish-looking parrot at that.'[1]

However low his expectations, at the end of that summer term, Douglas was awarded the school's Grindling Prize for History, having been placed first by Austin Lane Poole, the Oxford medievalist, examining Roberts's Grecians for him. Poole's comments on his performance and the senior history master's response were later recorded by Roberts:

'Well. I've brought a boy called Douglas out top, not I fancy an easy or agreeable character at this stage, but full of promise—by gum he is! He wrote an astonishing answer about Van Gogh.'—'Yes,' says I, 'I know where he got it from—the introduction to Van Gogh in the Phaidon Press.'[2]

On Douglas's end-of-year report Roberts had nonetheless commented: 'a most refreshing and original mind', capable of 'clear-cut and critical' written work. Douglas, he predicted, should get a University scholarship, and if he read and concentrated he could get a good one. His confidence was supported by Hornsby's comment on Douglas's 'consistently good and interesting' work in English, and the second history master, George Newberry's, hope that Douglas would keep up his first-rate work and not shy 'when the work is dull and difficult'. In fact, but for Roberts's encouragement and advice, Douglas could well have been leaving school at the end of this term.

[1] Norman Ilett recalls: 'KD was always on about his face—contemplating plastic surgery on his nose: pimples: *muscles*—generally rather body-conscious: typical enough, no doubt, of adolescents.'

[2] Douglas in a notebook recorded his reading of the Phaidon volume on Van Gogh during 1937–8.

In December 1936 he had made serious inquiries about entry to Sandhurst, and finding that it was financially practicable had written to his mother about the possibility. Roberts urged him to think about the army, if at all, after University.

Roberts's tutelage was affecting Douglas in more ways than the simple transmission of confidence and advice. Two books which the master had lent or recommended provided him with a new perspective and colouring for the outlook which he had already developed for himself the previous year. In Helen Waddell's *The Wandering Scholars* Douglas found a historical context in which to place his romantic and aesthetic view of the past. There he could read of Christian humanism as a succession of aesthetic moments enacted in the lives and discoveries of famous men, preservers of wisdom and seekers after beauty, inhabiting a world of change and death. In Dmitri Merejkowski's *Romance of Leonardo da Vinci* he found an image of the embattled culture hero, the Renaissance artist rediscovering the past in an alien world of superstition and philistinism. Supported by the scholarship of Helen Waddell, Douglas could affirm that summer in an examination essay on 'Leisure' that its best use lay in the study of history: there could be found the wisdom of the old heroes who taught the appreciation of the beauties of life. Douglas drew directly on Merejkowski in compiling a set of 'Notes and Ideas for Poems': a list of elusive images—'Leonardo's left-handed script'—mythological references, and direct quotation from the book. He also incorporated the R.A.F. motto, a glancing reference to *The Tempest*, and Owen's remark, 'The poetry is in the pity'; but only an allusion to Merejkowski, 'the old god found on the seashore', actually produced a poem, 'Triton', where Douglas could see this old god 'More clearly than I can see, / . . . you and you who stand there who really love me'.

Even while he was formulating this new mythology, however, Douglas kept up his interest in contemporary writing, acquiring Dylan Thomas's *Twenty-Five Poems* (1936) and Thomas Moult's *Best Poems of 1936* (1937). His notebook included notes on Eliot and comments on Pound's *Poems*.[1] His attitude had none the less remained unchanged; and on the end-papers of Michael Roberts's *Poems*, Douglas affirmed his credo in a poem dated August 1937:

COMMISSION

Be single like the seagull, who has come
Slanting on windy levels down the gnat's stratosphere
Who seeks worm citizen ploughed out of house and home
Thinks in his stomach once and furrows there.

[1] By April 1938 Douglas had published an essay in *The Outlook*, 'New Year', which quoted from Yeats's 'Sailing to Byzantium' and referred to Hopkins.

Not you nor Moses hurling ten written stones
To stand astraddle silhouetted places.
Lip flute or trumpet; music, never megaphones;
This way they turn more interested faces.

Love is King's English; lust its cockney accent,
Now leap and learn it, no need to decry then
The present age, when aitches are so lacking.
Speak to them splendidly; do not deny them

The sun, point him out ere the clouds climbs him.
Not their muck shew. You must demonstrate
Not stones but what's beneath. Set them amiming
The gods, each friend with friend and satiate.

Assuming the jaunty pulpit manner of his socialist contemporaries, Douglas
not only proves his powers of wit and assimilation: he appropriates their
style for the delivery of a message antithetical to theirs. From this élitist
viewpoint even the fashionable imagery of social observation is made to
express a decidedly upper-class superiority: 'Love is King's English; lust its
cockney accent . . .'

For as Douglas made clear in the marginalia with which he covered his
copy of Herbert Furst's quasi-Marxist *Art Debunked*, his was not a demo-
cratic view of art. If the size of the audience determined value, Douglas
claimed, then 'Walt Disney is the greatest artist the world has ever seen'.
His quest was for perfection in all things, enlightenment and cultivation:
qualities which cannot be measured by mass or number. And throughout
1937 Douglas sought them in the past. Alongside some notes on John
Stuart Mill he jotted the fragment:

over the painted stage, the symbolic figures.
This is an old language, dead
to most and thus more living
made among those few who recall it.
The allegiance of the rabble defiles that to which it is given.

Menippus was answered. Not just with a cynicism turned upon the present,
but with a new affirmation of superior vision.

5

I am writing during prep: in my study—a dirty little room which I will describe.
It is wooden mostly—partitioned off from the dayroom in which most of the
house work. It has a half glass door, and windows looking into the dayroom as
well as outside. All these are curtained with white stuff which has a green repeat-
ing pattern woven into it. The wooden and plaster walls are green (dark) up to

about waist high and then yellow plaster, or window. These walls are covered with initials and burnt lettering of various kinds (particularly the lower part of the door, which is brown). Indelible finger-marks of past owners are profusely distributed. I have a little table, a lot of books, an armchair, a deckchair and a settle. The wall is decorated with a large curtain (same stuff as the others) hiding where I wrenched away a hideous fixture school bookcase, and elsewhere with various small coloured reproductions of Van Gogh and one by Pollitzer. . . .

Also in the study are a card table covered with a rug of the Douglas tartan (mainly green), and a dirty fireplace with a fairly cheerful fire in it. Boys from other houses come periodically along the asphalt path outside in the dark and tap on my window and talk through it when I open it. Outside in the dayroom I can hear forms and benches creaking under people doing prep. . . . I hope you can see the study now.

Dominating the study was a large tempera picture by Douglas showing soldiers at bayonet practice: 'The composition, colouring, and technique are mainly modern, but the soldiers' attitudes and faces are intentionally reminiscent of Old French paintings, religious canvases and early stained glass.' Douglas had made extensive notes on early French painting in 1937, and although he wrote that his picture's dominance was intended to distract visitors from his study's dirt, it boldly proclaimed his desired blending of ancient and modern.

By the time Douglas gained his study in January 1938 he was enjoying the independence and prestige which he had missed at Edgeborough by leaving early. In November he had won his rugby colours after a match against St. John's, Leatherhead: a powerful force in tight scrums and fearless contributor to rushes although 'unable to get off his feet when dribbling fast' and handicapped by 'bad hands'. That autumn he had been invited to review for the school's official magazine, *The Blue*, offering measured and responsible criticism of a book about the school. Although he had not been made editor of *The Outlook*, everything he submitted, poems, linocuts, essays, and stories, was published; and in June 1937 his poem 'Caravan' had appeared in the Oxford undergraduate magazine *Programme*. He now had another swab, Jolyon Dromgoole, who remembers Douglas as a friendly and tolerant swabmaster, mainly requiring that he should keep his Corps equipment in trim. As Douglas had predicted, he was not House captain: that honour went to Norman Ilett, but room had been made for Douglas to be his deputy when John Adams, another of Middleton B's Grecians, was moved to a different House as captain. It was not Adams's decision, but Douglas made a point of calling on him in his new House to maintain their friendship and show his thanks.

If Douglas would have preferred the title of captain, between Ilett and himself there was no animosity. Not only was Ilett the more obvious choice,

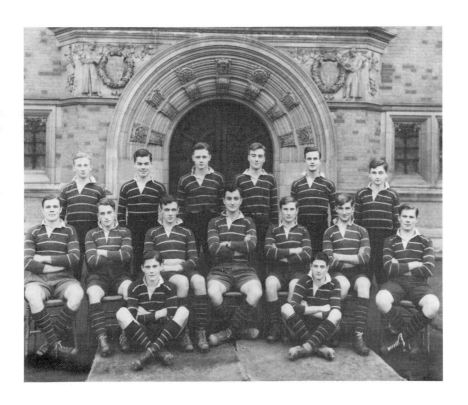

The First XV, Christ's Hospital, 1937. Seated, second from left, N. L. Ilett;
fourth from left, C. T. Hatten (captain); second from right, K. C. Douglas

he remained Douglas's closest friend, their talents and temperaments finely
matched. Ilett, two months younger than Douglas, was affable, relaxed and
easy to befriend, a boy who outmanœuvred authority rather than met it
head on. Beside him Douglas appeared prickly, rather daunting and difficult to know, but with a sense of humour which, Ilett recalls, 'in its way
was tremendous. I remember a walk to Horsham to buy Nat Gonella
records in which he talked all the time and I didn't stop laughing.'

Ilett could well have been Captain of School in his last year, 1938–9,[1] if
he had been less independent of mind: he was captain that year of rugby,
cricket, athletics, and fives. Without fondness for the Corps he became a

[1] Ilett remained at Christ's Hospital after Douglas had gone up to Oxford, a year early.

C.S.M. and with little appearance of effort gained an Open Scholarship at Brasenose for 1939. While Douglas was a tireless forward, Ilett was a wilful centre three-quarter; while Ilett played cricket all summer, Douglas swam; and although Ilett once came second in the Lamb Essay competition, he made no claim to Douglas's talents as poet and artist. Douglas was the better mimic, castigator, and raconteur; both of them impressed their contemporaries as imperiously articulate, and in acting they shared the honours. For House play in the Lent term of 1938 they collaborated on a dramatization of *The Housemaster* from Ian Hay's novel—having found that an acting version was not available because the play was currently on in the West End. Neither Hornsby nor Macnutt wished to produce it, so they did so themselves. Only one success of Ilett's may have given Douglas displeasure: Ilett, as a tenor in the school choir, was welcomed into the boys' concert party, 'the Blackberries': Douglas had to struggle for entry. For all his tuneful whistling, his voice was notably unmelodious—a quality which he continually demonstrated. Through their combined talents and success Ilett and Douglas became established as a renowned pair, whose fame extended beyond Middleton B.[1]

A part of Douglas's character remained unfulfilled by all his successes, as a story he wrote in an exercise book for 1937 suggested. The story starts with his memories of Cranleigh at the age of three, the world in which 'even the rain was interesting', then moves, more directly than his other autobiographical story, to his later childhood.

Then there had been Olwen, who had looked after him: he remembered her chiefly for the odd faces she made to amuse him, and the big bow which Olwen could pull, but which had been too stiff for his small arms. When he was four, his mother had been very ill. He never sensed anything wrong when she came back from hospital; and when his father, a hearty playmate whom he secretly feared and wholeheartedly admired, disappeared and Olwen too, he wept as much as his mother.

---

[1] Ilett later defined Douglas's character; for him

'he was not a popular figure, but the people (boys and masters) at Christ's Hospital who knew him well were very fond of him, and his talents were everywhere respected and admired. The stumbling blocks were his tongue, which hurt at times, his manners, which could be appalling, and his snobbery, which he tried to justify by arguing that grace and beauty belonged to the upper classes. None of these things could alienate friends (*male*, at any rate, who didn't have to cope with his amorous intentions) who understood his basic kindness, generosity, good humour, guts, genuine humility (surprisingly) and pleasure in the achievements of others—this is not a complete list. He was a great companion, when he had time for you, and he would give that time if he thought you needed it. He was extremely modest about his important attainments, but in other ways, an exhibitionist. He loved to perform: tap-dancing for instance— usually the gramophone ran down, or one of the steel caps would fly off his shoe. This would be but one more signal from a malignant fate—but a good laugh, all the same.'

Christ's Hospital

It was soon apparent that lack of a father meant lack of money, and after a curtailed prep-school career, Peter entered Christ's Hospital where, being somewhat old for his age, he attained a certain seniority by his fifteenth year.

He was now at the age of fourteen, tall (some five feet in shoes), and fair, with very white skin and large brown eyes,[1] long lashed. He sat now sprawled on a stone seat, whose white stone shone back the sun at him disconcertingly. Sunlight, the blue glare of the sky and far off cricketing sounds and dreamy ears, moving him to an inexorable feeling of melancholy and longing, which both compelled and denied analysis. He began stumbling in his mind after the ignis fatuus discontent, this definite and indescribable disquiet, and suddenly caught up with it: suddenly he knew that it was a desire to share beauty, the pleasantness of this summer afternoon, with someone else, someone to understand not this only, but every tossed thought and ambition. This would be a girl evidently: he pictured her for many days after that.

Making a break here, Douglas re-opens with the description of a visit by 'Peter' to Eastbourne Baths. Perhaps he was drawing on a trivial incident recalled by his mother, when at twelve he bumped into a sixteen-year-old girl at the swimming pool who, mistaking his appearance for his age, flirted boldly with him, to his puzzlement. Perhaps it was another incident he recalled, one which could carry the weight his story gives to it.

Walking along Eastbourne front in the school holidays, he looked carefully at the faces of the girls who passed him. Some freckled and pleasant, attracted him instantly: any one of these would have been his sympathiser, and he turned heavily into the swimming baths, wishing that one of these faces could have belonged to an acquaintance. The pleasant artificial smell of the baths dispelled his gloom immediately. He changed quickly and climbed to the highest diving board. Here he stood rigid with muscles braced, yet trying to look as though each sinew stood thus in his body always. Two old women on the balcony regarded him with obvious admiration and whispered comments. Below him a hirsute out-of-condition young man leaned smoking against a pillar and shook ash into the bath. He was not interested in divers; his piggy eyes were turned with X-ray interest upon the charms of the baths attendant. Peter dived. He kept his body scrupulously straight, looking down upon the water as the air sang past him. Only a sideways wriggle in the air enabled him to avoid an underwater swimmer who broke surface suddenly beneath him, and he swam painfully to the rail smarting from flat impact with the water. The underwater swimmer followed him. She was small

The story finishes here, but at a New Year's Eve Dance in 1937, Douglas met someone who promised to be the sympathizer he sought.

Back at school for the new term, safe in his study from the January rain outside, he found a letter waiting for him. He replied at once.

[1] Actually, Douglas's eyes were blue.

Keith Douglas

Dear Chris,

M.H.R. for your birthday and really thank you for your letter—it was lovely to find it waiting for me when I arrived in the evening and the rain. I shall love writing to you because we never had to make friends, we just were more or less immediately, and I know there's nothing I need leave out of letters to you. There are millions of things I can't tell mother and long to tell someone, so I shall never lack any material for letters. You are in for an interesting time. . . .

Chris, in spite of all your Pat Rats (or is it Wratts?) and Glessings, are you rather lonely? I wonder, because you and I may have a lot of things in common.

Having written ten pages, Douglas rewrote the last one in the morning, certain that Chris (or Kristin, as he came to call her) would have found what he had written first as silly as he, unless she read it at night: 'I don't know, but I seem to have an infinite capacity for dreaming stupid dreams at nights and evenings, and they get into the letters I write then.'

The rest of Douglas's letter had reflected not loneliness, but a captivating enthusiasm for everything around him. 'THIS IS A HELLUVA LETTER. TAKE YOUR TIME', was at its head. What he wanted to share with the sympathizer was his capacity for life, the fertility of mind which made the observations and images of his poetry. Part of his trouble in class had stemmed from a real inability to suppress the mass of responses he could not help making. It never resulted from vacancy.[1]

His thoughts wandered, and as always on summer mornings, he could not read the book, for listening to the innumerable noises which told him small descriptive stories; of a man walking in big boots along one of the asphalt paths, a violin unskilfully scraped in the music school, a tractor dragging the great roller over the cricket pitch.

Douglas is not working up details for this notebook fragment, he is drawing on an endless supply of material from his own experience. Here, the fragment's protagonist considers Bishop Stubbs, who spent his youth learning Anglo-Saxon, a 'weed': he prefers to look out of the window at the gardener:

he could see the brown little man his face hidden under a large hat, his bare arms moving industriously as he picked grass from the blades of the mower. The face appeared after a moment, as he turned to wink through the glass at Ian, a small merry countenance like a squirrel's.

For Kristin, Douglas turned such capacities into a sharing of his world and an interest in hers.

[1] Mrs. Douglas has also suggested that his tendency to hay-fever and earlier suffering from asthma made him uncomfortable indoors for long periods in the summer.

With the detailed description of his study, its pictures and stains, the model brigantine he had made and placed on the mantelpiece, Douglas gave her an entrée into his universe. Through his concern for dress, colour, and style, he would go out to hers:

The other thing I wanted to say was, to tell you about the sort of clothes I would design you, if I did design any. You could look (to use your favourite word), marvellous, if you would only wear the right clothes for your figure and colouring. I would hesitate to tell you in a way because you would be surrounded with boys in no time and forget all about me.

Having thus prepared the way with thoughtful charm, Douglas immerses himself in a set of specific suggestions, remarkable for their good sense:

First, never wear dresses when you needn't. Your figure is either willowy or skinny. If you wear a roughish but well-cut tweed coat and skirt, brown or dark green, plain or check (small check), you are willowy and lovely, an open-air lady immediately—lipstick and nail-polish to match would help. In your thin dress you are skinny and unhappy-looking. Go in for checks and autumn sort of woven scarves and you would be the best of yourself, and attractive. You may despise sporty people, but they dress well.

At this point he sketched Kristin in coat and skirt, with 'tough "golfy" sort of shoes', putting her in a wind, 'because you look best windswept', and apologizing for making it blow in two directions at once. Then he offered his general views on colour and clothing. He had given a similar defence of

59

simplicity to Noel Burdett while cycling home from one of their rides at Southwater. To Kristin he wrote:

You wear a pale blue polo sweater but you would look yards better in dark brown or green. Your colours are the colours of woods and fields in summer and autumn—open air colours—the best colours in the world. Chris don't be offended by all this, but I would love you to look as nice as I know you could. The reds and yellows you wear now aren't the good clean eternal colours that the medieval people and the Greeks—the best dressed the world has ever seen—wore. They weren't thought of until mass-production and state-run brothels were invented. Will you do this thing for me and dress like this, (if your mother will let you).

If I can do anything to look better for you, tell me when you write. Who knows, even I might look presentable with someone else's advice!

This sort of honest caring, offering advice as tactful as it is frank, Douglas never lost.[1] But his tact, depending as it did on frankness, was readily misunderstood: then he was all too successful at proving his insensitivity.

Douglas knew he had an ally in Kristin, someone to whom he could express his enthusiasms as freely as his dissatisfactions, and in the summer he wrote her a love poem:

> This season like a child on airy points
> Has crept behind you in an evening time
> To take you unawares and touch your hair
> With a gift of gold; or like a messenger
> Arrives on the scene saying a god's wants,
> To exile the dull colours and make us sublime. . . .

Their love is a 'country interlude', made poignant by an awareness of 'black days' which 'lean over', 'hours curtailed with fear'. Douglas was as much aware as anyone of the meaning of Europe's crisis that summer, but as lover and poet he responded like a good cavalier:

> A little forlorn magic has homed again.
> Take this, these limpid days will not be constant;
> They will forsake you, will not reappear.

If the lyricism of this poem, 'Kristin', derives from love, it was nevertheless a mood which had returned to his work in this last year at school.

'Commission' had found the point of contact between Douglas's boisterous assertiveness and the poetry of socialist contemporaries, writers like C. Day-Lewis and Rex Warner: now he seized on the opportunities for fanciful boldness and boyish lyricism in the poets of his decade. Reeds

---

[1] At Oxford he warned Raymond Pennock off a blue jacket, with a tact which Pennock still remembers warmly.

'huddle like chums' while he watches 'The busybody engine' in the distance, and hears the horse's hooves 'Smack on the odd stone' 'like a pistol'. There is impending sadness, but who is to tell when the divine nurse wakes up and 'takes away our toys' which kind of person will 'catch tears in his simple hand' ('Point of View'). A storm will 'Retire muttering into a smutty corner' and the sun return 'like a tired giant' ('Sonnet'); or the sun will arrive like a messenger, sending dull colours into 'exile' ('Kristin'). From this compound of wit and sympathy, Douglas made the poem which finally won his bet with Ilett and in March 1938 gained a place in *New Verse*:

DEJECTION

Yesterday travellers in summer's country,
Tonight the sprinkled moon and ravenous sky
Say, we have reached the boundary. The autumn clothes
Are on; Death is the season and we the living
Are hailed by the solitary to join their regiment,
To leave the sea and the horses and march away
Endlessly. The spheres speak with persuasive voices.

Only tomorrow like a seagull hovers and calls
Shrieks through the mist and scatters the pools of stars.
The windows will be open and hearts behind them.

The sea and the horses are those of his summer holidays at Bexhill; the marching and the regiment, the language of a dedicated O.T.C. sergeant; the loneliness an experience he well knew at the end of summer holidays. But from these experiences Douglas has made an identikit thirties poem: travellers, boundaries, companionship, the outdoor world, indoor cosiness, a refusal to be introverted and an inability to be extroverted, a sense of change and a hope for rest. He managed his change of identity so well that it is not possible to tell how much of it was tongue in cheek: in any case, a note of self-parody was part of the style he was imitating.

A month after the appearance of this piece, *The Outlook* published another poem in similar vein. Where Douglas brings enough of himself to 'Dejection' to make the poem live, here he employs the style as a cover from which he can speak more directly.

ON LEAVING SCHOOL[1]

Here where the years stand under us in the valley
We can look down upon their shops and vineyards
And honestly say, we had rather be like leopards
Let loose in one direction, who cannot be silly.

[1] In *The Outlook* the title was 'Sonnet: Here where the years stand'.

This simple evening moment, when the shallow
Echoes stagger against Big School, it is awkward
Realizing happiness seems just to have started
And now we must leave it, live like trees or charlock.

One of us will be the kettle past care of tinkers,
Rejected, one the tip-top apple, the winking
Sun's friend. It will be that way, and Time on our ground

Will sweep like a maid, and where we were be clean.
Shall we find room to laugh, if turning round
We see where we have walked, how wrong we have been?

Douglas had known since the beginning of the year that he was to try for an Oxford scholarship and in December had gone up to Merton for the few days of the examinations which were held in Christ Church Hall. After Christmas he learned he had been awarded an Open Exhibition in history at Merton, with an option to read English once he got there. The uncertainties of his future were settled; and in the same issue of *The Outlook* as 'On Leaving School', he published another view of departure. There Douglas explained how 'Going Away' (his essay's title) was part of 'the art of living': depending on timing, good judgement, and seeing, as it were, 'both sides of the coin'. To illustrate such art, he opened his essay with a specific departure, choosing neither the death of Socrates nor Orpheus *en route* for the underworld:

The man was large and pompous: he ought to have been called Mr. Troutbeck, or Purdle; no doubt he was. And as he said goodbye to his wife in the next compartment, I saw that his nose was very large. Large noses always tempt me, and as the train began to move, I said, 'Excuse me, sir,' and pulled this one. The train gathered speed, and he and the platform were hidden by a bend.

But how different it would have been if the train had stopped again after a few yards, as trains do, with Mr. Purdle free to storm up the platform behind his injured nose. The absurd episode would have been incomplete and disastrous, as many more serious have been for the same reason. For a great measure of the art of living lies in knowing when to remain and when to go away.

In July Douglas left Christ's Hospital, without having called 'Mr. Dandy' a drunkard or pulled Mr. Flecker's nose. He had, however, enjoyed a final scandal. With rumours of war causing the various arms of the forces to make preparations, Douglas wrote direct to the War Minister, Hore-Belisha, protesting at the Ministry's failure to equip the Christ's Hospital O.T.C. with gas masks. Thus he broke the rules of both the Corps and the school by going over the heads of the officer in charge and the headmaster. He was again summoned to be reprimanded, but this time he had behind him the security of his Oxford scholarship.

Christ's Hospital Grecians, May 1938. Second row, third from left, H. L. O. Flecker, headmaster; Adams, fourth from left; Hatten, front row, third from left; KD (in spectacles), back row, second from left.

Yet Douglas's departure from school had all the appearances of a model success. He had his colours for rugby and swimming, his contributions to *The Outlook* and *The Blue*, and his Open Scholar's prize; and in his final term he won the Lamb Essay medal with an essay on Sussex.[1] For all the unhappiness of his middle years at school, Douglas was leaving the place which had been his home for seven years, and it was a place where he had found appreciation. Roberts later wrote of him as 'the most brilliant and the most cantankerous' of his pupils; Hornsby, as one of the most difficult boys he was ever to encounter and one of the cleverest. In the 'House Notes' of the following term's issue of *The Blue* Middleton B recorded its loss:

[1] For the Open Scholar's prize he chose Francis Thompson's *Poems* and *The Oxford Book of French Verse*; for the Lamb Essay prize, Auden's *Poems* (1933), John Hampden's *Fifteen Modern Plays*, and Butler's *The Way of All Flesh*. W. R. Macklin, judge of the Lamb Essay competition, many years later remembered a phrase from Douglas's essay: 'the spinster faces of the sheep'.

Keith Douglas

Douglas has gone where he can work on the floor without either splinters or rebuke; no longer does the welkin ring with the strains of some almost unrecognizable ditty, and no longer does the homely smell of horse pervade our changing-rooms and dormitories. Only an odd spur or riding crop here and there remains to recall the glories of the past.[1]

On the day Douglas left, Hornsby went on his customary patrol round his House, clearing the débris of joyful departures. In Douglas's study he saw a bundle of old exercise books stuffed into a wastepaper basket. Taking them out he kept them for thirty years.

[1] The writer was Norman Ilett.

3

Oxford

October 1938 - June 1940

This then is the city of young men . . .
('Oxford')

I

At Merton Douglas was given a large sunny ground-floor room in Fellows' Quad.[1] On either side of the fireplace, a long window, with a window seat, gave him a view across the Fellows' garden. To one side of its avenue of limes was a fine prospect of Magdalen Tower: to the other side, Christ Church meadow; and to complete the scene Douglas had his 'masterpiece', a painting of race-horses, expensively framed and hung it above the fireplace, with a red candle in a bottle at either end of the mantelpiece. Having thus done justice to the elegance of his new surroundings, Douglas soon made them unmistakably his own by covering the other walls with his own pictures, and littering floor, chairs, and window seats with half-finished works. His apparent unconcern for their safety amazed his less obviously talented visitors, while his display of his own work could impress the unconfident as a sign of his self-satisfaction.

Merton presented a reasonably varied social population, with a proportion of its undergraduates coming from grammar schools. But Oxford in 1938 still seemed to offer the newcomer a choice between ways of life, defined by the public school boys who dominated its society. Those who wrote poetry or painted not only took delight in their release from compulsory games, they determined to look like poets and artists. Those who sought pleasure in rugby and rowing, boozing and rags, despised the artists and determined to look like hearties. However crude such distinctions, they were cherished by many as essential to Oxford's character; and in a world of chance meetings and new acquaintances social clichés die hard. By temperament Douglas had long refused to recognize such categories and Christ's Hospital had encouraged that refusal. Now he was in a place where his mixture of interests and talents was proof of his independence, attracting

[1] Now the office of the Domestic Bursar: number 2.2.

65

to him those who were unwilling to commit themselves to either orthodoxy.

Douglas cared about dress, clothing himself in a manner which was at once striking and in defiance of both the aesthetic and the hearty: a red shirt, cravat, and labourer's corduroys which squeaked as he moved, a hacking jacket and riding breeches, a gown and plimsolls. Such attire made him readily recognizable, even if his short sight and refusal to wear his glasses for reasons of vanity meant that he could not recognize you.

As expected, Douglas had transferred to English on arriving at Merton, and whatever his schoolboy feelings about Bishop Stubbs and Anglo-Saxon, he became 'captivated' by *Beowulf*. With Childe's translation of this poem and Saintsbury's *History of English Literature* on his shelves he happily argued the superiority of Henryson to Dunbar, for his 'greater grasp of word-music', and showed no distaste for a course which concentrated on earlier literature. His tutor, Edmund Blunden, found him considerate and attentive, working well at his weekly essays which were fluent and attractive, even if he 'did not care about novelty when he was finding his way'.

Douglas was fortunate in his tutor, for Blunden was not only known for his patient and scholarly concern for his undergraduates, he was a devoted old boy of Christ's Hospital. Showing great sympathy towards all his students, Blunden felt closer to anyone from his school and especially if that person were a poet. In May 1940, he wrote thanking Douglas for showing him a collection of his manuscript poems: 'We have had some pretty good poets, Peele, Coleridge, Lamb, Hunt, but the line must be extended! and I think you can do it.' Douglas, in turn, treated Blunden with a courtesy and sensitivity which impressed his fellow-undergraduates. Several have recalled how Douglas made a point of inviting Blunden to gatherings which the tutor would have been shy of attending without invitation.

A month after Douglas came up to Merton, Blunden suggested that he should meet another Oxford poet, Margaret Stanley-Wrench, who was in her fourth year at Somerville and had recently published a first volume. Douglas had little desire to meet Oxford writers, and his difference in standing within the University led him to approach her with diffidence.

Dear Miss Stanley-Wrench,
    Mr. Blunden, referring to you as the Senior Poetess in statu pu., a rather forbidding title, suggests that I, being about the most junior incipient poet, introduce myself to you. I said you would be too busy and know too many people already; and if you are and do, I shan't be particularly put out if you don't answer this. . . .

Further protecting himself with the postscript, 'You won't have to read my poems', Douglas made his invitation. Margaret accepted, and within a week he was invited back to Somerville: 'I shall be terrified of venturing within a women's college. Won't I be stopped and interrogated at the frontier?' On this visit, he read her poems and said that he did not like them, but he praised her drawings.

Margaret had found Douglas attractive company, writing to her mother after their first meeting that he was 'quite pleasant looking . . . very self-assured, writes poetry, paints remarkably well, has a distinct personality and rides and likes horses': such interests coincided with hers. After their second meeting, she gave a more detailed account to her mother:

> He is a very opinionated young man, but not unpleasantly so, because he has a lot of sense. He is remarkably mature and confident. He must be only nineteen, if that, but looks quite twenty or twenty-one, fair, with hair falling over his forehead in half curling locks, rather like a mane, a fresh complexion, in glasses, thickish brows, pleasant features, tall and long-legged. . . . He is very athletic looking, and evidently fond of sports as well as reading and so on.

As an independent woman poet in the largely masculine world of the University, Margaret was delighted by the way in which Douglas treated her without the slightest patronage, towards the end of her letter making an observation which was later to be echoed by two other girls[1] whom Douglas met and befriended at Oxford: 'It is a relief to find a man who is completely unconscious of sex difference and so completely at ease.'

For with certain girls Douglas was able to establish a thoroughly straightforward friendship. With Margaret he simply talked about painting and horses and occasionally went riding. Sometimes they would discuss poetry, but literature was never the centre of their friendship. Her friend, Jean Turner, whom he saw more of when Margaret was preoccupied with the business of a last term at university, did not write at all. Although Douglas steadily sent poems to various magazines, he had no desire to join a literary milieu. Had Blunden not introduced him to Miss Stanley-Wrench he could well have passed the year without the friendship of a single poet. John Waller had something of a literary circle at Oxford at this time, but although Douglas published in his *Bolero* and later in *Kingdom Come*, beyond a visit for tea and a party or two he saw little of him. John Hall included his work in the Oxford and Cambridge magazine *Fords and Bridges*, of which he was the Oxford editor, but Douglas met him only once or twice. Douglas made no secret of his writing, many of his friends remembering the sight of him intently revising and redrafting his work, but he met no one's expectations of a poet. Hamo Sassoon, a nephew of Siegfried Sassoon who had spent most of his school holidays with his uncle and was familiar with his dedication, recalls that to him Douglas, working away at a typewriter, appeared a poet by determination rather than by nature.

[1] Jean Turner and Joan Appleton.

While the company of poets did not attract Douglas, he joined the Mounted Section of the University's O.T.C., partly for the chance of free riding, as soon as he arrived at Merton, going with Sassoon to its 7.30 meetings a couple of mornings each week.[1] He also kept up his rugby, playing hooker for his college and befriending Raymond Pennock, also in the team. Pennock recalls that Douglas was always anxious to learn how he had played, being keen not to lose his place and worried about his eyesight: 'It's all right for you,' he told Pennock. 'You can see!'

Rugby players, O.T.C. men, friends met at the English Club or at lectures, college acquaintances, and as he became more settled, numerous girls, made up a steady stream of visitors to his room in Fellows' Quad. It was quite a meeting place, and as it was the best route for nocturnal entry into the college the visitations continued into the night. During the day at least, Douglas welcomed all who came, but not directly: he stayed stretched out on the floor, writing or painting, modelling or drawing, while the visitors entertained each other or looked after the girl friend waiting for him to finish whatever he was doing. Douglas loved being surrounded by people while he worked, the gregariousness heightened by jazz or classical music on the gramophone. Then he would shout at everyone to get out or suggest a trip to the Moorish for morning coffee and cream at three-pence a cup or an à la carte tea.

When he was not the silent centre of affairs in his own room Douglas was upstairs with Hamo Sassoon, 'another non-conversationalist', recalled a Merton acquaintance. There he found a much better fire than he could afford and company as undemanding as it was entertaining. Sassoon was as fanatical as Douglas about making things. With chalk collected from the Chilterns, and clay which, to the horror of a college scout, they prepared in chamber pots, they shaped masks and medieval figurines. While Douglas typed his poems, Sassoon sculpted, and in the intervals of their labours they did Swedish gymnastics on the floor, inviting visitors to join them in tossing about a medicine ball, doing press-ups, or standing on their hands. Visitors were also entertained by their game of classifying people into various types. One version of this, drawn by Douglas from a Christ's Hospital pastime, divided people into 'fiends' and others.[2] The fiends, taken from a wry misreading of Milton's 'the superior fiend', possessed a certain charm, lack of orthodoxy, and ability to be slightly incalculable. Recalling the game, Mary Oswin, a friend of Margaret Stanley-Wrench's,

[1] Sassoon also recalls that he felt Douglas, with his habit of leaving spurs and riding crop strategically placed on a chair, as he candidly explained, to impress visitors, had decided on the kind of poet he would be: one who was sporting and courageous.

[2] The game was an adaptation of one invented by John Adams. Norman Ilett recalls that at Housey the 'fiends' were the school workmen, 'especially those who worked in the Tube —the underground passage where the heating pipes were: Beelzebub, Moloch, etc.'

Self-portrait, 1939

gave as example of a fiend, Chico Marx. A second system, based mainly on facial types, divided into 'earwigs, spints, and bun faces'. A spint, Hamo Sassoon says, was someone who could get his trousers off without undoing the fly.

The return to Bexhill for Christmas and the usual search for rooms, as his mother had let the bungalow, painfully contrasted with his new life at Oxford. With grants which left him forty-three pounds after payment of college fees, he had money enough for term-time expenses: though he and Sassoon, who was not himself hard up, competed with each other over living cheaply. Sassoon remembers a diet of brown bread, brown sugar, and margarine, supplemented by occasional visits to the Taj Mahal restaurant where a huge bowl of rice left nothing to desire. But Douglas was hopelessly

Watching eights: Jean Turner, Mary Oswin, Margaret Stanley-Wrench

unrealistic about money. Midway between Robin Hood and Harold Skimpole, he was recklessly generous when he had it, and when others had it and he had not, he expected them to be the same. As he was generally without, the arrangement was not as equitable as he would have liked it to be.

The Christmas holiday that year Douglas and his mother spent with the Mileses, but thanking Margaret Stanley-Wrench for her card at the end of December he wrote, 'stranded at a Tea Room with nowhere to go until we find a house or a flat'. None the less, he returned for the Hilary term equipped with a 'lovat weskit' and red navvy's handkerchief so as to be suitably dressed to accompany Margaret and Mary Oswin to the University Drag's point-to-point.

The University had given him a way of life which he had long desired, and as often as possible he invited his mother to Oxford to share it with him. Like his other visitors she was generally left to entertain herself as she chose, but in Douglas's behaviour with her, Pennock recalled, there seemed a kind of pride, a proof of an understanding which did not need words. Hornsby also visited, finding Douglas's rooms 'indescribably untidy, paintings all over the floor' and Douglas lying in the middle of them writing or preparing to do more painting, 'unwashed, unshaven and frightful!' He invited Douglas to lunch, 'but not like that', and after Douglas had tidied himself up they went for an enjoyable meal, over which, Hornsby recalls, Douglas 'talked with zest and enthusiasm about Oxford, Blunden, art, games and Hitler'. Kristin also came once to Merton, but their friendship waned under the pressure of Douglas's new life.

2

In February Douglas met Yingcheng. Her father had at one time been Chinese Ambassador to Washington. Sophisticated and thoroughly westernized, she had come from Cheltenham Ladies' College to Lady Margaret Hall, and seemed older than most of the other undergraduates; though not yet twenty, she was a well-known and much sought-after figure in Oxford social life. She was secretary of the China Society, a University club which attracted dons and townspeople as well as undergraduates who, a few years earlier, would have supported the Spanish Republicans. Douglas was not interested in politics beyond the pleasure of general argument, but he joined both the Labour Club and the China Society for their excellent dances and good selection of partners. He asked if he could do Yingcheng's portrait. She agreed, and increasingly they were seen about together.

Yingcheng found Douglas interestingly unlike the other young men she knew at Oxford: a writer and artist whose certainty about what he would achieve through his talents contrasted with the casual, unmotivated assurance of her more privileged friends. The youthful pleasures of Oxford, which they could take for granted, Douglas approached with the enthusiasm of someone to whom such pleasures were obviously new. He was 'unconventional, strikingly individual', she recalls, and they had met at a time when she was undecided about whether she wanted to remain in the milieu in which she had been brought up. To Douglas she was a new kind of person, a prize infinitely removed from the Housey world he had unhabited only a few months earlier, and someone sensitive and intelligent. Later in the year, he drove to Christ's Hospital with Yingcheng in a red sports car, 'a sporty little Riley roadster that he and I chose secondhand'. It was an ambition, he told an Oxford friend, he had long waited to fulfil; to complete the effect, Yingcheng recalls, 'he made me wear a Chinese dress—determined to emphasize the exotic!' Middleton B was appropriately impressed, Hornsby, Ilett, and Mrs. Roberts all well remembering the stir the visit caused. And at Merton, the sight of Yingcheng patiently waiting in Douglas's room impressed his friends to the point of envy.

Three times Douglas painted portraits of Yingcheng, and he courted her as a poet in little doubt of his having rivals but hopeful that his poems would plead his cause.

> *To his lady, who must not be too critical,*
> *these verses of a bewildered poet.*[1]

> What in the pattern of your face
> was writing to my eye, which came at once

[1] Published by Douglas the following year as 'Stranger: For Y.C.S.' The version sent to Yingcheng is quoted here: it differs slightly from that in *Collected Poems*.

like a prisoner in your beauty's land
to find that venerable secret stand
somehow carved there, and ever since
has rested still, enchanted by the place?

Cast up along your eyes' dark shore
there, or in the carved red cave of lips,
my heart would spend a solitary spell,
delighted hermit in his royal cell.
For your eyes and precious mouth perhaps
are blessed isles once found and found no more.

You are the whole continent of love
for me, the windy sailor on this ocean,
who'd lose his ragged vessel to the waves
and call on you, the strange land, to save.
Here I set up my altar and devotion,
and let no storm blot out the place I have.

Gone is the alert Audenesque explorer of the school poems, and in its place an openly romantic poet who transforms the magic and shipwrecks he had found in Shakespeare's last plays into a landscape of love. However literary and full-blown his style Douglas established through his metaphors an unmistakable emphasis. This is a love which expresses its excitement through images of danger. This lover, shipwrecked, lost at sea, claiming triumph through dependence, insists that he is a Ferdinand on Prospero's island, for otherwise he is an enchanted Ulysses. Accompanying his poem with a letter, Douglas had opened: 'These lines, written by the famous poet in his youth, just before he went to the dogs over a woman, are more sincere than they sound.'

The edges of Douglas's character remained, and the new emphasis Margaret Stanley-Wrench placed in a letter to her mother in January: 'That Keith is as self-assured and self-possessed as any child, and pretty nearly as petulant', gave a view which increased in relevance. For as he committed himself increasingly to Yingcheng Douglas's character sharpened to the point where it was once more cutting. With Mary Oswin who first met him at the point-to-point, Douglas appeared 'rather cold and arrogant, class-conscious to the point of snobbery, and perhaps rather too prone to call people fools if he thought they were.' Her socialist ideals he considered either naïve or self-deluding: for him politics was a mythology and he could not stand the socialists' illusion that their mythology offered realistic, logical answers. Despite their wrangles Mary Oswin also recalls his gratitude to those who, like Blunden, helped him, and she recognized that he possessed a kind of authority: he seemed 'somebody, a personage',

Perhaps you would like Ophelia for your name?
Ophelia Sze; perhaps not. Personally although I admit
Margaret isn't good, Marguerite Sze sounds well enough.
The trouble with Margaret is that it is Marguerite faded,
all the scent gone & a poor dusty blossom altogether.

Do you remember which piece of wall we sat on,
where for 10 seconds you became one of the world's great
heroines? I shan't bother to go & sit there but my
shadow will be on duty for me. When you have given
me up and spoilt the few good bits there are left in
my heart, you will see that shadow every time you come
past late at night. Maybe it will come & block the way
of whatever man is with you, like the angel standing
in the donkey's path.

I suppose you have read A. E. Housman. If you
will take as from me the saddest and most moving
love poem he ever wrote, and read it well, you will
have much better what I want to say than I could
tell you.

I will forget you sometimes, & since I must be
sad sometimes, I may as well be sad about you,
and who knows what gracious experiences await me
when one is complete. There are so many for everyone

    Stars, I have seen them fall
    but when they drop & die,
    No star is lost at all
    From all the star sown sky.

Good old sky! I shall keep my eye on it.
             yours etc
              The old flame

P.S. buy me a telescope.

To Yingcheng, from the letter enclosing 'Stranger'

and if not exactly likeable, 'valuable'. After a violent quarrel with her
Douglas wrote 'Poor Mary', and published it to annoy her.

> Death has made up your face, his quiet hand
> Perfects your costume to impersonate
> The one who cannot enter this living land.
>
> And it is death who makes sure, and chances
> No tenderness in the recesses of your eyes.
> In the halls of your heart no spirit dances,

73

> But you are the house of sorrow. In you all
> Colours are dark and casemented for ever,
> No answering song inside the cold wall. . . .

Alongside such a mood, however, Douglas could express an increasingly hopeful lyricism. Watching 'That high-decked cloud adventuring along' in 'Spring Sailor', he can think of the 'marvellous story without words, and still / Beyond your speech', and respond to the melancholy of twilight without succumbing to unease:

> I will contrive to escape the dainty touch
> Of a day so heavy with the imagery
> Of longing. And the various eyes of earth
> Opening, the dreams ready for their rebirth,
> Even the gentle hands of earth for me
> Shall move without disquieting me much.

His poetry was better served by the impulse of abusing Mary, but his romantic dreams regained something of their earlier security, an immunity to the world outside, as they drew on his new-found sympathizer, Ying-cheng.

In the Easter vacation Douglas was spared the discomforts of a stay at Bexhill by travelling to France for a cycling holiday with Hamo Sassoon. Riding from Dieppe to Amiens and Soissons and then back via Paris, they made the last leg to Dieppe and the night Channel boat in one stretch. It was a simple holiday, most clearly remembered by Sassoon for the ride back to Dieppe, with him carrying their luggage for fear that Douglas's old bike would not otherwise make the journey; and their becoming separated in a crowd on the way to Amiens, to rejoin there by chance. When they met Douglas was not so much perturbed by the fact that he had left his money with Sassoon, as curious to learn whether Sassoon had followed the directions he had marked on stones along his route.

After spending their nights in chicken houses and by the roadside, at Soissons they put up at a good hotel. For the first time they ate a huge meal and drank champagne, their high spirits leading them to perform handstands and backflips at midnight on the steps of the cathedral where earlier in the day they had watched a stonemason at work. From such beginnings Douglas made a poem, 'Soissons'. There the city is an image of the Old World restored, a place where the white-hatted M. l'Épicier makes gargoyles 'from the selfsame stone / men used in the religious century'. Aquileia had monuments, Soissons a surviving tradition in which the cathedral, damaged in the Great War, 'in new masonry' could stand 'openly in this sunlit town'. Douglas and Hamo heard Daladier announce over the wireless that Germany had betrayed the Munich agreement; but writing of Soissons Douglas subsumed the reminders of war nearly as thoroughly as thoughts of shipwreck in 'Stranger'. The sounding of 'the equivalent of Lights Out' from the barracks of the Nineteenth Regiment is allowed to suggest the peace of evening more strongly than the presence of an army. There is an undercurrent none the less. What in Gorizia had been 'old wine with a new tang' now has an effect more of evasion than pleasure:

> Now the sweet-sour
> wine clambers in our heads. Go in. Tomorrow
> tiptoes with us along the dark landing.

And by the end of the poem Douglas has granted the omens their place.

> 'A Laon, belle Cathédrale,' making
> a wave of his white hat, explains
> the maker of gargoyles. So we take
> a route for Laon and Rheims leaving you
> Soissons, a simplified medieval view
> taken from a Book of Hours. How dark
> seems the whole country we enter. Now it rains,
> and trees like ominous old men are shaking.

Allowing the future to enter his poem, Douglas nevertheless makes from its menace a moving lyrical moment.

Learning, on their return to the University, that Hitler had denounced the Anglo-German naval agreement and the Polish non-aggression treaty, made this first Oxford summer look more like a last. With Yingcheng, however, bad news coming 'like black birds' on 'dire wings from Europe' could be defeated. In 'Invaders' Douglas outlined the dangers: she will not care for her beauty, he will not 'write a word to escape'. Their life will 'take on a hard shape', drained of sensitivity, and then, 'if we are spared we shall not arise / to hold the world up when it finally slips.' The world depends on their resistance, and this they must offer:

> So keep a highlight in your handsome eye;
> still be fastidious, and I will write
> some well-intentioned words. We with our heart
> still sensitive as air will do our part,
> always to think, and always to indite
> of a good matter, while the black birds cry.

It was easier, perhaps to face the ominous news than the immediacies of his relationship with Yingcheng. For in May he sent her a poem which replaced the committed lover with one whose courtship had been

75

forestalled by an emissary of Death, 'To a Lady on the Death of Her First Love'.

> O rich man, death, you sent your creature
> from your country, disguised with life, to steal
> a gem you never wanted. You cannot feel
> its worth. She yielded with the first gesture
> of her awakened hand. My darling—look—
>
> it was death's emissary who took your love
> to hoard it in the quiet land, nowhere.
> He followed death's instructions from the start,
> and when you said goodbye, he stepped apart
> delivering the stone to death, the rare
> bright plunder. Death retains the precious stuff. . . .

His service is still hers, 'for the little profit I enjoy of it'.

Most of the summer term Douglas spent lazing with Yingcheng on the lawns at Merton or in a punt on the upper reaches of the Cherwell. He day-dreamed, told her of plans for their future travels and his art, or said nothing at all.

> Please, on a day falling in summer,
> recall how being tired, you and I
> among the idle branches by the river
> and blind to propriety and passers-by,
> where leaves like eyes turn sidelong to the river,
> fell asleep embraced and let the shades run
> half crossing us, and half the vigorous sun,
> till he had almost climbed enough.
>
> ('Farewell Poem')

The tapestried sun of 'Youth' has come out of its picture to play its effects of light and shade upon real people, warming them to real indolence.

In the rest of his Oxford life Douglas had little interest. Margaret Stanley-Wrench occasionally saw him at lectures, commenting to her mother that he now breathed loudly, creaked his seat, and looked ostentatiously at her watch, broadcasting his boredom. Probably Douglas only attended in order to feel that he was keeping up with the work left undone elsewhere. With Jean Turner, at St. Hilda's, Douglas started a friendship based on a mutual, jocular rudeness; he found Jean a refreshingly open person. But he saw little of her, for all his time was Yingcheng's. By June he was anxious that they should become engaged, giving Yingcheng a silver ring, 'St. George and the Dragon carved in a shield shape', she remembers, 'that reached from knuckle to first joint—that I wore on my right hand'.

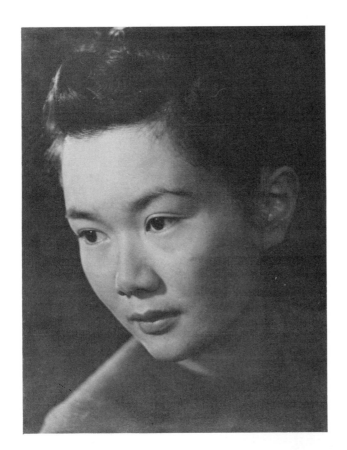

Yingcheng, 1939. (*Below, left*) In the garden of her Banbury Road flat;
(*right*) KD's watercolour portrait of her

At the end of the summer term, for what could well be their last chance to exploit happiness before the world 'hardened', Douglas suggested a trip to Paris. Yingcheng agreed but not with the same feelings as Douglas. For some time she had realized that his involvement was far greater than hers, but each suggestion she had made that they might separate for a while, had met with a blankness which proved Douglas's genuine incomprehension. She had met Mrs. Douglas; later, on moving from Lady Margaret Hall to a flat in Banbury Road, she invited her to stay. They got on well, and Mrs. Douglas had found no difficulty in understanding the source of her son's attraction; but she too realized the imbalance of feeling and could not think of a way the relationship could end gently. In Paris, Yingcheng hoped, the different environment would help to clarify her feelings.

Late in June they set off, as a foursome, with a Rhodes scholar and a New Zealand girl, Yingcheng helping with Douglas's hotel expenses but Douglas insisting on finding money enough for his ticket. The week was uneasy, and ended with Douglas returning to Bexhill and Yingcheng sailing, as already planned, for Bermuda. For Yingcheng, as she recalled, Douglas's weaknesses seemed exaggerated away from the Oxford scene. Not only had she found how much uncertainty was masked by his air of self-confidence, but how far his outlook clashed with everything familiar to her. Even his single-mindedness now seemed to her a defect rather than an asset. On seeing more of him she had come to feel that he was 'not a very male man' and seemed to enjoy depending on a woman.

For two months Douglas hoped that the end of their holiday had been no more than a temporary setback. In July he read in the library at Christ's Hospital, staying with his mother at Hadlow Down, Sussex, where she was companion to an elderly lady. In August Norman Ilett met him again at the Brodies' where he and a few others still at Housey were staying to work on a local farm. He remembers Douglas as 'very down' and a final 'come back and marry me' telegram he sent to Yingcheng. Hesitant over hurting him, she had replied to his letters from Bermuda, though Douglas felt that her letters spoke only of the good time she was having and 'how many handsome young men' were there. Yingcheng recalled: 'I hoped the long summer apart might solve my problem, but it proved harder than I had anticipated, so in the end I was cruelly blunt.' Her final letter, Douglas told Jean Turner in November, 'complained of me insulting her, said she had only been kind to me because she thought I needed encouragement as an artist, and now I could go to hell.'

Douglas had one more thoroughly unrealistic scheme, to take a winter semester in Munich, and he arranged with his college for a couple of terms off. But on 3 September Chamberlain announced that Britain was at war with Germany. Douglas was with his mother at the Mileses' new rectory at

Withyham in Kent. A friend of the Mileses, Stephen Hearst, recalls that after the broadcast he and Douglas sat on the lawn looking across the Sussex landscape, saying nothing. Douglas returned at once to Oxford. Among those who had come up to collect their belongings was C. T. Hatten, the former editor of *The Outlook* and captain of school in Douglas's last year at Housey. They had lunch together, Douglas telling him about his trip with Yingcheng, and in the afternoon visited the Cowley Road garage where Yingcheng had left the red sports car. Asking the girl there if she had news of Yingcheng, Douglas was told she was going to be married. Hatten remembers that he 'took this news with impassivity and then said to me, "Anyway, I had that week in Paris." ' On 6 September Douglas reported to No. 15 Reception Unit, in Manor Road, to enlist in the 'Cavalry of the Line'. Pennock was there, and Latimer, and two other friends from college. Afterwards they met in the Rector's Garden, and there, Pennock recalls, Douglas announced that he would join a good cavalry regiment and 'bloody well make my mark in this war. For I will not come back.' The force of his conviction impressed them and it was renewed when, passing a Great War memorial, he casually commented that his name would be on the next one.

3

Douglas, like other undergraduates in his age group, was not called up at once: so in October, for what promised to be a single term of University life, he returned to an Oxford already changed by war. Sandbags protected buildings and afforded shelter from expected air raids; and while there seemed to be innumerable civil servants, evacuated with their Departments from London, there were fewer undergraduates.[1] As his Merton rooms were in the part of the college taken over by the Ministry of Agriculture and Fisheries, he moved across the road, with most of his friends, to a crowded University College. If this meant the loss of his fine room at Merton, at least it removed him from its disquieting associations. But the continued presence of Yingcheng in Oxford gave little hope of forgetting.

Douglas, in fact, did not keep out of her way. He sustained a friendship which his friends felt, and Yingcheng knew, he would have been only too happy to see return to its former status. Within the first month of the new term, however, Douglas had plunged into a new relationship.

I knew my only chance of getting over this affair properly was to get someone quickly. Also I was determined not to fall flat for any one person. So I arranged all sorts of meetings, some through Yingcheng and some on my own. But unfortunately they rather fell through when I had that evening with you on Wednesday: and ever since I first heard of this bust up with Yingcheng I've been trying

[1] Hamo Sassoon was among those who had gone, though not to join the forces.

79

No............ Name _DOUGLAS K.C._ .... Corps _Cavalry of the Line_

PART I.

Questions to be put to the Recruit before Enlistment.

1. What is your full name and permanent postal address?
   1. _KEITH CASTELLAIN_
   (Christian Names)
   (Surname) _DOUGLAS_
   (Address) _THE RECTORY_
   WITHYHAM   Sx

2. In or near what Parish or Town were you born?
   2. In the Parish of _WITHYHAM_
   In or near the Town of _TUNBRIDGE WELLS_
   In the County of _SUSSEX_

3. (a) Are you a British Subject?
   (b) Nationality of parents at their birth.
   3. (a) _YES_
   (b) (Father) _SCOTTISH_
   (Mother) _ENGLISH_

4. What is your trade or calling?
   4.

YOU ARE HEREBY WARNED THAT IF AFTER ENLISTMENT IT IS FOUND THAT YOU HAVE GIVEN A WILFULLY FALSE ANSWER TO ANY OF THE FOLLOWING FOUR QUESTIONS YOU WILL BE LIABLE TO PUNISHMENT.

5. (a) What was your age (in years) last birthday?
   (b) Day, month and year of birth
   5. (a) _19_
   (b) _24th JANUARY 1920_

6. (a) Are you married? (b) How many children are dependent upon you?
   6. (a) _NO_
   (b) _NONE_

7. Do you now belong to, or have you ever served in the Royal Navy, the Army, the Royal Air Force, the Royal Marines, the Militia, the Special Reserve, the Supplementary Reserve, the Territorial Force (or Army), the Imperial Yeomanry, the Volunteers, the Auxiliary Air Force, the Army Reserve, the Air Force Reserve, the Militia Reserve or any Naval Reserve Force, or any O.T.C. or Cadet Unit? If so state particulars of all engagements.
   7. _CHRISTS HOSPITAL O.T.C. (Junior Div) Rank of SGT IC ADMINISTRAL. PL. 1934-36. Crop A 1936. OXFORD UNIV: O.T.C. HORSED CAV. SQDN. 1936-9_

8. Have you truly stated the whole, if any, of your previous service?
   8. _YES_

9. Are you willing to be vaccinated or re-vaccinated?
   9. _YES_

10. (a) Are you willing to enlist for General Service?
    (b) Are you willing to serve outside the United Kingdom?
    10. (a) _YES_
    (b) _YES_

11. Are you willing to serve upon the following conditions until the end of the period of embodiment of the Territorial Army, provided His Majesty should so long require your services, which means that you will be required to serve for so long as His Majesty should require your services in connexion with the present emergency for which you are enlisting, and that if you are still serving at the termination of the period of embodiment you will be discharged as soon as your services can be dispensed with thereafter?
    11. _YES_

12. Are you in receipt of a disability pension?
    12. _NO_

13. Have you received a notice paper stating the liabilities you are incurring by enlisting and do you understand and are you willing to accept them?
    13. _YES_
        YES

I, _KEITH CASTELLAIN DOUGLAS_ do solemnly declare that the above answers made by me to the above questions are true, and that I am willing to fulfil the engagements made; also that I understand that, should my health fail or should I sustain an injury during military service, I shall not be eligible for consideration for pension or gratuity on account of disability unless the disability is directly attributable to the conditions of Military Service.

Keith C Douglas ....SIGNATURE OF RECRUIT.

G.E. Allsbrook ....Signature of Witness.

OATH TO BE TAKEN BY RECRUIT ON ATTESTATION.

I, _KEITH CASTELLAIN DOUGLAS_ swear by Almighty God that I will be faithful and bear true allegiance to His Majesty King George the Sixth, His Heirs, and Successors, and that I will, as in duty bound, honestly and faithfully defend His Majesty, His Heirs, and Successors, in Person, Crown, and Dignity against all enemies, and will observe and obey all orders of His Majesty, His Heirs and Successors, and of the Generals and Officers set over me.

CERTIFICATE OF MAGISTRATE OR ATTESTING OFFICER.

I, _John Compton_ do hereby certify that, in my presence, all the foregoing questions were put to the Recruit above-named, that the answers written opposite to them are those which he gave to me, and that he has made and signed the Declaration, and taken the oath at _Manor Rd Oxford_ on this _7th_ day of _September_ 1939.

J. Compton 2/Lt for ASST. ADJT. { Signature of Justice of Peace, Officer, or other person authorised to attest Recruits.

NO. 15 RECEPTION UNIT

If any alteration is required of the Attestation above, a Justice of the Peace should be requested to make it and initial the alteration under Section 80 (6), Army Act. No other manuscript alteration to this Form will be valid, unless authorized by special War Office instructions. The Recruit should receive a Certified copy of his attestation on Army Form E.531A.

Form E531/1. Wt.26139/D1369. 200m. 9/38. D.P.W. T.51-2374.

to make myself fall for several girls—four in fact. I tried very hard because I was terrified of having no one, but it didn't work. As soon as I got away from each of them I knew it was no use. But I never tried to fall in love with you.

The confession was to Antoinette, a younger contemporary of Ying-cheng's at Cheltenham, and introduced to Douglas by her. The previous July she had been presented at Court, and had come up to Lady Margaret Hall that October, to read modern history. Slim, with reddish hair, green eyes, and fine-textured skin, Antoinette seemed to friends at her college and Douglas's friends alike the epitome of the upper-class English girl; she was to recall that to Douglas, who always looked for 'more exotic and clear-cut lines', she was 'unpaintable'. Her family background was artistic and cultivated. Her father, a judge in India, was to become well known as an art historian, and her guardian Douglas described in a letter as 'incredibly rich' and 'someone in art circles'.

But if Antoinette's background naturally equipped her for Oxford, years at boarding school and a 'strong Victorian upbringing' had left her shy and rather quiet in new surroundings, particularly with men. She was attracted to Douglas by the same qualities as had earlier drawn Yingcheng to him. They had in common the lack of a settled family background, Antoinette's parents being in India, and it was this, she later felt, that brought them close. Certainly, as Douglas expressed his new-found commitment, it was her sympathy which he emphasized: 'When you said you would see me again, and listened to my not unusual hardluck story, you gave me something I've never had from any girl before, a sense of your sympathy.' In the margin Douglas added: 'This sounds awfully like a married man being unfaithful to his wife, but I can't help it.' As he had confessed earlier in this letter, he needed 'someone like you so badly that if you *are* kind to me I shall repay you the only way I can, with complete devotion.'

By the middle of November Douglas again considered himself engaged; and in answer to his mother's understandable qualms he set out to prove his clear-headedness:

I think Antoinette and I have thought of everything you put down—and since we look like having to be engaged for at least three years, we ought to be quite sure of our minds at the end of that time. . . . What with the things Dadda did that were mistakes, and the mistakes of other people which Antoinette has heard about, and the mistakes I made with Yingcheng, we have had plenty of things to think of that we will not do. . . . It is possible I could meet someone who was both very intelligent and very original and very beautiful, and in love with me; and that such a person would suit me better. But it is very unlikely indeed that I should meet a person like that, and not certain they'd suit me better if I did. Antoinette is not by any means unintelligent or bad looking. She dresses very well, has been an art student and done ballet.

Writing, about the same time, to Jean Turner, he protected himself with a more dismissive tone, well aware of the precipitousness of his new attachment:

I am well, but don't think I shall be for long as I have Groups in a month, and also I am (and don't you tell anyone AT ALL) engaged all over again. She is probably going to chuck me quite soon, but at the moment parental and guardian opposition are stimulating her to stay engaged. Once again I have ensnared a member of the upper ten, a last year's deb. with the imposing christian names of Antoinette Gabrielle. She is very determined at the moment that my brokeness shall make no difference, but let her once meet again the vastly rich young gentleman whom I have cut out, and off I go in quest of further beauty. . . . I feel much less left out in the cold being engaged, and at the same time there is no prospect of getting married for at least three years, by which time the thing will obviously have gone up in smoke, so I'm not really so very tied down, or up.

Conscious of the scepticism of those around him at Oxford, part of Douglas clung all the tighter to the hope of his new relationship, as a proof that the dream which Yingcheng had damaged was not in itself destroyed. He supported his case with reason: 'I have never till now been so utterly carried away with love, and yet able to consider difficulties and disadvantages quite coldly.' By the end of this letter to Antoinette, the paradox had become more hazardous: 'I know I am content to be lost in love, and passionately anxious to continue as lost for ever. It's like being picked up by a huge hand or a wind out of heaven and moved helplessly.' What the clear reasoning proved was his urgent need of new commitment. Rationally, he saw what was entailed in his loss of Yingcheng: it was not the girl he had loved but his own ideal of her, and 'when the bust up came, it was the disappearance of my dream which filled me with misery'. A page later, however, he assured Antoinette that 'my heart hasn't hardened in the least towards my original dream which you fulfil.'

On the edge of his letters, Yingcheng remained. She was after all a mutual friend, a presence hardly to be ignored, but to express his new feeling of commitment Douglas had to explain her away; and in doing so he reached at least part of the truth.

In Paris, at times, it was a wonderful adventure, and I enjoyed it. But what I enjoyed was being in Montparnasse, the haunt of Romance, among artists and Bohemians to be as Bohemian as any of them, and Yingcheng was a piece (a big piece, but only a piece) of the Bohemian atmosphere: it was the same, on a larger scale, as when I took her to Christ's Hospital.

Another time he wrote of himself as 'made up of two very different parts: I'm almost two people.' One wanted 'exoticism, travel, adventure'; it had a 'terror of perishing into an ordinary existence', and wanted 'an ideal

Antoinette and KD, November 1939, with (*below*) the back of an envelope KD addressed to her at Lady Margaret Hall

companion in these adventures'. This was why he loved Yingcheng, 'and why I still love the person I pictured her to be in my imagination, when she was away'. The other part was 'tired of fighting, wants to be settled, to have a real aim for the rest of my life'; and it too wanted a companion, 'to whom I can give all my love without fear of being hurt, who will need my protection and consideration'. In Antoinette, he affirmed, the two parts had come together. Yet in the mood of his letter announcing to Jean Turner his engagement the two sides had remained apart, identified with different persons: 'I don't think I shall ever get married, because the person I want would have to be a cross between Kristin and Yingcheng, which is obviously impossible.'

For the rest of the term, Douglas saw to Antoinette's education. She recalls that he presented himself to her as the ordinary man, one who could expose the stupidities of the social world to which she belonged and mix equally on every level of society. His talk was constantly about his school, its routine and character rather than his troubles there, and about the blindness of people with money. But he had other subjects: Antoinette recalls that Douglas urged her to read Siegfried Sassoon, and in particular his *Memoirs of a Fox-Hunting Man*.

As part of her education Douglas introduced Antoinette to a group of artists from the Ruskin and the Slade School of Art, which had been evacuated to Oxford from London.[1] These friends inhabited a network of rooms above some shops in Broad Street, approached by going down Saunders Passage, into the Town Ditch, and negotiating twisting flights of unlit stairs. On arrival the welcome was warm, particularly from Evelyn, the flat's official tenant, the girl friend and later the wife of Michael Young. Douglas had talked to Evelyn of the difficulties of holidays in other people's houses where his mother was companion or housekeeper, and she 'mothered' him as she did any other visitor in need. Michael and Evelyn, however, were only the centre of a world comprising a floating population of art students, and the occasional undergraduate. From the attics above their rooms unknown persons would descend by ladder and go about their business. Food was generally available, and music, and in the kitchen was a zinc bath for anyone who needed it. One visitor recalls sitting through a whole meal in the kitchen at Saunders Passage before discovering that someone was having a bath beneath the table. Antoinette remembers that on their first visit Douglas teased her by saying she could only be accepted if she had a bath in the kitchen while others looked on. Fortunately Evelyn's memory of her is of 'an elfin face and a lot of black velvet in the candlelight'.

[1] Douglas occasionally drew at the Ruskin, and took out at least one Slade student, Deirdre Newstubb.

Despite her background, Antoinette had only a small allowance, so their entertainment generally consisted of long walks, coffee at Fullers, a drink at The Bear, or, as she recalls, 'eating economically Indian at the Taj Mahal and Chinese (cabbage substituted for bean sprouts) in a little place in a passage off the High'. They also saw innumerable films and a few plays, Douglas writing to his mother before Christmas of having been to *The Importance of Being Earnest* (with Gielgud, Edith Evans, and Gwen Ffrangcon-Davies: seen from the second row of the stalls); *Design for Living* (with Rex Harrison, Diana Wynyard, and Anton Walbrook: witnessed from shilling seats after queueing for hours); the film *Algiers*, which Douglas was seeing for about the fifth time;[1] Charles Laughton's *Jamaica Inn*, which disappointed him; and *Carnet du bal*: '*Four Feathers* is here next week—I suppose you couldn't get here for it?' His taste for films was insatiable, and catholic—from *The Cabinet of Doctor Caligari* to *Fantasia* and Garbo's *Ninotchka*.

On his return in October 1939 Douglas had joined Alec Hardie and Edmund Blunden in a plan to publish a miscellany of Oxford writing. Much of this first term was given over to meetings, generally over tea at Fullers, discussing the miscellany's contents with his co-editor Hardie, Blunden, the other members of the editorial committee, Roger Lancelyn Green and Daphne Aye Moung, and the eventual publisher, Basil Blackwell. By design, the miscellany was anti-militaristic, even anti-serious, offering an indication that the simple and civilized pleasures of life still mattered. An article on amateur drama in Oxford was obtained from Nevill Coghill; one on an obscure villager who translated Sanskrit, from Basil Blackwell; and one on a kind of moral rearmament from E. R. Appleton. The volume, to be called *Augury*, was with the printers by the end of the second term, its preface explaining that the book was planned 'in the hope that it would show not only some degree of merit and thought still existing in Oxford, but also some way through the seeming morass of public ideas.' The editors, pleased that most of the 'stark and bitter' verse contributions were too bad to print, affirmed: 'The poets in this anthology are not with the times, but in most of their thoughts they hark back or forward to a better age.'

These sentiments were matched exactly in the poems Douglas contributed to the miscellany. 'Villanelle of Spring Bells' showed the pleasures of a traditional poetic form in the expression of a traditional theme:

> Bells in the town alight with spring
> converse, with sweet concordance of new airs
> make clear the fresh and aged sound they sing.

[1] Norman Ilett, who had come up to Brasenose, 'went to see the ridiculous film *Algiers* with them—it left me cold, but they were stirred by it.'

'Stars' celebrated the martial order of the heavens. *'Pas de Trois'* finely recreated the power of dancers to appear 'like gods miraculously borne' before offering them as an image of past craftsmanship and leisure:

> Theirs is a craft of quiet:
> they are shades of an old time
> when you could hear, no riot
> intervening, intricate and frail rhyme
> and music . . .

And he included one of two poems aroused by music. The one he chose, 'Haydn—Military Symphony', introduced 'two grenadiers, scarlet and tall / Leisurely fellows . . . The idle lords of all / The park', to suggest that they, 'Like all authentic heroes are unreal', and advise the reader to follow them:

> For you perhaps to step behind these two
> May shew such dead romances can revive,
> The painted backcloth quicken and be alive.
> You will look out upon this painted view
> Of madmen in a non-existent place.

The other, 'Haydn—Clock Symphony', led the reader into a magical eighteenth-century ballroom where he moved in eternity:

> No wonder you have the carriage of a god,
> For here you are the man who in your sleep
> Walks in the corridors and in the deep
> Recesses of your mind; where you have trod
> The polished ground of dreaming every year.

The visitor must leave, for 'Time's alive' and he is 'Death's servant': but once he forsakes that service, he will return.

The spirit of 'Commission', with the poet offering music and not megaphones, had found renewed purpose in wartime Oxford, and another scheme which took up a fair amount of Douglas's first term emphasizes that he was not alone in sustaining it. With Blunden's active support, Merton Floats and University College Dramatic Society prepared two works for performance in the Clarendon Building on the fifth and seventh of December. The choice could hardly have been more pointedly pacific and backward-looking: Fielding's burlesque of high-minded tragedy, *Tom Thumb the Great*, and Dryden's paean to common sense after an age of war, *The Secular Masque*. With Michael Young, Douglas painted scenery for the masque, made papiermâché masks for it,[1] and at one time thought he might also have a part. Blunden, known as 'a pacifist in a Sam Browne', played the role of Chronos.

---

[1] They collapsed before the performances.

'Though I had purposed merely to address, / Pen and imagination would digress',
wrote KD on the verso of this envelope sent to Blunden in December 1939

The preparations for the plays and the miscellany brought Douglas back
into closer contact with his Merton friends and he once again played rugby
for the college, sometimes persuading Antoinette to watch him. Margaret
Stanley-Wrench had gone down and Jean Turner, despite Douglas's offer
of twenty pounds to assist her to return, was no longer at St. Hilda's.
Douglas spent an increasing amount of time with Norman Ilett, Raymond
Pennock, and Abu Taylor, a Nigerian at Merton. Pennock remembers
going to dances in the city with Abu and Douglas, in defiance of college
regulations, and how, when discovered by the proctors, they left Abu, a
law student, to debate the legality of the matter while he and Douglas
escaped. Thus only the one fine was incurred, Abu's, which the three of
them split. In a letter to Antoinette Douglas recorded a riotous drinking

session which concluded with Abu playing the piano in Pennock's room, while Ilett, Pennock, and Douglas danced and tap-danced wildly.

After that we all reeled out again, said goodnight to Ilett, and went off down the High, along the Corn singing and crashing into policemen and soldiers. We ended in the milk bar, where we sobered up, and where a pathetic old man sold us obsolete Communist propaganda, and I gave a shilling to him.

But the letter explained that the riotousness and the drinking had been designed to cure unhappiness brought by 'a chance remark of yours about me feeling pleased with myself'. The cure failed, and the incident was one of many in a term in which Douglas was prey to his own powerful emotions, his 'moods', as Antoinette called them. After Christmas he confessed in a letter to Yingcheng that he 'more or less lost all self-control last term, did no work of any kind, ate and drank far too much, and hardly took any exercise.'

Such pressures lie behind most of the letters he wrote to Antoinette this term. While the explanations showed Douglas working out his own character, the affirmations of love most readily became requests for help. Encouraged by night-time reverie, and often, the drink of the preceding evening, he allowed sentiments to pass which he would normally have censored. Setting out in one letter from the suggestion that each should try to understand what the other wanted—'The more hints we can give each other the better time we can have'—he then moves to a recurring theme:

And I can't help thinking that I haven't got an awful long time before I leave this lazy life, possibly for good. And I shall leave you with it, to my successor, unless we're changed somewhat by then. I feel rather one of many with you at the moment, and I don't quite know why. In fact I feel very at-a-loose-end, and I don't want to. If I ever get near a firing line, I want something to fight for. Not a country, not my family, not even a girl entirely—just the chance of a life worth living afterwards. I'm one of many in too many ways, and yet I'm desolate

Here the writing faded, his pen running dry; then having added 'and isolated', with a new line and a bold, decisive hand, he concluded: 'And Christ, am I sentimental?'

4

By the end of the term the war had shown little evidence of threatening action. The air raids had not come, and since the Germans had overrun Poland, nothing momentous seemed to have happened. The undergraduates, and Douglas with them, were to return to Oxford, probably to complete the academic year.

Douglas spent the Christmas vacation first, with Antoinette at her grandmother's, then with his mother at Hadlow Down, and then with Alec Hardie in Hampshire, where he enjoyed a 'most Scottish and cheerful

New Year' which included 'reels, sword dancing (on the sword cane)' and singing. There he also had great fun driving the Hardies' car at speeds of up to 76 m.p.h., Back at Oxford he got straight down to work: 'I read 47 pages of Milton today (triumph)'; started film reviewing for *The Cherwell*; gave riding lessons, attended classes at the Ruskin, and continued with preparations for the miscellany.

With Antoinette, however, his relationship entered a new phase. The explanations which had earlier supported declarations of love became more self-contained. On 17 January, he wrote that 'so far from being near' their 'tether's end', he thought they showed signs of 'beginning to get acquainted':

I think you understand quite a lot about me and I'm beginning to get some inkling of the way your mind works too. One thing about me is this. I lived alone during the most fluid and formative years of my life, and during that time I lived on my imagination, which was so powerful as to persuade me that the things I imagined would come true. So far I have been looking for them to come true exactly according to the way I had imagined. I am beginning to find that things don't happen like that. If they *never* happened in the least like I imagined it would be easy to take a new line—but sometimes they do, for a little, so I have to keep my eyes skinned.

Acknowledging that her description of him as 'self-centred' was a triumph of understatement, he added: 'I am hopelessly, and by now quite involuntarily and even unwittingly submerged in myself, swamped by myself, tied to myself. If we break up now the little way that I have got away from this curse will be quickly retraced.'

A week or so later he wrote to Antoinette's parents in India explaining: 'We have broken off our "engagement" as such, because we prefer, after thinking it over, that there should be nothing whatsoever to bind us but our own liking and sympathy.' To help their understanding, Douglas added a frank self-portrait:

By now I expect you'll have heard a variety of assessments of my character, to which may I add my own? I spent a fairly stormy career at school and most of my holidays were alone with the result that I came up here a very defiant and rude person with vulnerable but concealed feelings and the wrong attitude towards most people. I shall never get over the idea of the world in general as a powerful force working for my hurt: nor would I wish to, for this conception of things saves me many disappointments. I am over-critical of everyone—luckily of myself too, though I do my self-criticism in private.

On reading over what he had written, Douglas confessed:

I must say I think it sounds rather a conceited letter: I wonder if you'll think so—I believe if so Antoinette and a lot of other people will agree that I am conceited. Myself, I believe I alternate between extreme conceit, and an extreme inferiority complex. During intermediate periods I am however normal and tolerable. I hope you'll meet me at one of those times.

The 'inferiority complex' Douglas had explained in letters to Antoinette. It was towards women, not men, and arose from a fear that he was too unpleasant for them to want more than an intellectual relationship with him. But once it had arisen, it could extend to his behaviour with everyone.

As Douglas and Antoinette moved through this second term, it was primarily protection against the consequences of losing her which he sought. But as she settled into Oxford she became increasingly aware of their incompatibility. That he needed understanding rather than censure when he got into 'a totally seething state' while others indulged in 'ordinary silly converse'; that he had 'an aversion to parties and the people who go to them' which he had 'carefully built up for some years' in order to spare himself 'a good deal of fruitless longing'; and that he was 'very much more emotional than most people seem to think', explained his social behaviour but could not cure their differences. Occasionally his humour showed through, as when he insisted on doing a Latin translation for her tutorial so that she could come to a party. Delivered at the last minute, to her surprise, and her tutor's entertainment, she found that some dignified emissaries had been given thick Welsh accents. More often, however, Douglas was truculent, showing little of the vitality and sense of fun which had long attracted people to him.

Yet during this term and the Easter vacation Douglas had established another friendship in which good spirits remained uppermost. In the preparations for *The Secular Masque* he had met two sisters, Betty and Joan Appleton, whose family lived in John Masefield's former house at Boars Hill, and like many others, he became a frequent and welcome visitor.

Betty remembers Douglas's capacity for making his companion feel that for the duration of an outing, she was everything that mattered to him. Another day his mood might change, but 'if he felt you mattered, he made you feel so special that you were all that mattered that day.' Like Antoinette, Betty sometimes accompanied Douglas to films he was reviewing. On one occasion, she recalls, the film was so bad that he wrote up the Eldorado ice cream advertisement as the best item of the evening. Another time, a group of them went to see an Ivor Novello musical, and Douglas, who was evidently bored, passed along the row a sketch of the female lead who sang out of the corner of her mouth. It was funny enough for the party to be thrown out for their rowdiness.

Behind such simple pleasures, however, lay Douglas's conviction, remembered by both Betty and Joan, that he would be killed in the war. He was not melodramatic about it, merely detached; and quite seriously said to Betty on several occasions, about his impulse towards being engaged: 'Someone must have my pension.'[1] But with the Appletons, his emphasis remained positive: he should best use what time he had left.

Douglas spent much of the Easter vacation with them, Antoinette being in Scotland, and Joan recalls his arrival on the last day of term:

Betty brought KD to Hill Crest by car; as he crossed the lawn, the picture he called his 'masterpiece', and baggage in hand, Bridget (my younger sister) told him it was my birthday. KD said 'Happy birthday!' and put the picture into my hand. This kind of generosity was typical—he had it in his hand, so he gave it to me.

In the course of his holiday Douglas borrowed a bike and cycled to Sussex to see his mother. When he returned to the Appletons', soaked to the skin, he carried a shoe box full of primroses, picked with his mother, for the house.

At Hill Crest Douglas worked at drawings of angels and riders on white horses for a broadsheet Mr. Appleton was having printed. He designed a new cover for the miscellany, and made linocuts as illustrations. The proofs arrived, 'and it all looks very nice but VERY thin'; and he collected his poems together—'I almost have enough to publish now.' He had sent seven poems to Antoinette's parents in support of his self-explanation, and among them was a piece called 'Do not look up', reiterating the command of 'Invaders': 'Do not look up against this fluid sky: / though flames and Lucifer fall down again / you must persist in what we always said. . . . ' The sentiments were echoed elsewhere. Oxford, in 'An Exercise Against Impatience', 'experiences a difficult time', but thought could still work, 'a hidden creator like the silkworm. It is this / to which I cling, and think will save us all.' Here even the burden of survival is removed, for 'if we die / those we have met or heard of will not be cold / they are as suitable as you or I.'

Beside such poems, however, the collection Douglas made at the Appletons' revealed work in a different vein. While he had striven to sustain his relationship with Antoinette, the hazardous emotions of the past twelve months had driven his poetry with a new force. In May *The Cherwell* published a poem announcing that 'time has reached a round number'. His hope of 'happiness and renown' is lost, a 'sacred lady who needs no art' has given place to a mocking idiot, and with her death his innocence perished.

---

[1] As he had not been supporting his mother before the war only a wife would be eligible for it.

> Then she is gone. I still remember
> my early promise, looking for
> obliging fame to make amends,
> and here my last existence ends.
>
> For I can't feed hope any more
> and Time has reached a round number.
>
> ('A Round Number')

In an Oxford magazine of 1940 this must have looked like a fashionable literary game with poet, *femme fatale*, and *Zeitgeist*, but 'A Round Number' had been part of a poem in two sections called 'Despair' which made clear the source of such feelings. It opened:

> Foul as a yellow ferret
> you who were the rose the fragrance lingers.
>
> Who were the rose a royal
> bloom of polite love, oh how you change
> flower to animal . . .

Yingcheng had not only remained within Douglas's view as a friend—he had taken her to the Cheltenham Gold Cup meeting and to visit the school she and Antoinette had gone to—in January his letter to her had explained his inability to forget her. The intensity of his need for Antoinette was proof of the loss he had suffered and the short-lived security of their relationship offered little reassurance, for, merged with the aspirations and failures of his new love, Yingcheng's continued presence could be traced in his art. Poems of vindictive despair, reproach, emptiness, resignation, hope for recovery, and nostalgia dramatized the range of emotions engendered by her loss. 'Reproach' offers a woman who is as beautiful as she is false, the enchantress of Ulysses and deceiver of Troilus, to whose unfaithfulness the poet cannot do justice in words.

> Cressida could not match you, but I pray
> you'll feel Cressida's ruin and decay
> who was known for a strumpet, and outcast.

In *The Cherwell,* beside his love poem dedicated to Yingcheng, 'Stranger', Douglas placed his translation of the fifth Ode from Horace's first book where the rejected lover thinks of his 'poor gull' successor and is grateful for having survived love's shipwreck. The poet of 'Absence' waits in a moonlit garden, its voice sighing:

> She is not here and you who come instead
> show by your attitude she's dead.

In 'Leukothea', this experience of loss through death is dramatized. Here the lover worships the buried body of his mistress, finding even the grass above her grave 'a strange plant, precious as emeralds'. In a dream, the truth is revealed to him:

> Last night I dreamed and found my trust betrayed
> only the little bones and the great bones disarrayed.

Stranger.

While Douglas made such metaphors from his loss of Yingcheng, else-where he wrote more directly. The lovers of 'Farewell Poem' are 'broken apart and not aware', keeping pain prisoner and talking wryly. The poet of 'Shadows' moves through suggestive metaphors of 'forgetful caves' and a corridor of trees where 'memory easily makes graves / for dead sorrows', to a confession which carries the sound of his own voice:

> . . . It is sacrilege of course to speak,
> but I am here for silence: I had heard
> the property of the place to heal,
> and have come here not to feel

93

a wound winter and summer have not deterred
from aching. And I find this charm as weak.

In February, however, Douglas had published a poem which not only
described a crisis: it suggested a means of recovery.

SANCTUARY

Once my mother was a wall;
behind my rampart and my keep
in a safe and hungry house
I lay as snug as winter mouse:
till the wall breaks and I weep
for simple reasons first of all.

All the barriers give in,
the world will lance at every point
my unsteady heart, still and still
to subjugate my tired will.
When it's done they will anoint me
being kinder if they win.

So beyond a desperate fence
I'll cross where I shall not return,
the line between indifference
and my vulnerable mind:
no more then kind or unkind
touch me, no love nor hate burn.

'Invaders' had seen hardness as the enemy of the lovers, an insensitivity
to be fought, and with help, defeated. It was now the protection Douglas
sought and in poem after poem he proved that he had found it.

How silly that soldier is pointing his gun at the wood:
he doesn't know it isn't any good.
You see, the cold and cruel northern wind
has frozen the whole battalion where they stand.

That's never a corporal: even now he's frozen
you could see he's only a commercial artist
whom they took and put those clothes on,
and told him he was one of the smartest.

('Russians')

Making his poem from an incident reported from the fighting between
Finland and Russia,[1] for three more stanzas Douglas drew a grim vir-

---

[1] A campaign in which, Joan Appleton recalls, Douglas would have liked to join the
Finnish forces.

tuosity from designedly bad writing, proving with each false tone his refusal to make contact with the scene he described.

It was fitting that the poet who had written '·303' at fifteen should turn to war for the expression of his cynicism, but 'Russians' was only the opening salvo for a counter-attack launched during the last two terms of this Oxford year upon his own positive and romantic hopes. 'The Creator' directly answered the heavenly harmony of 'Stars', with stars which 'in bone idle groups . . . stupidly linger'. 'Soissons 1940' redefined his view of the city's timeless peace as 'a mental tower restored only to fall'. Beside the poignant lyricism of his earlier 'Soissons', he now placed both a Yeatsian irony—'The devils pilloried in that holy wall / must smile to see our faith broke to the wide'—and his own, Menippean cynicism:

> You who believe you have a kind creator
> are with your sire crowding into twilight,
> as using excellent smooth instruments
> material man makes himself immense.
> Oh you may try, but can't deny he's right
> and what he does and destroys makes him greater.

Instead of the delicate magic of the dancers in '*Pas de Trois*', he offered a new ballet. First, a dance of spring which is described through the clichés of the conventional balletomane—an anti-poetry, similar to that of 'Russians':

> How cleverly the choreographer
> and costumier combine—
> the effect's fine and the young lady's line
> impeccable. . . .

Then, a different dance:

> But here they come, again, I'm certain, or
> is this not the fair
> young sylph? I declare
> she has a dead face and a yellow eye
> and he has no limbs—how dreadfully spry
> he is on his stumps;
> he bleeds, but he jumps
> ten feet at a prance.
> I don't like this dance.
>
> ('A Ballet')

Writing of 'The Poets', Douglas no longer stressed their possession of truth but their rejection by every element of society:

Keith Douglas

> . . . not even the wantons
>
> roll eyes in our direction. For we are hated,
> known to be cursed, guessed to be venomous;
> we must advance for ever, always belated.

Even this small consolation of advancing for ever was absent when Douglas published in a June issue of *The Cherwell* an elegy on a hypothetical poet, 'The Deceased'.

> He was a reprobate I grant
> and always liquored till his money went.
>
> His hair depended in a noose from
> a Corona Veneris. His eyes, dumb
>
> like prisoners in their cavernous slots, were
> settled in attitudes of despair.
>
> You who God bless you never sunk so low
> censure and pray for him that he was so;
>
> and with his failings you regret the verses
> the fellow made, probably between curses . . .

Cynicism had again brought new impulses into Douglas's poetry and where at school it had been identified, even when it was poetically creative, with an alien modern world, it was now more readily accepted as a part of his poetic make-up. He had not offered the clichés of the first stanza of 'A Ballet' as the collapse of an imaginative vision but as elements of diction, poetically useful in their own right. The free rhythms and emphatic, collo-quial tones of 'The Deceased' were a new and liberating way of saying something which mattered to the poet; and in this poetic upheaval, Douglas had also found new room, in 'A Mime', for his humour:

> Time and Death, villains in the wings,
> stretch out their fingers parallel
> at me. Death says: 'If I don't get you,
> then Time aha will presently upset you—
> you'll find how soon his famous spell
> will coil you in successive strings.'
>
> 'But Sir,' says he, old melodramatic Death,
> 'May I be the first one after all,
> and Time young man will spare you, for
> the young fill my fastidious maw

more tastily. Revel and grow tall,
and rest you merry near your last breath.'

Finally, he had not lost his capacity for lyricism, and for a preparatory
farewell to Oxford he wrote, in 'Canoe', his most poignantly lyrical poem
since his arrival in the city.

Well, I am thinking this may be my last
summer, but cannot lose even a part
of pleasure in the old-fashioned art of
idleness. I cannot stand aghast

at whatever doom hovers in the background;
while grass and buildings and the somnolent river,
who know they are allowed to last for ever,
exchange between them the whole subdued sound

of this hot time. What sudden fearful fate
can deter my shade wandering next year
for a return? Whistle and I will hear
and come another evening, when this boat

travels with you alone towards Iffley:
as you lie looking up for thunder again,
this cool touch does not betoken rain;
it is my spirit that kisses your mouth lightly.

5

In May, after the repeated ruptures and recoveries of the previous months'
incompatibility, Antoinette told Douglas that she could stand his jealousy
no longer. She remembers a long scene outside Lady Margaret Hall in
which he threatened to shoot himself, and there the relationship ended.
By the end of the month Douglas was writing of the view of 'The Happy
Fatalist': he is not 'that hopeless castaway he sometimes appears' and he
does not trust in nothing.

He rather believes in the most evident and omnipotent deity of all, whose ways
are inscrutable, who moves in a wonderful but not wholly mysterious way, and
who is as fundamentally just as any other deity has ever been.

Some people, Douglas says, may think the fatalist cold and inhuman, but
in his unusual rationality and impartiality, he is 'inhuman and superhuman',

and what he loses in the enjoyment of high hopes, 'he gains in immunity from despair'.

The remarks were made as editor of *The Cherwell*, a post Douglas had held since the start of the Trinity term, and their philosophy was a response to Dunkirk. The German forces, having already overrun Norway and Denmark in April, had broken through the defences of the West on the 10th of May. By the 26th the British Expeditionary Force was encircled at Dunkirk. And only now did the reality of the war strike home in Oxford, generating a mood remembered by some undergraduates as almost approaching hysteria and one which seemed at the time expressed in a series of publicized suicides. At University College there was a shooting incident, later described by one of Douglas's Merton colleagues, Douglas Grant:

A pacifist stole a sniper's rifle from an armoury and lay in wait at the top of the College tower. He fired three times, and I turned round at the first shot to see a friend clutching his belly as the blood gushed through his fingers on to the path. He fell dead on the spot, and two other men were wounded.

Alec Hardie remembers coming across Douglas in the quadrangle immediately after the incident, and being surprised how badly shaken he seemed.

Much of Douglas's term was taken up with editing the weekly. The previous term, as co-editor to David Beaty, he had rebuked the apathy of the undergraduates in an article on 'The Undergraduate Fallen From His High Estate', and in his first editorial he had declared his allegiance:

Here the follies of youth and the idiocies of old age flourish as nowhere else: and winter, which damps youthful activities without much impairing the indoor life of old age, has departed . . . meanwhile we are pledged to youth this term as a matter of duty.

A week later he was affirming that an incident in which tomatoes were thrown at a socialist May Day procession, despite its bad taste, represented an energy 'which seemed to have left the University'. For the next weeks Douglas tried to stir his audience from their apathy by publishing an attack on the undergraduate, by Walter Douglas of the Ruskin, and by writing scurrilous reviews: 'The job of producing at the Playhouse seems usually to be allotted with beautiful impartiality to the best boy of the week, or drawn out of a hat.' He also proffered his old reactionary mythology, partly it appears in the hope of provoking a response:

. . . In this golden New World it no longer matters if a man is born of an ancient family, with an ancient tradition of authority and service. . . . Birth no longer is the hallmark of a gentleman: money alone now marks him out. The hustler, spy, popular novelist, are men of the hour.

('The Station to Which We Are Called', 15 June 1940)

In his first editorial Douglas had proclaimed it his intention to produce a 'consistently improving' *Cherwell*, but it was an uphill task, as he noted on 25 May in 'Editor's Folly':

Every week the editor is more and more struck with the futility of writing anything at all in this paper. Every week he must sit opposite a typewriter which is too heavy to carry about out of doors, and compose poppycock, which is read by very few and deserves to be read by fewer, very often.

In the previous term, he and Beaty had announced a special poetry number; when it appeared it contained six poems by Douglas—three under his own name, two under his pseudonym 'Peter Hatred', and one anonymously. Having published during his editorship a number of poems attributed to Shotaro Oshima, Douglas had to protest that these were not by himself. Part of the trouble was that Oxford was thin in established writers, many of those, like John Hall, who would have sustained its literary activities having been removed by the war. Another part was Douglas's distaste for followers. A new generation of poets had arrived at the University in October 1939, Drummond Allison, Michael Meyer, John Heath-Stubbs, and David Wright, but they were not to make their presence felt until the following year when Sidney Keyes came up and they formed a self-contained group; and apart from Michael Meyer who was to join him as assistant on *The Cherwell*, Douglas knew none of these poets.[1]

A few *Cherwell* mainstays remained: Geoffrey Matthews, Charles Monteith, John Russell, Lance Thirkell, Paul Rosenthal, and, of course, David Beaty. There was also an emergency supply of poems deposited by Blunden. Few new poets were found, however, perhaps because, as Alec Hardie recalls of their work on *Augury*, Douglas still returned poems with rejection letters which pointed out the artistic and personal deficiencies of their authors. Yet on occasion Douglas could appear a courteous and encouraging editor. One of the few new poets he found for *The Cherwell*, Gordon Swaine, recalled:

Our initial meeting couldn't have been more casual: it took place in the street, the Turl, outside my College. I rather diffidently showed KD my poems and the illustrations (linocuts by Jocelyn Jacoby of the Slade). He liked them, asked for more, and published about a dozen of the poems in the rest of that term.

It was his public role as spokesman, however, which took most of his time. *The Cherwell* of 1 June had reported a Union debate in which

---

[1] Meyer, Heath-Stubbs, and Wright all have no memory of Douglas ever meeting Keyes. Francis King, however, thinks he met them together once. Douglas's work was nevertheless sufficiently admired by them for it to be included in their anthology *Eight Oxford Poets* (1942).

Beverley Nichols gave a lesson to the undergraduates and his frivolous fellow-speakers, Mgr. Knox and Gillie Potter, on the need for a sense of the solemnity and danger of the times. Nichols was ragged for such mis-judgement and responded with an attack on the undergraduates in a Sunday newspaper. On 8 June, Douglas, as editor of the only undergraduate weekly to have survived the war, made his reply. The undergraduates, having already registered for military service, were trying to keep the character of the University alive: they did war work in vacations and even the con-scientious objectors would do more dangerous work with ambulances than those who had volunteered early to secure military office jobs. Far from being somehow responsible for the current disasters, everyone under twenty-one 'in this curiously arranged country' was 'legally a zany':

. . . for some time yet we shall continue to hear the slurs cast on us, until the chances of war have made us deaf to them. The thought that we shall fight to save these futile critics so that their futile criticism may outlive us is one of the greatest burdens and discouragements we have to bear.

Douglas was not by nature temperate. Raymond Pennock remembers an occasion on which he ran up the stairs to Pennock's rooms in Merton, and not noticing that the outer door was closed, ran straight into it. Having heard the noise and Douglas's steps rapidly descending the stairs, Pennock looked out to see him rolling about on the ground, clutching his nose and cursing. For a good ten minutes the cursing continued, then Douglas got up, climbed the stairs, and to Pennock's relief, knocked and entered without the least emotion.

Cant infuriated him, but to hear cant about the war in which he would participate and in which he was convinced he would be killed had an irony which he could not tolerate. In his first *Cherwell* editorial, he had attacked those who believed 'that we are fighting a race of sub-men, of whom every member from birth is certainly a brutal moron'. In this summer term, David Beaty recalls being at the cinema with Douglas when they witnessed the usual newsreel in which an aerial dogfight was concluded with the German plane spinning to the ground in flames. The audience cheered. Even in the semi-darkness of the cinema Beaty could see that Douglas was trembling with rage. He climbed on to his seat, shouting at the audience, 'You shits! You shits! You shits!' until he was forcibly removed by a doorman.

Publishing few of his cynical poems in *The Cherwell* Douglas gave his readers little evidence of such feelings. An editorial of 18 May, however, had written of the contributors to *The Yellow Book* in terms which matched his deeper feelings better than did happy fatalism. They are no longer masters of the art of living but people working 'in a feverish hurry against Time and Death'. Beardsley's art

made ordinary things precious and sinister, imbued with all the unhealthiness and hectic quality of the movement itself. And unhealthiness, the last energy of high fever, is the mark of all typically decadent art and writing. Those who could not bring themselves to be unhealthy, succeeded with hardly an exception, only in being sentimental.

If the unhealthiness of the necrophiliac lover of 'Leukothea' seems too literary to carry the 'energy of high fever', Douglas's emphasis upon brutal detail in 'A Ballet' and 'Russians' suggested a more thoroughgoing decadence. Cynicism and violence were associated in four stories Douglas published in *The Cherwell*.

At school he had already linked physical violence and cynicism, in '303' and a short story, 'Drunk'. Now, this story, which ends with a young man falling downstairs and breaking his neck on the way to collect the news that he had won a poetry competition, was printed in a context where it appeared unexceptional. Beside it in the issue of 27 April, 'Coutts' concluded with a madman being scalded to death, and 'A Present for Mimi' retold the story of Van Gogh and Gauguin to savour the macabre present of an ear in a matchbox. On 4 May 'The Gnome' echoed Merejkowski's story of 'the old god found on the seashore' by bringing a gnome into a suburban garden in order to relate how he was shot to death for his strangeness.[1]

A draft for a second war poem closed the gap between cynicism and brutality:

John Anderson with stubborn mind
advancing in the first wave of the attack
took one in the face that came out behind

his creative brain split and he fell back
rolling in the dust (for it was summer there)
the blood fell out and turned his tunic black . . .

Zeus looks on, convinced that he has seen Anderson die before, 'at Troy and twenty battles since' and he 'cannot abide' this corpse's stare. The draft ends with his summoning of Apollo to 'take him away and conceal him somewhere'. The emphasis is crude and consistently ironic; yet by the time Douglas left Oxford in June he had rescued from this unpromising material a remarkable poem.

[1] Norman Ilett suggests that the story is based on the *Punch* joke, 'There's a curious bird on the lawn . . .'

In the crude opening stanzas Douglas found a diction of euphemism and pedantic detail which precisely recorded an absurd heroism:

> John Anderson, a scholarly gentleman
> advancing with his company in the attack
> received some bullets through him as he ran.
>
> So his creative brain whirled, and he fell back
> in the bloody dust (it was a fine day there
> and warm). Blood turned his tunic black
>
> while past his desperate final stare
> the other simple soldiers run
> and leave the hero unaware.

Deploying the clichés of John Anderson's 'desperate final stare' and 'the bloody dust' to dissociate the poet from what he portrays, Douglas builds up an ironic context through which the poem develops. Like the euphemistic description of Anderson's being hit and the pedantic reference to the weather, they establish Anderson's own detachment from the reality of war. Thus associated with *Boy's Own Paper* heroics and scholarly manners, he is no more of a hero than a man who walks under a bus. This very immunity from reality makes possible a transformation:

> Apt epitaph or pun
> he could not hit upon, to grace
> a scholar's death; he only eyed the sun.
>
> But I think, the last moment of his gaze
> beheld the father of gods and men,
> Zeus, leaning from heaven as he dies,
>
> whom in his swoon he hears again
> summon Apollo in the Homeric tongue:
> *Descend Phoebus and cleanse the stain*
>
> *of dark blood from the body of John Anderson.*
> *Give him to Death and Sleep,*
> *who'll bear him as they can*
>
> *out of the range of darts to the broad vale*
> *of Lycia; there lay him in a deep*
> *solemn content on some bright dale.*
>
> And the brothers, Sleep and Death
> lift up John Anderson at his last breath.

By the end, ironic diction has given way to dignified elegy, the power of poetry performing the ritual move towards peace which Anderson's innocence has deserved. It is an extraordinary and moving change of direction, in which Douglas finds his cynicism no longer ground to be held, but rather, a route to be traversed, to find on the other side a new affirmation.

At the end of June Douglas left the University, having made his reputation as one of its most promising writers. If his more recent and impressive work had yet to be published it was perhaps because he had more ambitious plans for it. He had sent Blunden the poems he had typed up during the Easter vacation at the Appletons', and on 21 May Blunden returned them with the assurance that 'you have produced a most attractive series of poems' and asked him whether he intended to try to publish them as a book. On going down Douglas deposited the whole collection with Blunden, adding copies of his latest work, in the hope that his tutor would find a publisher for them.

Early in July Douglas visited the Robertses for the first time since he had brought Yingcheng to Housey. He was staying with the Brodies for a last few days before call-up, and from Southwater he wrote a farewell letter to Yingcheng. His tone had a new resignation. 'I still fall tremendously in love with people while the circumstances are right and romantic, but you're the only one who survived the light of reason.' He had been too involved to exercise much charm over her,

any more than any but the most self-controlled person could look his best walking a rickety bridge across 900 feet of space. I knew what I was in for if I fell and that made me too nervous to behave ordinarily. . . . I think more than likely we shan't meet again, so this signs me off except as a literally distant acquaintance.

On the 17th his mother and Norman Ilett saw him off at King's Cross for a journey to Redford Barracks in Edinburgh. On enlistment the previous September he had ambitiously stated his preference for 'Indian Army, Infantry; Royal Scots; Black Watch'. The choice was delayed, for Douglas was to join the Third Horsed Cavalry Training Regiment. For N.C.O.s, however, the regiment had members of the Royal Scots Greys.[1]

[1] A presumably apocryphal story of Douglas's, relayed by Hamo Sassoon, tells how he had been accepted into the Scots Greys. He arrived for an interview with the regiment's colonel having equipped himself with the full regimental uniform. 'Why are you wearing that?' asked the colonel. 'Because I like it, sir!' announced Douglas.

4
Sandhurst and Wickwar
July 1940 - June 1941

a subtle process worked out to minute detail
(January 1941 to Jean Turner)

I

Two days after his arrival at Redford in the pouring rain of 17 July Douglas wrote to his mother enthusiastically. The uniform was 'most handsome', the ordinary Troopers 'very decent' telling newcomers what to do and expect, the facilities good: spring beds, beer room, smoking room, restaurant, and theatre for concerts. Douglas had returned to the communal living known to him since the age of six, and he described his 'bedroom' containing twenty-four beds as 'about the size of a Housey dormitory'. To him military activities were familiar, and people he knew in the Mounted Section of the Oxford O.T.C. had joined the regiment with him.[1] They trained with the rest of the new Troopers and received the same pay of fourteen shillings a week for the same duties, but the Oxford contingent remained together as a recognizable group, destined for commissions. Their privileged status was particularly apparent to Edward Malins, who had been a master at Christ's Hospital during Douglas's last years at the school and soon arrived at Redford as an ordinary Trooper. He had seen Douglas's poems at David Roberts's and knew of his rebellion, and to his surprise discovered that Douglas was enjoying the training and was frankly ambitious to do well in his new life.

Douglas cultivated all the simple soldierly virtues. To come to attention and salute with the vigour and precision of a Guardsman was a skill he wished to perfect. For two hours each night he 'boned' his boots, softening the leather by working in a specially-made mixture, one component of which was horses' urine, and smoothing it with the back of a toothbrush. When, some months later, Douglas met Raymond Pennock in Oxford he inquired whether he too boned his boots; on hearing that Pennock

---

[1] Not all of them: some went to another cavalry training establishment.

As a cadet, autumn 1940; KD's embellishments, including the halo

did not, Douglas affirmed that such things did matter.[1] In addition to caring for his uniform, Douglas devoted much time to cleaning and polishing his saddle, bridle, stirrups, and bit, the implements of his new trade.

[1] On one Oxford visit Mr. Appleton was so impressed by the shine of Douglas's boots that he took a photograph of them.

For he had joined not simply the army but the cavalry. His drill was on horseback and in his bedroom, for exercise, there was a full-sized dummy horse. Several members of the training regiment were ex-jockeys and others had been hunt officials, grooms, and horsemen. The Royal Scots Greys who trained them embodied and preached the values of the old cavalry army of Balaclava, and it was natural for one instructor to debate the relative merits of horse and tank and to conclude that the horse remained superior because it was quieter.

After six weeks of barracks life with no time for non-military activity other than a 'painfully moral romance' with a girl called Netty in an Edinburgh hat shop, Douglas left Redford with the rest of his Oxford group. His successes were clear from his record: 'Drill proficiency: Good, very keen. Keenness and cleanliness: Very good. Intelligence and character: Intelligent and capable. C.O.'s remarks: Capable and reliable.' The group, now joined by Malins and others who had been recognized as potential officers, was sent to the Army Equitation School at Weedon in Northamptonshire. Arriving there on 1 September, they started their education as horsemen all over again.

Riding instruction in the Mounted Section at Oxford had been tough. At their first sessions the undergraduates had been taught to strengthen the grip of their knees by being placed on a horse whose reins were tied and stirrups raised beyond reach of their feet. The sergeant started the horse with a slap and the novice fell off, remounting to the comment, 'Who told you to dismount—sir!' Later they had to take off their saddles at the trot and continue, holding up the saddle in the left hand. Now, while the Battle of Britain was being fought and won, Douglas at Weedon learnt to do impressive and seemingly impossible manœuvres on horseback, sometimes with drawn sword: advancing at the trot and the gallop, mounting a horse at the trot, learning to cut and thrust. Here he was expected to acquire the skills and the grace which made the cavalry officer: an opportunity remarkable in 1940 but one which perfectly suited his years of martial dreams. However, Douglas's self-taught horsemanship, his years of hacking and makeshift jumping, had produced only bad habits. Alongside comrades who had owned horses and had been riding and hunting all their lives, who were confident that their deficiencies came either from the novelty of the tasks or the foolishness of their instructors' demands, Douglas was exposed as 'rather an awful horseman.' The sergeant instructor, delighted by the discomforts of the officer cadets, seized on every chance to embarrass or humiliate them; the horses, one member of the Oxford group recalls, knew exactly how to discompose their riders; and if Douglas was not the only victim, he took his mishaps more painfully than others. David Lockie, another of the Oxford cadets—whose early difficulties Douglas character-

Joan and Betty Appleton at Boars Hill in the summer of 1940

ized in a sketch of a huge mare, Hilda, in full gallop, demoniacally switching her tail while her rider clung on, toes down and elbows out—simply did as best he could. Malins, who was later to join the Indian Cavalry, bore minor discomforts with refined indifference. Douglas earnestly tried to succeed.

A severe kick from a horse late in September gave him two weeks' respite from such travails. His shin was too badly injured for him to continue training but not badly enough for a stay in hospital, so Douglas spent the time on leave with the Appletons in Oxford, Joan acting as nurse to the open wound on his leg. It may have been while he recovered at Boars Hill that he turned to his recent Weedon experience to make a short story, but it was not of swords and charges that he wrote.

The story opens with the cadets gathered in a shed as a horse is led in, its leg just broken from a fall during training. As they watch a vet draw lines in chalk on the horse's forehead the narrator wonders whether the horse comprehends the procedure. A man in a white coat arrives and places a tube to the chalkmark and still the horse is passive, as though accepting a role in a ritual. The man strikes the end of the tube with the flat of his hand and the horse, with amazing suddenness, drops to the ground dead. Now the vet opens the jugular vein and standing in blood dissects the horse, explaining each of his actions.

'The horse has a small stomach,' said the vet: 'Look!' And he flapped the stomach in front of him, like an apron. The stench was unbelievable. Simon began to feel sick; his hand searched frantically for his pipe, but it was not in his pocket. He looked firmly at the wreck of the horse, the crowd of spectators, some craning their necks for a better view. The horrible casualness of the vet's voice grew more and more apparent; the voice itself in volume; the faces merged and disintegrated, the wreck of the horse lay in a flurry of colours, the stench cemented them into one chaos. He knew it was useless. His one thought, as he felt himself falling, was that he had let the horse down.

After his leave Douglas returned for another month at Weedon. His absence must have put him further behind the others in the skills of the cavalryman but he remained with the Oxford group until the end of October when they all left the Equitation School. On their departure the establishment was closed down for the duration of the war, and for the Oxford group this was more than a symbolic conclusion, for at Sandhurst, where they were to complete their cadet training, there were no longer any mounted units. Placed, on 1 November, in the Infantry Wing there, they were offered the chance of transferring to the mechanized cavalry, with the encouragement of an instructor who assured them that they would grow to love their tanks as much as they had loved their horses. Douglas was one of the few who followed his advice, and during the next three months of mechanized training in the R.A.C. (Inns of Court) Wing of the Royal Military College, he must often have regretted his decision, for he was not by nature at home with machines.

Studying the theory of the internal combustion engine for one week, doing practical work on it for a second, and driving it for a third, Douglas completed a carrier and light tank course with a Grade III pass, the lowest pass grade available. His driving was judged even weaker than his practical and teaching ability. Instruction in wireless produced no better results, for having achieved eight words per minute in Morse code Douglas earned the report that he had done satisfactory work but did not appear to be trying. To this criticism was added a comment which would have surprised those who had watched his care for martial dress in Middleton B and at Redford: the wireless instructor considered that Douglas should try to make himself look more presentable. A change had come over Douglas's behaviour as a soldier and with it came disenchantment with military life. Early in December he wrote to Jean Turner: 'We lost our horses only a month ago and that seemed the last straw. Until then I had a handsome chromium plated sword to play with and felt comparatively happy.' It seemed years rather than months since his 'previous existence ceased'; he felt that he had all the disadvantages of army life but 'at present, no advantages'. Even departure from Sandhurst seemed to offer no promise, for he was 'just about at the end of my hopes':

I can see nothing more attractive than active service and final oblivion, to which I quite look forward. I shall feel such a chap dashing about with stuff blowing up everywhere. I am trying to get East as soon as possible: and when I get there I shall make for the nearest harem and leave the rest to Allah.

At Redford and Weedon the Oxford group had received their share of rough treatment from N.C.O.s and instructors. They had little free time, and among their more frustrating duties at Weedon had been stable guard. This entailed not only the usual guard duties, but watching the horses in order to prevent them soiling the stable floor, by placing a shovel between the rear of the horse and the floor at the appropriate moment. Perhaps the humour of such a job diminished the annoyance and it was part of training with horses which Douglas enjoyed. At Sandhurst, however, their tasks were mechanical and no longer carried out as a small group privileged to learn the mysteries of an archaic cavalry world. Douglas was one member of a huge establishment which appeared to pursue a policy of messing about its cadets. To make matters worse, it seemed to him that most of the Sandhurst cadets had more money than he. As he wrote in December to Jean,

At least if I had as much money as most officer cadets I could hire or seduce an obliging young lady to spend my leaves with me. But I haven't even got anywhere to go if and when I get leave. . . . Here I just work, though in very luxurious surroundings, and hitch-hike to Oxford on Sundays. There I walk desolately about trying to find people in, until it's time to come back.[1]

Douglas had not previously written to Jean from the army and the dejection of his tone was prompted partly by his desire to regain contact with her. Hoping to provoke a reply he blended his expressions of misery with rudeness, a combination she would recognize as a plea for help. Having heard that Yingcheng was not to marry her 'smooth Bermudan' after all, he

[1] From Sandhurst Douglas also paid a visit to Christ's Hospital, where he met Hornsby, also on leave.

thought that she would most likely end up a 'society wife', so she 'broke my heart for no reason at all, blast her'. Blunden was sending his poems to T. S. Eliot,[1] 'and in fact the whole silly business continues'. Jean, he supposed, would be 'leading a helpful existence' at St. Hilda's, 'coping efficiently with about six things at once. I'm afraid you were born to be so. . . .' She was so 'ruthlessly sensible' that no one dared to approach her. To have fallen in love with her would have been lovely, he said, because the women he generally chose were 'idiots' and Jean was 'the only female friend I have, whom I like just because it's pleasant to be with you, and not for obvious masculine reasons.'

By the time Jean's reply reached him Douglas had missed her on a visit to Oxford and the Michaelmas term had ended. Still feeling thoroughly lonely he tried to find a way of meeting:

if you can get here from wherever you are, before the Sunday after next, let me know. I can escape next Saturday afternoon, and I shall probably be free on Sunday but don't know yet. After that I'm free on Wednesday next week. If I get a week's leave, would you come and spend it or some of it with me, if I could find anywhere? This is not an improper proposal, particularly—but I may well have to spend my leave alone otherwise.

Instead of leave, and before hearing from Jean, Douglas moved with his squadron to a tank gunnery course at Lulworth Cove. There he found 'the filthiest scruffy hole' he had ever fallen into, a 'concentrated army nightmare':

We're put on a charge for having a bath. We have to scrub out lavatories. We have to sweep rooms, clean washbasins, make beds. We have to walk everywhere through at least a foot of mud. Everyone either swears at us or is very grim or morose. We have to walk three hundred yards through a bloody blizzard and queue up for twenty minutes to get a plate of dirty grease and a few lumps of offal or gristle, as the case may be.

Douglas defined such treatment as a 'subtle process' designed to reduce 'what might have been quite a good person' to a 'malevolent idiot'. When he received his report from the Gunnery Wing, the reductive process had evidently been successful. Although he had acquired a 'satisfactory knowledge' and should make a 'useful tank commander', Douglas had gained a mere pass and seemed 'a sound and reliable type but not very quick mentally'.

The end of the gunnery course coincided with the start of the Hilary term and having heard again from Jean Turner, Douglas at last had the chance of a meeting. This time, however, his invitation carried a warning:

---

[1] Douglas had acquired Eliot's 'East Coker' in September.

Please do something for me: whether you know about my affairs or not you know I'm stuck for a girl at the moment. Well for God's sake don't let me try to make love to you. You're the only girl I like enough to hope it won't happen. It always ends in a muck-up. So don't let me start.

Within a week they had met and the dismal tone of his previous letters had gone:

My dear Jean, I thought you were a goodish person but I must say I didn't think you were as good as all that: you seem to have blossomed out. David [Lockie] was most emphatic in your praise. And I was more content just wandering about and being rude to you than I've been for months.

For this last couple of weeks at Sandhurst, Jean provided the certainty of female companionship which he had lacked since Redford; and at the end of his cadetship he now had the prospect of leave and a twenty-first party in Oxford arranged by Jean for David Lockie and himself.

On 1 February Douglas passed out from the Royal Military College. His troop, '33 (Weedon) Troop', had gained the highest marks in the written examination and the entire cadet body was summoned by the Commandant to congratulate them. In fact, Edward Malins recalls that three well-off members of the Weedon group had succeeded in bribing a corporal to let them see the papers before the examination. At five o'clock that evening Douglas started a week's 'beautiful orgy of sentimentality' in Oxford with his belated twenty-first party. Held 'above the Noted Snack Bar' in the High, the party made a fitting conclusion to a period in which Oxford had remained Douglas's only real home.[1]

It was also a period in which his military performance had reached its nadir. His leaving report from Sandhurst had placed him in Category C as someone who, his commanding officer considered, should 'look to his appearance' and although he had plenty of brain did not always show it. In the opinion of his squadron leader Douglas was 'not a very impressive personality' and could do better 'if he tried to be more aggressive'.

2

On 7 February, leaving behind his tin hat and respirator and sending a stream of telegrams in search of them, Douglas set off for Ripon and his new regiment. During his course at Sandhurst he had given a revised list of preferences, 'Yorkshire Hussars; Shropshire Yeomanry; Royal Wiltshire Yeomanry', in January altering his third choice to the '22 Dragoons'; but his posting was to the regiment he had placed first on his arrival at Sandhurst, the Second Derbyshire Yeomanry. A new regiment, constituted in

---

[1] Mrs. Douglas and Mrs. Lockie attended. Iris Murdoch was among those invited, but she has no recollection of the event.

July 1939 as an offshoot of the Derbyshire Yeomanry, it possessed a certain character through the senior officers drawn from the parent regiment. Before the war, to join the Yeomanry was thought a privilege,[1] the annual camps and meetings forming an important part of county life. Most of the senior officers hunted, shot, or fished, and brought with them into the regiment their local social hierarchy. They were gentleman soldiers, proud of their amateur status and suspicious of the bureaucracy and ambitions of the professional army. As an embodiment of such traditions, Douglas had a commander, Colonel Barnes, who always carried a shotgun on manœuvres, firing it from the turret of his armoured car whenever he saw game.

Both parent regiment and offshoot had been mechanized before the war and not only had this dislodged some of the more deeply entrenched cavalry prejudices, it now gave the new regiment a sense of purpose. When Douglas joined them, the Second Derbyshire Yeomanry were beginning to look like a possible fighting force. Starting the war with first a drill hall and then a derelict factory for depot, and private cars and requisitioned buses as their only mechanized transport, they now had a tolerable depot at Ripon race course, its Totalisator building for headquarters, and fifty Guy armoured cars which had been delivered, appropriately, on 5 November 1940.

At once Second Lieutenant Douglas set about establishing his position as troop commander. Before his arrival the troop sergeant had held this post and it was not long before they clashed. Ordering a parade at a certain time and place, Douglas found that his troop did not turn up. The sergeant explained that one of the gun barrels was sweating and had to be cleaned at the last moment. Douglas described this to Jean Turner as 'the crucial point'.

If I had let him get away with it, I should never have caught up again. So I had a good snap at him, which required some courage, as he knows much more about a lot of things than I do and so I'm dependent on him over car maintenance etc. However I snapped my snap and smoothed things over as soon as I saw he'd got it straight, so I hope to God I won't need to do any more snapping.

For good measure he gave the sergeant an 'incredibly authoritative tactical lecture' to establish his superior knowledge of some areas of military practice. To Jean, however, he added that he found the sergeant an 'excellent chap' and thought the rest of the troop 'very amiable and cheerful', 'though two of them think by numbers, and with a good pause between each thought'.

[1] From 1903 to 1904 Douglas's father had been a member of the West Hertfordshire Yeomanry.

I'm getting very fat again due to eating & drinking
such a lot to keep warm, and getting no exercise. We had been
snowed up until today, + though I've done a lot of standing
about in it, I haven't done much walking. We did a scheme
(the Squadron) for the Commander in Chief Home Forces,
Genl Brooke. The Great man did not actually speak to
anyone himself, but the Divisional General, McCreary asked me
a lot of questions, in fact I was the only person in the
Squadron who was spoken to at all. I answered them all
satisfactorily & the Colonel (our Colonel) was tremendously
pleased with me, as he had expected me to be frightened of
all the Red Hats. As I was able to bob down into my turret
again the moment they asked me anything I didn't know, &
so I was disguised in thousands of scarves, overalls, glasses and
earphones, I felt quite safe.

I have bought for 11/3 some beautiful blue overalls.
So in battle order I now appear like this

I must stop & get on with
various other letters — I believe
reply to Lacey

I forgot to post a

Love
Keith

To his mother from Ripon, March 1941

At Ripon for only six weeks, Douglas saw little of the town and found
only frustration in Harrogate, where he danced with someone who looked
'marvellous', talked sense, danced better than anyone he had danced with
before, and turned out to be married. 'Why do I always pick those sort of
people? There must be an unmarried, unengaged edition, but where do

they hide?' Then, early in March, the regiment moved south to join the Southern Command, now under Montgomery. Although they knew their eventual destination would be abroad, for the present they were to continue training in Gloucestershire.

Regimental Headquarters was at Wotton-under-Edge, and C Squadron was billeted in Wickwar. They held their mess in the White Horse Inn, which, despite its name and fine situation in a cleft below the parish church, was an unloved establishment. Douglas slept at the opposite end of the village's long High Street, at Hope House, the home of the bank manager, Mr. Thayer. The Thayers, who were recently married and had not had soldiers billeted on them before, were relieved by the quiet politeness of Douglas and the fellow-officer who shared a back bedroom with him. The two officers were rarely in the house, however, for under the more rigorous routines which Montgomery had brought with him to the Southern Command, they spent long days racing round the narrow lanes in armoured cars, maintaining and repairing their vehicles when there were no manœuvres, and going on a squadron run each day before breakfast.

From their first day in Wickwar, when Sir Derrick Gunston, who was living in a cottage next door to the Thayers,[1] invited Douglas and his fellow-officers for drinks, the squadron had managed a busy social life. As visiting gentlemen the Yeomanry officers were welcomed into local society, which centred on the Duke of Beaufort's hunt, and received a steady succession of invitations to dinner parties, dances, cocktails, and rides. For several of Douglas's fellow-officers such a life meant a return to normality after the privations of their earlier training, but for him it was new and discomforting. Though never excluded from invitations—for, as one of the more senior Derbyshire Yeomen later commented, 'Douglas was the kind of person you could take anywhere'—he had little desire to participate.

Occasionally he did join in, and he did so with half-hearted irony. Writing to Jean of a visit to the Cheltenham Gold Cup meeting, where he was surprised to find in the members' enclosure about twenty people he knew, he commented: 'I must be getting quite a socialite.' He reported that he was going to a dance at the Bath Assembly Rooms with several 'ornaments from *The Tatler*' and predicted that he would probably spend the evening combing his hair in the gentlemen's lavatory, unable to keep pace with his company. His fellow-officers were impressed by Douglas's efficiency and conscientiousness as a troop leader, and his sense of responsibility in trying to persuade another officer to co-operate with a squadron leader whom he disliked; but they felt that he kept himself separate by what one of them described as his 'aggressive poverty'. If he could not afford their pleasures, they would happily pay his way, but he preferred to be something of an

---

[1] He had handed over his house for use as a transit hospital.

outsider. While David Lockie recalls Douglas showing him his poem 'The Prisoner'[1] at Sandhurst and discussing it with him, most of his friends in the Derbyshire Yeomanry did not even know he wrote.

At Wickwar, instead of dancing and paying social calls, Douglas spent evenings exercising a polo pony, and week-ends trying to get to Oxford. Largely for the purpose of such visits he became joint owner of a Bugatti, run with the help of squadron petrol; and with this advance on his Sandhurst hitch-hikes, he visited Jean Turner at St. Hilda's or the Appletons at Boars Hill. His customary, and welcome, announcement of his arrival was a phone call to the Appletons which opened with the question, 'Am I going to sleep in this phone box or stay with you?' In Oxford he simply walked around, or swam at the Cowley Baths, and if he could find an opponent he played squash.

With this measure of freedom the one serious shortcoming in Douglas's life remained the lack of girl friends. At Sandhurst he had perhaps taken out a girl called Mary Steedman,[2] and in Oxford he saw Natasha Litvin (who later married Stephen Spender) a few times. She recalls their meeeting on a bus and Douglas offering to help her distribute copies of *Horizon*. He seemed 'likeable and giving a feeling of suppressed energy', and she remembers 'noticing so often his open charm seeming to cover a sort of sensitive vigilance (*not* egocentrically so; I mean, rather, receptive).' Douglas sent Natasha a beautifully made Valentine card but got no further. At Wickwar he saw something of the seventeen-year-old daughter of a farmer, Margaret Robinson, and he made constant appeals to Jean to visit him there for a week-end, as harmlessly as she wished. She was unable to come, but a sixteen-year-old girl he had met at the Appletons', Bunny Agarwala, whose father was a high court judge in Patna, did take up his invitation. Visiting a friend at Wootton, she came over with another girl to make up a foursome with one of Douglas's fellow-officers, for an evening ride in the Bugatti.

While Douglas was at Wickwar the German air offensive which had been quiet during the winter began afresh. Douglas already had first-hand experience of an air raid, for a bomb had hit his block at Sandhurst, and he had helped to extricate the injured. Now he watched from a distance as Bristol was lit by fires which seemed to stretch across the whole of the city and the sky was coloured with flares and anti-aircraft fire. The prospect of his squadron being quartered for a week in the city, when they could have returned each night to Wickwar, had infuriated him shortly after his move south; though he did expect it to give him a glimpse of 'all this British

---

[1] See below, p. 119.
[2] There is a passing reference to her in a letter, as someone with whom his mother might be able to stay in Camberley.

heroism'. As it happened, not a bomb was dropped on Bristol during that week. There were, however, stray German planes around Wickwar. One dropped a single bomb on the headquarters at Wotton, without causing serious injury, and another came down in a field just outside the village, sounding to Douglas as though it was on top of them. A third crashed in a near-by field and Douglas visited the wreck sometime later to find the remains of the crew, 'which stank', and one of them 'hung in a tree some yards from his own head'.

Yet when he wrote a short story of war during his stay in Gloucestershire, it was to the Great War that he turned. With an irony similar to that of his earlier stories, 'The Weapon' reverses the myth of the Angels of Mons. God, seeing the suffering in the trenches, descends to earth to end it, but the blinding light attending His arrival is taken for a secret weapon and the two sides slaughter each other with more murderous fire than before.

3

During his first year as a soldier Douglas had published only two poems, and those in *The Cherwell*.[1] That small output fairly reflected his state of mind in the months following his entry into the army. What he had written, however, had curiously reflected the phases of his army training. As a cavalryman at Weedon, Douglas celebrated the end of the whole illusion of 'chromium and machinery' in 'The News From Earth', a thoroughly literary poem, as backward-looking in its style as in its relation to Douglas's achievements at Oxford:

> And every luxurious beast with purple eye
> in the hot East you shall espy
> his second ornamental age begin.
> See with alchemic horn and golden skin
> the heraldic Unicorn at leisure lie.

There are 'sea nymphs and mermaidens', gods leaping down to earth, Cupid leading 'lusty youth to bed', and Zephyr swimming to meet his comrades; and Douglas decorated his manuscript with their pictures. Enjoying a harmless literary fantasy, he even brings Pan out of retirement, to 'address his pipe' for his last performance in Douglas's poetry.

In the dispiriting months at Sandhurst, Douglas wrote on the more mundane subject of his own ability to face action in the prescribed military manner. 'This severe building and barrack square / with the guns of Waterloo exactly as they were' should make him copy the lieutenant 'who cried Floreat Etona to his friend' before tumbling heroically in the dust.

[1] 'Extension to Francis Thompson' and 'The Marvel'.

But how could I achieve that grand moustache
or such élan without a sabretache
or dying, left that fervent glare, or at
the sudden cue, have all my last words pat?

Then, whatever will restrain
the coward closely reasoning in my brain?
I think only that I must try to see
the whole performance and what the end will be.

Casting himself as 'John Anderson' Douglas is at once too involved in his
question and too flippant to make a serious poem. Sending a copy of 'Sandhurst' to Alec Hardie in April, he commented: 'though the sentiments are
true they are not very original and the verse isn't very inspired after all.'

Douglas had not lacked encouragement during these eight largely unpro-
ductive months. On 15 October Blunden had responded with unqualified
praise to two poems Douglas had sent him:[1]

It's not much good *my* praising you, for I am considered antediluvian, but I'll
say the two you sent me, in different ways are the best verse I've seen lately outside the Old Masters. In time these admirable unions of wise humanity and
strong fancy will be properly appreciated.

On 16 December Blunden reported that the 'Works', the collection of
manuscripts Douglas had left with him, had been sent to T. S. Eliot.
Although Douglas mentioned this to Jean as 'the whole silly business',
when he received Eliot's reply at Ripon in February, he was delighted:
'Coo! I had a letter from T. S. Eliot today—quite nice on the whole—
promising young man—send some more when you've written it. How much
can I sell his autograph for?'

Eliot had read the collection 'several times', he said, and with 'continued
interest':

They seem to me extremely promising, and I should like to keep in touch with
you. I should much like to know whether circumstances permit you to keep on
writing at the present, or whether we must expect a silence of indefinite duration.

My impression so far is that you have completed one phase which begins with
the very accomplished juvenilia and that you have started on another which you
have not yet mastered. Of the first phase I feel that, as might be expected, there is
a certain musical monotony in the rhythms. That does not matter in itself because
it is a good thing to go on doing one thing until you are sure that its use is exhausted, but from the point of view of collective publication it is... [2] and I think
you have definitely an ear.

---

[1] Blunden does not name them: they were possibly 'The News From Earth' and
'Extension to Francis Thompson'.
[2] The words 'a very good monotony' are crossed out by Eliot, who inserted in the
margin, 'The typist has dropped something.'

What I should like to see is the second phase which you have begun developed to the point of formal mastery, and meanwhile I think that it would be useful to get poems in periodicals outside Oxford. There are not, of course, many periodicals now in which to publish verse, but I shall be very glad to draw the attention of the editors of *Horizon* to your work.[1] If you are still writing I should like to see something.

About six weeks after this encouraging letter, Douglas received an invitation from Alec Hardie to participate in a sequel to *Augury* which he hoped to publish with John Lehmann. Replying with 'Sandhurst' and four Oxford poems, Douglas admitted the low state of his work: 'Herewith what poems I can find. I am afraid I can't rise to anything new at the moment.' After two months at Wickwar, however, Douglas was able to send Eliot four new poems. Returning to his poetry, he now drew more productively on his current mood.

> I who could feel pain
> a month, a month ago
> and pleasure for my mind
> and other pleasure find
> like any dotard now
> am wearily sat down,
> a dull man, prisoner
> in a dull chamber.
>
> You who richly live
> look at me, look at me;
> stirred to talk with you
> I say a word or two
> like an effigy.
> What answer will you give?
> Will it wake the drugged man,
> I wonder if you can.

Where 'Sandhurst' had failed by being too directly related to its author, the impersonal form of 'Song' gains Douglas distance enough from his personal feelings to make a poem.

In a rambling piece called 'The House', Douglas first explored the several relationships of the poet to his creations, then gave an account of poetic sterility. Its cause was the presence of 'a young lady / whom I admit I knew once, but had heard / declined in another country and there died.' The country of her demise could well be Bermuda. Only by exorcizing her would he be able to expect 'the beautiful stranger, the princess' who is perhaps both the real woman he sought and the creative impulse he had lost.

[1] It is not known whether Eliot made good this offer; none of Douglas's work appeared in *Horizon*.

Sandhurst and Wickwar

None the less, it had been to Yingcheng that Douglas addressed the one really significant poem he composed at Sandhurst; there, through his art, he achieved a kind of exorcism.

THE PRISONER

Today, Cheng, I touched your face
with two fingers, as a gesture of love;
for I can never prove enough
by sight or sense your strange grace,

but mothwise my hands return
to your fair cheek, as luminous
as a lamp in a paper house,
and touch, to teach love and learn.

I think a hundred hours are gone
that so, like gods, we'd occupy.
But alas, Cheng, I cannot tell why,
today I touched a mask stretched on the stone

person of death. There was the urge
to break the flesh and emerge
of the ambitious cruel bone.

The Prisoner.

As in Douglas's first poem to Yingcheng, 'Stranger', the expression of love conceals a vulnerability, and now this is released. But it is not Yingcheng's loss but the shift of perception which concerns him: the awareness of a puzzling process whose course he traces with disquieting detachment.

At Wickwar, on the end-papers of a copy of Christopher Caudwell's *Poems*,[1] Douglas drafted another poem about mortality. It began as a free exploration of the metaphorical possibilities of Time as a predator:

> . . . his saliva masticate the flesh,
> of animals, buildings and material things.
> Similarly in his vast intestine swims
> the windy thought and unnutritious speech
> love, even durable memory and each
> word, every gesture Time includes
> whose slow digestion no hard piece eludes . . .

For over twenty lines Douglas develops variations on this metaphor without being inhibited by the demands of structure. Then he locates abruptly the human significance of his image:

> So Time has used his rodent teeth
> on us to eat your love and my hope
> till both [?]. But in his innards shape
> new love, new hope, despair and new hate
> Even while I so desperately wait.

The poem has swung from its general theme to the poet's immediate feelings. Again Yingcheng seems to linger behind it, and as in 'The House' her presence leads Douglas to step right out of his poem to speak directly of himself.

From these freely developed metaphors, Douglas shaped a poem, 'Time Eating', which debates the balance between the destructive and regenerative powers of Time. In spring Time restores the flowers it destroyed in autumn and for every dead man it can create another. The source of growth, Time can bring the child to 'mansize'; and yet, while it creates, it destroys. Time's 'ruminative tongue will wash / and slow juice masticate all flesh'; 'thought and ambition melt' and 'even the world will alter' in Time's belly. For three stanzas Douglas maintains the formal metaphysical tone, while gradually developing a more negative view of Time's activities. He then releases the emotional force of that view:

---

[1] Douglas left the book with Mrs. Thayer.

> But Time, who ate my love, you cannot make
> such another; you who can remake
> the lizard's tail and the bright snakeskin
> cannot, cannot. That you gobbled in
> too quick, and though you brought me from a boy
> you can make no more of me, only destroy.

The abstractions of the poem's argument reach a conclusion which denies their calm. Here, what had been no more than a personal confession when Douglas first drafted the poem, has become the anguish of the individual.

In May Douglas had written another, more simply celebratory metaphysical poem, 'The Marvel'. It was the product of a week spent on the coast at Linney Head in Wales, attending a gunnery course in a mood antithetical to that of Lulworth Cove. The squadron had driven there in bright sunshine, travelling over the Brecon Beacons with their cars spaced a hundred yards apart as a precaution against air raids. For the whole week of firing at targets out to sea or sitting on the sand dunes lazily recording the accuracy of fire, the sun had shone, and after their duties the squadron had returned each night to fine quarters at Stackpole Court.

> A baron of the sea, the great tropic
> swordfish, spreadeagled on the thirsty deck
> where sailors killed him, in the bright Pacific,
>
> yielded to the sharp enquiring blade
> the eye which guided him and found his prey
> in the dim place where he was lord.

The eye acts as a magnifying glass, a marvel of nature, whose impact on the poet is increased by the mundane purpose for which it is employed:

> With it a sailor writes on the hot wood
> the name of a harlot in his last port . . .
>
> And to engrave that word the sun goes through
> with the power of the sea
> writing her name and a marvel too.

In 'Extension to Francis Thompson', the first of his poems to be published that year in *The Cherwell*, Douglas had listed various phenomena which revealed the wonders of creation, and although he suggested a quasi-religious source for their power to 'embody the celestial thing', he concluded that analysis was 'worshipping'. If he had not performed any analysis in these two Wickwar poems, he had exchanged his Oxford exploration of imaginative worlds for an observation strengthened by detachment.

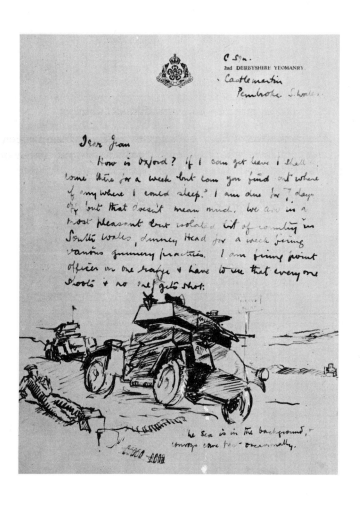

To Jean Turner from Linney Head, May 1941

4

Returning to Wickwar from Linney Head in the middle of May, Douglas
had expected to move with the regiment to Surrey, as the first step towards
going abroad. They had long known that Wickwar was only a temporary
base and at last it seemed that they were to start their further travels. On
17 May, however, Douglas was sent on a course at Karrier Motors in
Birmingham; returning after a week he found them still at Wickwar.
Through his absence he had missed a chance to place his name on a list of
volunteers for the Indian Army; a few days after his return, he learnt

however that one of the officers who had applied had changed his mind, so he could put his name down. At the beginning of June he heard that his application had been successful, and was granted a week's leave prior to joining a course in preparation for India. Douglas took the leave in Oxford, and where his previous visits had depended for their success on chance meetings, this time he had arranged company.

In Birmingham during his course Douglas had met a girl called Diana. She was only sixteen and shared none of his interests, but she was pretty and had an attractive innocence. Unlikely as their relationship was, he could offer her a good holiday in a romantic city and with her to provide the partner he needed he could act out his dream of Oxford in what could well be his last stay there. On one of his earlier visits, writing the celebration of Oxford which had eluded him as an undergraduate, Douglas had invoked not only the 'legendary figures', the old, who looked for truth, but the young:

> At home, as in no other city, here
> summer holds her breath in a dark street
> the trees nocturnally scented, lovers like moths
> go by silently on the footpaths
> and spirits of the young wait,
> cannot be expelled, multiply each year . . .
>
> This then is the city of young men, of beginning,
> ideas, trials, pardonable follies,
> the lightness, seriousness and sorrow of youth . . .
> ('Oxford')

Trying to impose a romantic conclusion on his association with the city, with a recklessness which was both produced and protected by the uncertainties of his future, Douglas told Diana he would marry her. They even went to the Registry Office for a marriage licence, but it was closed. Immediately after his leave, he offered the customary rationalization in a letter to Jean:

Diana and I are engaged, but I hold out no hope for the engagement, from either end. It is simply for these reasons, that we really would like to get married, and are in love, and that being engaged gives a very slender extra chance to both of us, to exercise a certain amount of self control and wait. But it's a long time, and she's very anxious to get married and start having babies straight away.

By the time he made this announcement, in the middle of June, Douglas's military future had been settled, though not as he had expected. The Indian course was cancelled, and instead he was to be posted immediately to the Middle East, to await the arrival of his regiment. 'With any luck', he expected to be in action within 'two or anyway three months'; and then, he wrote to Jean, 'the simplest thing would be to get conveniently incapacitated, come home, and ignore the war in Oxford.'

After two weeks with the 55th Training Regiment, R.A.C., at Farn-

On leave in Oxford, May 1941

borough, Douglas invited his mother and Diana to see him off at Southampton. He was not to see Diana again. As he acknowledged in a cynical letter eight months later, the engagement had been a dreadful mistake. By 25 June, Douglas was on board ship, as part of Draft Serial RWF/KY/F.

In a last letter to Jean Turner, he examined his prospects with the protective facility he so often employed when writing to her:

Meanwhile I am for the wars, when the various officials and the convoy system meet at a point. I think on the whole the feeling of uncertainty is pleasant. I leave behind the requisite sweetheart, mother, friends etc. to mourn my loss, and enemies etc. to be glad of it. Perhaps some of them will still hold these official positions when I come back.

Before leaving, Douglas had written a final poem, as far from this letter as it was from Brooke's 'The Soldier'; for like Brooke Douglas was exploiting an important moment to make a poem which could provide his own elegy if he should not return. What he wrote, however, offered neither consolation nor uplift, and it made no attempt to draw the poem's emotion towards its author. Instead, with a clinical calm which was more disturbing than any show of emotion, it described his part in a natural process:

> Remember me when I am dead
> and simplify me when I'm dead.
>
> As the processes of earth
> strip off the colour and the skin:
> take the brown hair and blue eye
>
> and leave me simpler than at birth,
> when hairless I came howling in
> as the moon entered the cold sky.
>
> Of my skeleton perhaps,
> so stripped, a learned man will say
> 'He was of such type and intelligence,' no more.
>
> Thus when in a year collapse
> particular memories, you may
> deduce, from the long pain I bore
>
> the opinions I held, who was my foe
> and what I left, even my appearance
> but incidents will be no guide.
>
> Time's wrong-way telescope will show
> a minute man ten years hence
> and by distance simplified.

Keith Douglas

Through that lens see if I seem
substance or nothing: of the world
deserving mention or charitable oblivion.

not by momentary spleen
or love into decision hurled,
leisurely arrive at an opinion.

Remember me when I am dead
and simplify me when I'm dead.

Remember me when I am dead
and simplify me when I'm dead

So as the processes of earth
Strip off the colours and the skin
removing the brown hair and blue eyes

leaves me more naked than at birth
When hairless I came howling in
as   the moon   come in the cold sky
and forming my skeleton perhaps
so stripped, a learned man will say
he was of such a type, & intelligence, no more.

so when with ten years collapse
some superficial memories, you may
remember not that once I wore

these clothes but that my taste was this
and said not that on such a day
but so dressed habitually

there   Time's wrong-way telescope will show
Remember no careers or kin   a minute man 18 years hence
but who was the   but by the distance simplified

                                              And you'll tell them if I have been
so   in a year or 2   Substance or shadow in its worth
particular memories, you may   descend heaven or oblivion
remember the pain I bore
                                              Thus judge it not by hasty spleen
the opinions I held, if was kind or no   or love into decision hurled
and what I left behind, even my appearance ~   but at leisure make your opinion
incidents serve as guide   Remember me when I am dead
                                              & simplify me

5

Palestine and Egypt

July 1941 - October 1942

To do this is drilling the mind, still a recruit
for the active expeditions of his duty
('The Hand')

I

The voyage to Egypt did not seem at all like 'being at war' to Douglas. Writing to Jean Turner from Freetown harbour that it had so far been 'interesting and mildly exciting', he referred only to porpoises and shoals of flying fish and the monkey he had bought from a bumboat to entertain them while confined to ship in the sweltering heat. But the cabin he shared had a window on to the boat deck, and an electric fan. At Durban he enjoyed ten days' holiday in an atmosphere which reminded him of 'American society films'. In a 27 h.p. Studebaker, hired with friends made on board ship, Douglas had raced round the night spots after days spent lazing on the beach. At the Hotel Edward, the Stardust, the Athlone, the Roadhouse, the Dollhouse, and the Blue Lagoon they danced, in the intervals retiring to the car to eat toasted egg and bacon sandwiches by moonlight. He thought South African taste in dress appalling, running chiefly to pink, and the accent more like someone imitating an accent than using a natural form of speech, but considered that South African hospitality could not be bettered.

For the last lap to Suez the holiday mood was sustained as they travelled on an 'almost luxury liner' in the company of about two hundred women on their way to work in hospitals and offices in Egypt. Among them was Mary Benson, who remembers talking a lot to Douglas because he seemed rather lonely and younger than most of the other officers. He repaid her attention by one night reading her Donne and, after their arrival in Egypt, sending her copies of nine of his poems.

Disembarking on 24 August, Douglas travelled with a friend he had made in Farnborough, John Bethell-Fox, also a subaltern, to the R.A.C. base depot outside Cairo. There he found that he was not to await the Derbyshire Yeomanry, but with Bethell-Fox was to join another yeomanry

128

regiment, the Nottinghamshire (Sherwood Rangers) Yeomanry, then in
Palestine. As he was not due to be posted until 24 September, Douglas
spent a month at the R.A.C. Schools and base depot, passing his leisure
time swimming and discovering 'what a bloody town' Cairo was.

Out of his voyage towards war Douglas had written a 'Song' telling of
doom, but it was not the soldier's fate which concerned him: the poet's
doom was to venture too far from the 'hot coast' of a love whose 'southern
virtues' had bewitched him.

> Yes, for I am doomed my dear
> and I have jilted myself and you;
> soon when the sea's embalmed me
> I'll fade into the deceitful blue,
> for the poisonous sea and a cruel star
> the one by day and one at night have charmed me.

Here his fate is in little doubt, but within a month of this poem of 12
September, Douglas had turned again to his voyage to write a poem,
'Negative Information', in which the omens were ambiguous. His point of
departure is the search for patterns which had preoccupied him ever since
as a child of four he had told his mother that the shapes in the sand of the
beach must have a meaning.

> As lines, the unrelated symbols of
> nothing you know, discovered in the clouds,
> idly made on paper or by the feet of crowds
> on sand, keep whatever meaning they have,
>
> and you believe they write, for some
> intelligence, messages of a sort—
> these curious indentations on my thought
> with every week, almost with each hour, come.

The impressions, however, fail to add up. On board ship, 'the fantastic
moon / in the Atlantic . . . the phosphorescence, the ship singing a sea-tune'
had raised them above their circumstances, making them seem 'like spirits
attendant on the ship / now at the mast, now on the waves', who might
almost 'dip / and soar as lightly as our entranced sight'. Beside this there
was the news of war which made no impact:

> And in general, the account of many deaths—
> whose portents, which should have undone the sky,
> had never come—is now received casually.

In his letter to Jean from Freetown about the flying fish, Douglas had
half-humorously referred to their destined role: 'We are beginning to look

like heroes already—considerably thinner and pleasantly tanned.' To his mother, between Durban and Suez, he had written of the journey:

The last lap is as unlike being at war as any of the others. Action must still come as a hell of a jolt. Particularly after the peacetime atmosphere of Durban . . . The war sounds to be in a more hopeful stage at last, but I think this lot have a hot time ahead of them before the pendulum swings over.

In 'Negative Information', he had made a poem of this sense of unreality, its lovers 'careless of these millions of wraiths',

> for as often as not we meet
> in dreams our own dishevelled ghosts;
> and opposite, the modest hosts
> of our ambition stare them out.

The balance between life and death, tilted towards death in 'Time Eating' and 'Simplify Me When I'm Dead', has been restored, but only by 'levity' and 'indifference':

> To this there's no sum I can find—
> the hungry omens of calamity
> mixed with good signs and all received with levity
> or indifference by the amazed mind.

2

Bethell-Fox went alone to join the regiment at the end of September, for Douglas, having contracted *otitis media* at the swimming baths in Cairo, was moved, in great pain, to a hospital in Palestine. There, surrounded by survivors of the fighting in Abyssinia, Greece, and Syria, 'bandaged and riddled with bullets . . . all with a thousand gruesome tales to tell', he planned a novel to be set in Oxford: 'I know nothing about anything else though of course there are vacations.' Mentioning his project in a letter to Jean, he felt too tired to say more than that it was based on a 'rather Charles Morganatic' idea, with a 'slightly adapted and more normal' Hamo Sassoon for hero. He wrote later that he had given it up before writing a word.

Douglas felt a fraud in hospital, beside the war wounded, and as his infection took time to heal he worried about falling behind those with whom he should have joined the regiment. When he was moved in late October to a convalescent depot, however, he gained the consolation of a companion in the same circumstances, John Masefield,[1] who should also have joined the regiment earlier but was recovering from pneumonia and sand fly fever. He also found a way of life which well suited him. Douglas

[1] Though he was 'not in the least poetic', John Masefield was a nephew of the Poet Laureate, whom Douglas had heard speak at Oxford.

had liked what he could see of Palestine from his hospital window. Now, on the coast at Nathanya, he had four miles of deserted sandy beaches, interspersed with clusters of rock, and the 'incredibly blue, clear, warm Mediterranean' where he could pass his time walking and swimming. Writing to Jean on his last day at the depot, 27 October, Douglas acknowledged the potential tedium of such an easy life and mentioned his misgivings about being away from the regiment, but he also revealed that his few days of leisure in the open air had, as so often happened, produced poems.

He had not previously written to Jean of his poetry, and now he approached the subject with a diffidence heightened by the consumption of a whisky and ginger ale, 'which drink will be my ruin if I can ever afford as many as I want', a bath, a good meal, and 'quite a good film':[1]

Well I have been walking beside the sea waves and have rather unoriginally been inspired, presumably by the waves etc. to produce three rather unoriginal poems. There are millions of mosquitoes in this room.

His rapid change of subject indicated a mood which Douglas acknowledged at the end of the letter: 'I can't think why this is such a facetious letter.'

The poems certainly did not merit his dismissive comment, though he could well have been encouraged to write them not just by the sea and time for thought, but by news he had had from England. Early in September John Hall had written to Mrs. Douglas that he was planning a selection of work by three poets, possibly to be published by John Lehmann. Finding in her son's poetry 'a perfection which is extraordinary among the poets of his generation', Hall asked if Douglas would join with Alan Rook[2] and himself in the volume. Mrs. Douglas sent Hall the manuscript of poems which had been left with Blunden, and on 17 October Douglas wrote to Hall from hospital. Mentioning that he had already agreed that work of his should appear in Michael Meyer's *Eight Oxford Poets*, he accepted Hall's offer of publication, providing a list of his poems for possible inclusion. He enclosed two pieces, 'Song' and 'Negative Information', and details for a bio-biographical note.[3]

The first of the Nathanya poems, 'The Hand', set out a new view of the period of waiting described in 'Negative Information'. Here, however,

---

[1] *Three Loves Has Nancy.*

[2] Rook, who had departed from Oxford before Douglas's arrival, had been in the evacuation from Dunkirk. He became one of the war's most published younger poets.

[3] 'My full name is Keith Castellain Douglas, my ancestry Scottish and pre-revolution French. . . . I am interested in clothes, drawing and painting (my own and other people's), horses . . . music, ballet, stage design.* Recreations, tap dancing, rugger, water-polo, competitive swimming. That should be enough.

* 'Present work—2nd Lieutenant Royal Armoured Corps.'

Douglas proposed a course of action. The poet was to train himself in perspectives, like the artist who uses the hand as a means to their discovery; and from this examination of shapes and patterns he was to try to discover 'arguments / whose phases . . . tend / to the centre of reasoning, the mainspring'. Douglas's manner was frankly didactic, offering as an exercise for the poet the metaphysical procedures he had employed to more serious effect in his Wickwar poems. Perspectives and arguments provide a new alchemy, one which is not only 'not difficult to teach' but whose processes, unlike those in 'The House', are logical rather than magical. All this, however, is only a preparation for activities which have lost none of their magnitude:

> To do this is drilling the mind, still a recruit
> for the active expeditions of his duty
> when he must navigate alone the wild
> cosmos, as the Jew wanders the world:
> and we, watching the tracks of him at liberty
> like the geometry of feet
> upon a shore, constructed in the sand
> look for the proportions, the form of an immense hand.

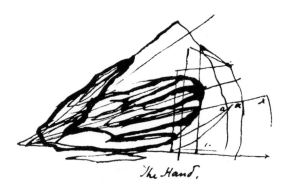

The Hand.

If Douglas has shifted his emphasis from imagination to intellect, replacing a princess with 'proportions' and magic with squad drill, he still foresees a quest of immense romantic proportions. This Darwin aboard *The Beagle*, noting and measuring, is preparing for an encounter with the Ancient Mariner.

Following the directions of 'The Hand', Douglas's second poem looks for a pattern in a change of perspective. Its subject was something he had seen on his walks at Nathanya and described to his mother in a letter of 26 October: 'There is a sort of sea-kingfisher here, brilliant blue on the back and orange underneath, with a long black beak. They appear by themselves and always sit very upright.' Such simple observations were transformed in the poem into a concentration upon the bird, of such intensity that the bird's passage evokes a deeper process.

THE SEA BIRD

Walking along beside the beach
where the Mediterranean turns in sleep
under the cliff's demiarch

through a curtain of thought I see
a dead bird and a live bird
the dead eyeless, but with a bright eye

the live bird discovered me
and stepped from a black rock into the air—
I turn from the dead bird to watch him fly,

electric, brilliant blue,
beneath he is orange, like flame,
colours I can't believe are so,

as legendary flowers bloom
incendiary in tint, so swift he
searches about the sky for room,

towering like the cliffs of this coast
with his stiletto wing
and orange on his breast:

he has consumed and drained
the colours of the sea
and the yellow of this tidal ground

till he escapes the eye, or is a ghost
and in a moment has come down
crept into the dead bird, ceased to exist.

From this poem Douglas made a third, 'Adams'. He generally worked by paring away material from an extensive first draft, and even completed poems like 'Time Eating' and 'The Marvel' could be radically cut later. Yet, having flawlessly encompassed the movement from possession to loss within the single sentence of 'The Sea Bird', he tried to extract another, more hazardously ambitious poem from the ground it had gained. Using the first four and a half stanzas of 'The Sea Bird' virtually unchanged, he

seized on the menace previously hidden by the bird's absorption of life.
The power which, in the bird, could be perceived with poise by the poet,
in a man threatens to destroy him:

> . . . as legendary flowers bloom
> incendiary in tint, a focal point
> like Adams in a room.
>
> Adams is like a bird;
> alert (high on his pinnacle of air
> he does not hear you, someone said);
>
> in appearance he is bird-eyed
> the bones of his face are
> like the hollow bones of a bird.
>
> And he stood by the elegant wall
> between two pictures hanging there
> certain of homage from us all;
>
> as through the mind this minute
> he draws the universe
> and like our admiration, dresses in it,
>
> towering like the cliffs of this coast
> with his stiletto wing
> and orange on his breast;
>
> sucked up, utterly drained
> the colours of my sea,
> the yellow of this tidal ground;
>
> swallowing all my thought,
> swallows all those dark fish there
> whom a rock hides from sunlight . . .
>
> Till Rest, cries my mind to Adams' ghost,
> only go elsewhere, let me alone
> creep into the dead bird, cease to exist.

Emotion accumulates such force that its impact can be resisted only by
wrenching the poem free of it. If this is 'drilling the mind', there was no
hubris in Douglas's ambitions for it on the 'active expeditions' of its duty.

3

The military metaphor at the end of 'The Hand' was given a specific meaning when on 28 October Douglas set off from the convalescent depot for Karkur camp to join the regiment which he assumed would take him into action. There had never been any question of the role his draft was to play. Since Rommel's arrival in the Middle East in March 1941, Britain's commitment to the fighting there had been steadily on the increase, and the mass of reinforcements whose arrival coincided with Douglas's, along with the lack of success achieved in the limited Allied offensives 'Brevity' and 'Battleaxe', in May and June, clearly pointed to a large-scale offensive. When Douglas joined them, however, the Sherwood Rangers Yeomanry boasted three tanks. That the regiment might be dispersed was a more immediate possibility than battle, and as they waited to be mechanized, they passed the time firing Browning guns on the ranges and learning how to make Molotov cocktails. Yet it was a regiment which had already seen action in three different roles in three countries.

The Sherwood Rangers had left England when Douglas was at Oxford writing 'Russians' and the war seemed at its most 'phoney', and they had departed as a fully equipped, horsed cavalry regiment. Not only were they led by a county aristocrat, Lieutenant-Colonel the Earl of Yarborough, M.C., on whose Brocklesby Park estate they had sometimes met before the war, they had entrained from the station nearest to his home. One of the officers at least, Major Player, had sold three of his most valuable hunters to the army for a fifth of their value in order to take them with him as his own chargers; and their first casualty, suffered during their train journey through France towards Marseilles, had been a horse. At a railway station somewhere in France it fell sick, so the waiting room was requisitioned and Corporal Harrison, armed with several bottles of brandy, remained there with the animal until it was cured. He then phoned the Duke of Gloucester, who had once met the horse, and ordered a carriage for its safe transport.

The regiment's destination had been Palestine, and as Italy and its North African colonies had not as yet entered the war, their task was more a matter of policing a territory for which Britain was responsible than of facing the Nazis directly. So their first action was a cavalry charge with drawn swords down the main street of Jaffa, to rescue police cut off in a riot. When civil order returned to Palestine the Sherwood Rangers lost their occupation. Their colonel returned to England and the officers' wives who had followed their spouses to Palestine departed. Despair came when the regiment lost their horses too. Under a new colonel, E. O. Kellett, Tory M.P. for a Birmingham constituency, they were to train as motorized infantry.

However, the capture of Tobruk by Imperial forces in January 1941 brought the regiment into action before they were motorized. As part of Tobruk's defence forces, while Douglas was racing round Gloucestershire in his armoured car, after a crash course in gunnery the yeomen rapidly taught themselves to handle the ancient coastal batteries left behind by the Italians. For five months they manned shore batteries, fired anti-aircraft guns on board a monitor, formed an airfield defence force, and sniped at German aircraft with rifles. Heavily bombed, possessing little equipment and having had only makeshift training, they bravely took their bizarre part in the fighting until, in July, they were relieved by a Regular regiment of gunners.

Another contingent of Sherwood Rangers had meanwhile served as coastal gunners in Crete. Trapped there by the German parachute invasion, a party of three had made its way on foot across the mountains to reach Turkey after a series of voyages in small Greek vessels.

Unfortunately for Douglas their varied exploits had given the regiment a character with which it was difficult for him to make contact. Leaving England in January 1940, the Sherwood Rangers had suffered neither the social discomforts of mechanization nor an influx of non-cavalry recruits. Two years abroad and the small scale of their fighting had deepened the regiment's sense of itself as a unit isolated from the rest of the army. From the outset the regiment had had the character of a club, in which it was difficult enough for those who had joined in September 1941 to find acceptance; arriving on his own at the end of October Douglas's individuality was exposed. Ironically, the very qualities which had marked him out from the aesthetes and intellectuals at Oxford now measured his distance from these cavalrymen, who formed a more tightly enclosed social group than the Second Derbyshire Yeomanry. Douglas neither hunted, fished, nor shot; he knew no one in Nottinghamshire and nothing of the regiment; the qualities for which his school was famous—intellectual excellence, classlessness, and its place in the mercantile history of London—meant little to these country gentlemen; and Douglas was incapable of the one role which might have brought him comfort in the regiment—anonymity.

His main discomforts stemmed from his contacts with senior officers. In his own squadron, where most of his time was spent, Douglas was in fact fortunate. Major Stanley Christopherson, the squadron leader, was a gentle and fair-minded young Wykehamist, whose tolerance and self-effacement Douglas soon recognized. But Christopherson was not from Douglas's world, seeming to him almost to have stepped from the pages of Saki; and the endless social connections and easy manner which had enabled Christopherson to slip so readily past the distinction made in the regiment between pre-war yeomen and others, aggravated Douglas's wish to make clear his own difference. The squadron's unofficial second in command, Lieutenant Garrett, had spent his whole life with horses and horsemen, and appeared to be knowledgeable and successful on every level of regimental life. There seemed little Douglas could do to make his own presence felt.

Shortly after Douglas's arrival, however, John Bethell-Fox was transferred to his squadron and their acquaintance, which had started in Farnborough, developed into a friendship.[1] Douglas had at first been put off by Bethell-Fox's outspoken, uncompromising manner, but on discovering his background he had found in it a source of understanding and attraction. Born in Germany of a French mother and British officer father, who died when he was eight, he had been brought up in the bourgeois milieu of a large French provincial town and after running away to sea had joined the ranks of the professional army before the war, rising to his commission in the Royal Tanks. To Douglas, a career so different from the orthodox county background of the other yeomen proved Bethell-Fox's individuality and helped towards the discovery of a very real sensitivity. It also meant that they shared a mechanized training, knowing more about their present and future duties than cavalrymen who had left England with horses.

With the two most senior officers below the colonel Douglas had little contact, but their presence disturbed him. Major Player, heir to the cigarette fortune, possessed a charm which Douglas saw as feudal. Alone among the pre-war yeomen Player did occasionally speak to the newcomers, but his manner seemed to Douglas like that of a squire asking after the health of his tenants' children. 'Sweeney Todd', whom he later described with sufficient venom for this pseudonym still to be necessary, Douglas recognized as a man devoted to his regiment, but whose view of command was that of a small boy playing with lead soldiers. Kellett, the colonel, was a natural focus for Douglas's dissatisfaction. A man who carried an aura of pomade wherever he went and whose fastidiousness in dress extended to making the bows of his shoe-laces fall in loops of identical length, Kellett might simply have passed Douglas off as scruffy; but in addition to finding him untidy he found him a nuisance. For during his first weeks with the regiment Douglas insisted on bringing to the notice of his colonel every shortcoming he found and each thought for its improvement: to the amusement of his new comrades a steady correspondence developed between them. The ambitious and immensely self-confident Kellett was the last person to tolerate the criticisms of a newly arrived subaltern. Meeting on equal terms, two such powerful characters could hardly have co-existed

---

[1] Of their meeting in Farnborough Bethell-Fox recalls being struck by 'Keith's very fierce independent air', his dark Derbyshire Yeomanry uniform, and the tight way he pulled in his Sam Browne belt.

happily—one fellow-officer thought Douglas and Kellett shared a 'feline' quality—but the gulf which Kellett understandably saw between himself and his junior officer, made their exchanges unwelcome to him.

After a month with the regiment, Douglas was writing to Jean in a tone which is hardly surprising:

I am bored stiff, being now isolated in sand to all intents and purposes—although we live practically in a village full of the most delectable cafés (of the continental type), where the troops are allowed to disport themselves, our kindly and (you can bet) beloved Colonel has forbidden officers to go there. The man could perhaps be forgiven for being an unimaginative fool in matters of that sort, if he were any use on the military side. But any of the Second Lieutenants knows four times as much as any major in the regiment, twice as much as a sergeant, twice as much as a trooper, and ten times (at a moderate estimate) as much as the colonel.

Douglas's judgement was not merely a product of his spleen, for in one sense second lieutenants probably did know more than the others, having, like himself and Bethell-Fox, received a mechanized training before departing from England.

In the rest of his letter Douglas extended his tirade in a way which he knew Jean would understand.

In spite of living in unnecessary isolation, under canvas, with the most primitive sanitation, inefficient cooking and no proper light anywhere, I am charged almost exactly twice as much as when I lived in civilian billets in England and lived in a pub, and three times as much as in the palatial Training Regiment mess in Farnborough. Mess bills in Egypt were as high, but at least we got something in return. I don't know what I'd do if I drank or smoked a quarter as much as the others —but I shall drink and smoke if the third indulgence isn't provided soon.

No one writes, playing rugger in the dust is vile, and the engagement to Diana was a mistake:

Diana has only written twice and I am inclined to cross her off (which to tell the truth I am glad to do with such a clear conscience). . . . She is a very kindly placid sort of girl but I never meant to get engaged to her, and only did so as a shock absorber to reproachful tears.

Diana in fact remained a faithful correspondent, as Douglas was later to acknowledge.

In this state of mind Douglas reported that he had 'heard again via mother from T. S. Eliot' about the poems he had sent from Wickwar. Eliot, he said, 'wishes me (dear unimaginative man) to give more attention to ineffectual adjectives.' Douglas would probably have reacted adversely to Eliot's letter in any mood; for in place of his previous warm encouragement and talk of publication Eliot commented that 'Song: Dotards . . . ' was 'very nearly written', and that the other poems seemed to him 'to need a good bit of work'. Eliot had taken up points of detail in the margins of the manuscripts but these were generally routine and to Douglas's eye probably looked downright pedantic: when he revised these poems he took no notice of Eliot's suggestions.

Playing rugger, soccer, and hockey and riding two or three evenings each week, Douglas was officially preparing to take part in the desert fighting. When, in the latter part of November, the Imperial forces relieved Tobruk he wrote to his mother ruefully wondering if there would be anything left for the Sherwood Rangers to do: 'I should look silly if I came home without even going into action.' Writing later of the contrasts he had found on a December trip to Syria, Douglas returned to thoughts of action, suggesting that the soldier visitors who reflected the 'two-faced' nature of the country would soon be at war:

> . . . though foreigners we surely shall
> prove this background's complement,
> the kindly visitors who meant
> so well all winter but at last fell
> unaccountably to killing in the spring.

('Syria II')

Despite his dissatisfactions, Douglas identified his fate with that of the regiment which was simply waiting for its equipment to arrive before joining in the desert war. This was why he had been posted to the Middle East and it could only be a matter of a few months before he met the experience which had occupied his thoughts ever since September 1939.

In the meantime, Douglas saw as much as he could of his new surroundings. One of his frustrations was the colonel's restriction on travel, but he saw enough to praise at least one aspect of the Middle East:

Haifa and Tel Aviv, and for that matter, our village, are well supplied with girls, whose appearance here is ordinary but who would make the occupants gasp of any room they entered in England. There are people who keep saying you can't beat English girls—but for sheer beauty, no English face or figure can compare with almost any Arab child, any Egyptian or Syrian girl (provided she hasn't run to fat and sallowness, as some do).

The trip to Syria had been a week-end's circular journey, to Ryak and back, with his troop in a two-ton truck. Douglas was an enthusiastic traveller, and writing to Jean after his expedition he judged that it would have been worth a journey of a few thousand miles. The mountain views improved on any description and in the village 'that men still call Tyre' he had seen ships 'like swans asleep, though perhaps not as colourful as Flecker's'. Beirut was impaired by blackout restrictions but the journey on to Zable and Ryak and then back through Damascus to Nazareth was no disappointment. There were even fewer signs of tourism than he had expected and blown bridges and the scars of the earlier fighting in Syria did not hamper their journey. Finally there was the Sea of Galilee, with fresh, clean water and, despite 'about one fish per square foot', lovely to bathe in.

The poem Douglas made from his trip, 'Syria', was a delicate celebration of what he had seen:

> It is not snow on the green space
> of hilltops, only towns of white
> whose trees are populous with fruit
> and girls whose velvet beauty is
> handed down to them, gentle ornaments.

At first he had simply defined the country's duality in which 'devil and angel' did not fight but remained interdependent, making a simple and rather literary traveller's poem.[1] Syria, however, had provoked a deeper and more personal response, and he revised the poem's second half. Already, in his first stanza, Douglas had evoked a sense of hostility before describing the hilltop towns:

> These grasses, ancient enemies
> waiting at the edge of towns
> conceal a movement of live stones,
> the lizards with hooded eyes
> of hostile miraculous age.

In his first version he had left this as one half of the country's nature. Now, however, he drew from his awareness of this hostility a distinctly personal understanding:

> Here I am a stranger clothed
> in the separative glass cloak
> of strangeness. The dark eyes, the bright-mouthed
> smiles, glance on the glass and break
> falling like fine strange insects.
>
> But from the grass, the inexorable lizard,
> the dart of hatred for all strangers finds
> in this armour, proof only against friends
> breach after breach, and like the gnat is busy
> wounding the skin, leaving poison there.
>
>   ('Syria I')

If the poem suggests that Douglas had maintained his barrier of indifference it makes clear that he understood its cost.

[1] Published in *Collected Poems* as 'Syria II'. Questions of order and dating are dealt with in the notes.

While he was seeking relief from the tedium of waiting for mechanization and action, his situation in the regiment failed to improve. At one point, John Bethell-Fox remembers, he and Douglas had applied for transfer from the regiment after a battle with the colonel had led to their being singled out and refused week-end leave, 'with no reason given'. Kellett, Bethell-Fox recalls, 'dealt with us as if he were placating some difficult shop stewards'. At the end of December Douglas's uneasy life with the regiment at Karkur came to an end. Without his having made any move himself, he was posted to a camouflage course near Cairo. If Kellett had arranged the posting in order to cool Douglas down, he had prescribed a cunningly effective medicine. For within twenty-four hours of his arrival at the course Douglas had reason to think longingly of Molotov cocktails and rugby in the dust.

4

After a series of mishaps *en route* Douglas arrived, on 28 December, at a 'Godforsaken spot' about twenty-six miles from Cairo. Breakfast the next morning he found 'literally filthy', and with a Mertonian he had met at the camp, he filled a complaints book with 'vitriolic but constructive suggestions'. Nothing was heard in reply until a few days later when Douglas was involved in a more serious incident.

As he drove one morning to Cairo, to collect pay for a friend, an Arab ran out from behind a stationary lorry, directly in front of him.

He ran right across me, so without braking fully I swung in towards his starting point to give him more room. Unfortunately he had seen the truck too late and tried to run back. I hit him with one mudguard and broke his left foot more or less clean off under one wheel. He had burst some small artery in his stomach and vomited blood all over everyone but we got him off to hospital within five minutes and made out an accident report.

The Arab died in hospital. There was no question of negligence, and the accident report was accepted; but the major in charge of the course summoned Douglas and threatened him with court martial for making personal use of a War Department vehicle. When Douglas replied that the truck was in his charge and he had authorized the journey, the major brought up the constructive vitriol in the complaints book; he had heard that Douglas was a leading light in complaints about the mess, and he was going to take over the truck.

A few days later, Douglas found that he had been made orderly officer without the customary three days' notice. He had tickets for a concert by the Palestine Symphony Orchestra, so he arranged for a deputy to perform his duties and went. That night the major inspected the guard, the deputy

141

failed to turn it out, and Douglas was again summoned before the major, to be told that he was responsible for the guard's absence and would be reported to the colonel of his regiment as lacking any sense of discipline. Douglas countered by demanding a speedy return to his regiment, where he would tell the colonel the true story. The result was that he was relieved of a further week of orderly duty which had been imposed on him, and given back his truck. Apart from the road accident at its source, the whole affair typified the time- and energy-consuming conflicts with authority which Douglas unerringly attracted.

Seeing the month's course through to completion, he found release in visiting Cairo most evenings and every week-end. Several of his Oxford acquaintances were in the city; but Douglas preferred more cosmopolitan and female company. In Palestine with the regiment he had complained to his mother of the expense and tedium of spending evenings in night clubs with his fellow-officers while the country was 'stiff with fantastic refugee genii and all kinds of amazing people'. He had hoped to gain local contacts through an aunt who had lived 'off and on in Haifa for ten years', but when his mother forwarded the addresses provided by the aunt they were all of English people.

In Cairo, however, he made the acquaintance of a French-Egyptian-Jewish family, the Manis. The main attraction was one of the daughters, Renée, but Douglas put up little resistance to the Levantine custom of bringing boy friends into the family. Like many only children who had spent years at boarding school, he found the rivalries and rituals of a large family continually fascinating. There were five Mani daughters: the fiancées of two had been killed in air crashes, and one had been forced to give up training as a ballet dancer because of an accident. Of the three sons, one had died.

The atmosphere of gloom is not so noticeable as you might expect, and they are all most generous and amiable, but naturally subject, individually to fits of utter depression which make my own efforts in that direction look very amateur.

With the Manis Douglas attended a Jewish wedding, finding it 'a fantastical sort of musical comedy' with impressive moments and splendid singing. With Renée he danced, drank coffee, and ate enormous quantities of strawberries and cream, which were plentiful and cheap. Renée he found 'very sweet' but marked by 'twenty-seven years, sundry almost incredible misfortunes and an attempted suicide'.

At the end of January, having kissed all five daughters and their mother good-bye, Douglas returned to the Sherwood Rangers. He was glad to be back, and the warm weather and opportunity to ride one of the regiment's seven horses most evenings added to his pleasure. With his pay and his mail coming through and Renée planning a visit, even the 'isolated and sandy spot' which the regiment inhabited seemed tolerable. Above all, although they had received no further equipment, the turn of events in the desert made it look certain that they would soon be on the move. On 21 January Rommel had broken out from El Agheila on a new offensive which took him to Derna on 3 February. While such events were hundreds of miles distant from the regiment's camp in Palestine, each development in the fighting made it clear that new units would be called upon and the Sherwood Rangers knew their turn must soon come.

Settled once more with his regiment and having put the frustrations of his course behind him, within two weeks of his return Douglas faced another change in his circumstances. Early in February he had written to Margaret Stanley-Wrench that he was now an expert *camouflageur*, 'though (of course) no one is in the least interested in my qualifications, or in having anything camouflaged'. The fates took about ten days to respond. On 16 February he wrote to his mother:

My latest trouble is an attempt to seize me away, by Division as a Camouflage Staff Officer. In spite of the possibility of extra pips, I don't want to go, and my fate at the moment depends on whether the Colonel can make them change their minds.

Within a week Douglas was writing from a new address, Division headquarters:

At the moment I am in a hopeless situation and don't quite know how to get out of it. I have been arbitrarily made a Camouflage Staff Officer. This doesn't mean any promotion, although I believe I get extra pay. It's not even anything to do with the result of my course.

Douglas's first intention on arriving at the headquarters of the Tenth Armoured Division in Palestine, was to get away again. He found that there was no office for him and the car and driver he was supposed to have did not exist. Others might have delighted in such a posting all the same; but Douglas wrote to Christopherson telling his squadron leader of his ridiculous position and asking to be recalled to the regiment. Meanwhile Douglas saw 'G.S.O.s 1 and 2, a Colonel and a Major', neither of whom had any idea of his duties, 'their line being "It says in black and white that you ought to be here, *and* you've done a camouflage course, so *obviously* you've got to stay."' For three days Douglas had been completely ignored; he decided that if in two more nothing had happened he would ask for an interview with the general.[1] If he did not secure permission to return to the Sherwood Rangers he would threaten to resign his commission. As Douglas

---

[1] General J. G. W. Clark, with whom Edmund Blunden, as he wrote to Douglas later this year, had 'walked the trenches by Gauche Wood'.

had heard that officers were in short supply he felt that this should have the desired result; if not, he wrote to his mother, he would sooner resign 'than sit here drawing extra pay for doing nothing when I could be with the Regiment'. Waiting for the general's reply to the request for an interview, however, Douglas wrote of another plan: 'I'm trying to fix to be sent up the desert on my own and hope to attach myself rather unofficially to a fighting unit and see what I want to.'

Within a week Douglas had 'interviewed the General' and it was this last plan to which he held. For although Douglas recalled that Kellett had assured him, on his unwilling departure, that he would see the general and arrange for his return, the general told him that Kellett had said nothing. Douglas assumed that Kellett wanted to get rid of him, and when, on 25 February, Christopherson wrote 'a very nice letter' assuring Douglas that he would not rest until he had got him out of the job which did not exist, Douglas commented to his mother: 'I'm afraid he's in for a pretty restless time.'

It was not only that Douglas had no wish to be on the staff in a pointless job; the move had taken place 'just when I particularly wanted to be with the Regiment', when they were about to move towards the fighting. If Kellett did not want him Douglas would have to make his own arrangements to 'see what I want to', and the general had given him some grounds for hope.

Meanwhile I shall try and escape to the front line somewhere, by myself, which has provisionally been granted without any definite when or where. Then make sure that when I come back I have some claim to a cushy job.

Early in March Douglas's assessment of the fortunes of his regiment was proved correct. Setting off in Rommel's direction the Sherwood Rangers moved by train to Khatatba in Egypt. There on 30 March they received one Grant tank.

5

Even a batch of letters from England did little to lighten the mood of Douglas's week at Division headquarters. A letter from Yingcheng suggested to him that she was turning into 'an unintelligent gusher', getting 'worse and worse' and becoming 'quite society'. He told her so in his reply. One from Blunden provoked the comment that Blunden seemed unaware of modern airmail services. Several from Diana suggested that she was being 'a good deal too devoted for my conscience . . . I think it's an awful pity she picked me. No one *ought* to pick me, not exclusively.' And news from his mother that *Eight Oxford Poets* had sold out in three weeks only proved to him that its poetry must be 'lousy'. Had Douglas heard the latest news from John Hall of their *Selected Poems* he would have found little to surprise him; for on 5 March Hall returned Douglas's manuscripts to Mrs. Douglas, explaining that John Lehmann did not want the book.

Despite the gloom of his letters, Douglas had spirit enough for an incident recalled by J. E. Morpurgo: a Housey acquaintance who met him in Palestine for the first time since school.

We found ourselves . . . playing rugger for a very scratch side against an even more scratch side. We were ordered to play centre-three-quarter, something that neither of us had ever done before. Keith let it be known to our opponents that I was wearing a Richmond jersey (it was in fact my old House jersey) because my modesty would not allow me to wear my England colours. He emphasized the subterfuge without words by himself wearing a plain blue jersey and white shorts and insisting that Douglas was a good Scots name, and once on the field we did nothing fast except talk, to the entire confusion of the opposition who were lured into belief in our skill to the tune of some 30 or 40 points.

With the hope that he would at some time be permitted to 'escape to the front line' by himself, Douglas resigned himself to his temporary freedom, explaining to his mother that he might as well make the most of it. His living conditions were 'luxurious', in a square white house with balconies, situated in a Jewish country town where 'disgusting quantities' of cream, chocolate, and cheese awaited his consumption. In his first days he had made a friend at the local Royal Air Force station who arranged for him to fly to Cairo 'on duty' virtually whenever he liked. Finding that these trips were generally in trainers, Douglas also had hopes of a few flying lessons. He had time to see more of Palestine, and on one occasion took a trip up the Jordan valley to visit a Jewish communal settlement at Givat Brenner, where he was impressed by the happiness of the children.

Such journeys, however, were only a way of filling in time, offering no real answer to the purposelessness of his existence. On 18 March he was already writing to Jean that he had been bored so long he felt as though he could never be interested in anything again; and this way of life was to last for nearly three months. In the middle of March, the edge had been taken off Douglas's trips to Cairo by a letter from Renée 'extolling the virtues of platonic friendship'. But his visits to the Manis continued and for company in Cairo Renée was replaced by a Turkish girl and two friends of the Manis, one an Iraqui girl, the other Turkish. On a visit to Tel Aviv, however, Douglas had met a girl who attracted him in a more serious way. Unfortunately his visits to that city were infrequent, so for the present she became a subject for his imaginative schemes:

If I come to see *you*, I shall be quite single-minded about it, and shall make all my arrangements for those few days centre round you—you will be the focal point of my world for that time and I hope you'll live up to it and spend as much time as possible with me. I hope I shall come for three or four days. During that time, let's go to your Cellar again, let's bathe, and one evening dress up as finely as we can and go to a dance.

Douglas had met Olga at the Kedem bookshop, where she was over-worked and underpaid. She was alone in Palestine, having heard nothing from her Latvian-Jewish family since the Russian invasion of 1940. Older than he, at twenty-seven she had a protective veneer of sophisticated cynicism, which even Douglas found impressive. After their first meeting, he had written: 'I hope you aren't entirely made of india-rubber. I have a rubber outside myself, but the inside is of more sensitive and fragile material, so be careful.' Olga puzzled him. Her seriousness, which had established a feeling of intimacy on their first evening out, had not only led him to direct his romantic day-dreams towards her, it had left him uncertain about the status of their relationship.

In his first letter, he explained that if he asked her to spend his leave with him, she should be prepared to go out and have a good time, 'but *not*, as the Americans say, to Give Me Your All—you can have your sleep'. Then he launched into a long personal confession:

I am sentimental, as you say all Englishmen are, and therefore although I'm dis-illusioned, I'm not cynical. Most of all I am never cynical about making love. If I tell you between two kisses that I love you more than anyone in the world—you can believe me. But not for long—love comes in waves, it can't be kept burning at the same pitch for years, or it just burns you up altogether. But friendship can: I have few enough friends to be able to count them. To most of them I don't write more than once a year, and they write back to me less often than that. But I know that if I walk round a corner one day, anywhere in the world, and meet one of them, we shall begin exactly where we left off at our last meeting.

Douglas needed a confidante, he needed a friend to whom he could talk intelligently and Olga was both intelligent and interested in poetry,[1] and he needed a replacement for Yingcheng. Which role Olga would play, or whether it could be all three he was not yet certain, but a move to the Cairo area, late in May, shelved the question.

Douglas was still with Division headquarters, but now they had found work for him.

I am the only subaltern in this emporium—the exception to prove the rule that no-one does any work at a Div.H.Q. and everyone gets paid three times too much. I lecture all morning and paint things all afternoon, while the others snore through the heat of the day, and then do office work in the evening.

[1] Douglas sent her copies of 'Search For a God', 'Russians', and 'The Marvel' with his first letter, adding: 'My poems aren't written in thumping dactylic metre like your friend Thomas Hood's, so perhaps you'll not like them.'

For another three weeks he endured such a life, driven by his frustration on one occasion to hurl a typewriter to the ground because its letters were sticking, its spacing awry, and its bell silent: 'I shall probably get more fits of this.' He was short of money, at one time receiving only four pounds a month because the Pay Corps decided to claim arrears, and short of clothes, a pair of corduroy trousers, two pairs of drill, and three shirts having been stolen from his bag on the back of a lorry. Since March he had known that the Second Derbyshire Yeomanry were on their way to the Middle East, with no chance of his being recalled to them, as he had volunteered to leave them for the Indian Army. In May, the arrival and prompt departure from Cairo of Hamo Sassoon re-emphasized his lot: 'he is luckier than I am and will be used at once on his own job'.[1]

However, there were compensations. Douglas's first stay in Cairo in September 1941 had been that of a newcomer; apart from the camouflage course, during which he had other preoccupations, his subsequent visits had been brief and generally spent with the Mani family or in the passing entertainments of the week-end visitor. Now he was able to visit Cairo two or three times each week, and being welcome to stay overnight in the flat of an Oxford acquaintance, David Hicks, he made the city the base for his civilian activities. By this point in the war Cairo had become quite a thriving literary centre. In the late autumn of 1941 Lawrence Durrell, Bernard Spencer, and Robin Fedden had started the poetry magazine *Personal Landscape*, publishing its first number in January 1942. The contributors were mostly exiles from Greece and elsewhere on the Continent or civilians trapped in Egypt by the war: George Seferis, Elie Papadimitriou, Olivia Manning, Terence Tiller, Ruth Speirs, and Robert Liddell were among them. There was also the 'Salamander Society', with its own review *Salamander* and its followers who met on Sunday mornings at the house of Keith Bullen. *Salamander* had its own cosmopolitan flavour, with the French poems and translations of Raoul Parme and Edgar de Knevett, the work of the Italian, Jean Moscatelli, the Yugoslav, Ivo Barbitch, the Armenian, Arsène Yergath, and the Egyptian, Ahmed Rassim: John Cromer and John Waller were the main British contributors.

Douglas could readily have gained entry to either world, and now, having heard from his mother that John Hall's selection had found a publisher,[2] he could have done so with confidence. Bernard Spencer shared David Hicks's flat, and with him Douglas got on well, but Douglas made no contact with

---

[1] Within a month Sassoon was back near Cairo, in hospital at Heliopolis, having been wounded at 'Knightsbridge' with the First Royal Tanks. He remembers Douglas visiting him in hospital.

[2] Hall wrote to Mrs. Douglas on 8 May 1942 explaining that Reginald Moore had offered to publish a volume by Hall, Douglas, and Norman Nicholson (Alan Rook had found a publisher independently), in Bale & Staples's new series, The Modern Reading Library.

Personal Landscape during this stay.[1] *Salamander* he could have joined through John Waller, to whom he had written a month earlier, having seen Waller's work in a local publication. That letter, however, suggesting that they should meet for dinner and mentioning his hope to escape the camouflage job 'as I prefer being an ordinary regimental officer', had indicated Douglas's view of two local publications, with fine candour:

I am sorry you allowed yourself to take part in producing such a shocker as *Orientations*. It is worse than anything in that line I've ever seen which is saying something. It should have been edited by Geoffrey Grigson. . . .

I see *Parade* awarded you an honorary hockey blue in rather a clumsy sentence. What drivel some of their 'Poetry' letters are.

Salamander may well have been better than the two magazines Douglas mentions, but he had nothing to do with it. Only a few weeks after his first meeting with David Hicks, however, Douglas began publishing work in *Citadel*, a largely literary monthly which Hicks edited from the Anglo-Egyptian Institute where he lectured. Douglas had mentioned in the letter to Waller that he had not written anything 'for some time', and these first contributions, in the July 1942 issue, were the Weedon story of dissection and the poem 'Syria'.

Hicks's flat, shared also by a journalist who had been a machine-gunner in the International Brigade, made a base camp rather than a club, and from it Douglas set out to enjoy the pleasures which he preferred. David Hicks kept a diary at this time and its brief notes on Douglas's visits record his preoccupations:

May 21   Keith Douglas arrived (last seen in 1939)
   23   Douglas came to stay; Fortunée with him
   27   dined with Douglas, then went to Groppi's, met his two nice Turkish girls
   30   dined at New Star; Fortunée with Douglas
June 2   Douglas came (a number of others staying)
   7   breakfast with Douglas at Groppi's; met Fortunée's sister and Fortunée came
  10   party, Douglas came
  14   Douglas joined us at swimming pool at Pyramids

In a report to his mother on his current life Douglas placed a similar emphasis:

I spent a pleasant evening dancing with the Turkish girl in open air under a full moon—it was lovely and cool and as jasmin is in season I bought a wreath and hung it round her neck—it is much fresher than jasmin scent . . . spent a very

---

[1] At the end of May Douglas described Spencer to Jean as 'a minor poet who once edited things with Spender—but to do him justice, has forgotten it'. Hicks, like others in Cairo at this time, recalls, however, that Spencer and Douglas became good occasional friends. Spencer died in 1957.

riotous evening with David and the others last weekend, when I ate half a chicken in an Arab restaurant . . . also a very nice sort of treacle sponge.

To Jean, writing on the same day at the end of May, he offered a more Leporello-like account: 'Renée, incidentally, is succeeded by Olga (Latvian, Palestine Area), Fortunée, Reman, Marcelle, Pilar (Cairo Area, Iraqui, Turk, Turk, Spanish). So the situation is well in hand.' Perhaps Fortunée and one of the Turkish girls were the friends of the Manis? Perhaps Reman or Marcelle had been her Cairo successor? In his letters Douglas gave few of the girls more detailed treatment.

Pilar had 'lovely hands and reasonably nice eyes and hair; but seems much affected by the semi-darkness in which her family always seems to live.' Douglas wanted to do her portrait but thought her a difficult subject because her attraction lay in her expression when she spoke. Marcelle was recovering from the loss of her fiancé in Paris. Having written to him for several months without reply, one day she simply received a parcel containing all of her letters, each stamped '*Décédé*'. One of the Turkish girls could have been the 'Turkish Delight' Douglas discussed in a letter to Olga in May:

The question of the Turkish Delight still is not solved. What can I do, not to hurt or insult her? She is intelligent and would be a delightful acquaintance and a good friend but she expects me to sleep with her, even if I only visit her for an afternoon. And I think she is in love with me, she doesn't seem to make a habit of sleeping with people. Myself, I need to sleep with someone sometimes, but I hate the idea of 'using' her, because she's really too good a person to be used, and ignored the rest of the time, and anyway I feel pretty low if I sleep with someone I'm not in love with. I wish the most natural desires and functions weren't rendered almost monstrous by the ridiculous arrangements of society. When I think what it is like to be really happy, and how little is necessary to make us happy, it's quite absurd to see how seldom anyone is happy.

But we should not always be so serious and introspective in our letters.

Olga, as the tone of Douglas's letter suggests, had settled into the role of friend and confidante. Douglas now teased her for being 'as ever . . . so serious and monitory' in her letters but he still responded with the same blend of self-protection and directness: and Olga could draw him into subjects which he did not normally discuss:

You want to know if I believe in anything and imply that you believe in nothing. Well, I do believe in something, and I have come to the conclusion that the particulars of my creed shouldn't be examined too often. If you have something valuable, keep it in a safe place and look at it only occasionally, to see if it is all right. If you keep taking it out to play with it you'll break it or lose it sooner or later.

On 15 June Douglas's brief period amid the pleasures of Cairo came to an end, though not as significantly as is suggested by Hicks's cryptic diary entry for that day: 'KD off to the desert.' While Douglas was in Cairo the Sherwood Rangers had moved closer to the desert war. With Rommel evidently preparing a new offensive during April, they had even been given three light tanks; at the end of May, however, when the German attack came, the regiment had suffered the strange fate of first having their few tanks taken away from them and then being moved closer to the fighting. Sent west of Sidi Barani to act as an 'emergency force', they arrived to discover that they were not required there and were sent back to 'Charing Cross', ten miles south of Mersa Matruh. One week later, tankless, they were ordered to complete their brigade training, and on the sixty-mile rail journey south to Amariya were bombed and strafed by German planes. Thus, their first experience of battle as a tank regiment, like their first wartime casualty, occurred on a train. It was towards their training area that Douglas had moved, still as a member of Divisional Staff.

Within six days of Douglas's move Rommel entered Tobruk; on 29 June the Axis army was at Mersa Matruh and the first day of July saw their forces at El Alamein, facing the Egyptian border. Now began the period known as 'the Flap', when Arabs re-wrote their shop signs in German, and British expatriates boarded eastbound trains. Cairo, the bureaucratic centre for the front to which British military force was most deeply committed, prepared for the enemy: at night the sky over the city was lit with fires and smoke. G.H.Q. was burning its records.

6

Douglas was in the desert for no more than two weeks; at the start of July moving, with his camouflage job, to Alexandria. Once more he had no duties and not only lived free of the restrictions of camp, but had lodgings overlooking Stanley Bay. At the changing rooms on the beach there, only a day or two after his arrival, he met Joe Arsenault, whom he had not seen since they had both been in the second row of the scrum at Christ's Hospital. They arranged to meet that evening in the Monseigneur Club and Arsenault, arriving early, was greeted by a shout from the bar; it was Norman Ilett, recently arrived in Alexandria as an officer in the 15th M.T.B. flotilla, the last naval unit left in Alexandria after 'the Flap'. Shortly afterwards Douglas turned up, to join them for the first of several evenings together.

Norman was likely to be in Alexandria for some time, and Arsenault had free time at the moment, his regiment, the 44th Tanks, resting at a nearby camp after the loss of every one of their tanks in the recent fighting. A day or two after their first meeting Douglas and Arsenault met again at the

KD on the beach at Stanley Bay, Alexandria, and (*right*) Milena

beach for a swim and a drink. There they saw two attractive girls being saved by a huge Australian from the annoying attentions of an Egyptian; Douglas and his friend offered the girls their company and asked them to look after their cameras while they swam. (The camera Douglas possessed was one of the few perquisites of his post as *camouflageur*.) The girls invited them home for tea, and afterwards repeated the invitation for the following Wednesday. Douglas, with more time on his hands than Arsenault, soon became a regular visitor.

Of the two girls, Milena and her cousin Clara, it was Milena towards whom Douglas directed most of his attention. The same age as he, Milena bore an air of competence in every situation—she was the last person, in fact, to require assistance in dealing with a troublesome man on the beach, and the last person to refuse it. As she worked only from nine till three, running the Alexandria dockyard office of Saccone and Speed, who supplied the Navy with wines and spirits, she had time enough to spend with Douglas and he was only too pleased to spend time with her. Milena, who spoke French, Italian, and Arabic with the ease of someone who had spent her life in Alexandria, as well as English (with an 'absurd accent', wrote Douglas), was perfectly placed to introduce him to this new city. Her father, a native of Gibraltar, welcomed everyone she brought to their home at Rouchdy Pasha[1] and her mother, an Italian, was soon darning and ironing Douglas's clothes and feeding him from the family's rations.

Out of these weeks of mainly leisurely life in Alexandria Douglas wrote

[1] 352 Avenue Fouad I[er].

two poems in which the elusiveness and personal discoveries of 'Syria' gave way to simple description. In 'L'Autobus' he observed a motorbus from 'the school of the Incarnation', making 'bulldog grunts in its nose' as it turned into the Saturday traffic, and thought of the ancestors of its school-girl passengers: 'perhaps Odysseus' bondwomen . . . variegated women of the ports / and seabounded villages'. Allowing his fancy to develop without pressure in the leisurely movement of the six-line stanza he had most used in his romantic poems at Oxford, Douglas found room to think of 'eyed ships' and 'the wine-dark sea's white towns / famous for beauty and nefarious arts'. His other poem, 'Egyptian Sentry, Corniche, Alexandria', remained within the world of the modern city where

> The moon shines on the modern flats
> where sentient lovers or rich couples
> lie loving or sleeping after eating.
> In the town the cafés and cabarets seating
> gossipers, soldiers, drunkards, supple
> women of the town, shut out the moon with slats.

Beside this world there is the sentry's life of poverty, but the very extremity of its sensations, its 'stinks and noises', its filth, have engendered a blank placidity. To the sentry:

> There is no pain, no pleasure, life's no puzzle
> but a standing, a leaning, a sleep between the coasts
>
> of birth and dying. . . .

But if Douglas remains safely within the broad contrasts seen by the visitor, his poem exists to celebrate the sentry's passivity. For in the man's simple acceptance he perceives a dignity more immediately human than that of art:

> Everywhere is a real or artificial race
> of life, a struggle of everyone to be
> master or mistress of some hour.
> But of this no scent or sound reaches him there.
> He leans and looks at the sea:
> sweat lines the statue of a face.

Douglas did not put much of himself into either of the poems, but the sentry, immune to the frantic life around him, and the school-girls, 'ignorant of the love or pain / to come', share a freedom from the troublesome emotions with which he was all too familiar; that he should write of them with such detachment perhaps suggests he had reached an impasse in more than his poetry. There is a kind of placidity to the two poems which could well have grown out of the turn his life had taken in Alexandria.

Before Douglas had arrived in the city he had simply been passing the time, either pleasantly or infuriatingly, until he could take himself to the front. Nothing had happened to change the absurdity of his military situation. While his camouflage job remained meaningless, serving only to keep him away from the action he had expected ever since he left England, each passing week made it clearer that events in the desert were building towards a climax. Early in August Joe Arsenault had returned with his regiment to the desert and the first El Alamein. Later that month Norman Ilett, who sometimes accompanied Douglas on his visits to Milena's parents, the Pegnas, had been in a raid up the coast. He recalls that 'Keith tried to get my C.O. to smuggle him to sea with us on the Tobruk raid. At that time he'd no experience of action and wanted to see it. We couldn't do it, of course.' There had been sufficient likelihood that Ilett would not return for him to give Douglas all his spare cash, three pounds, to spend if he failed to appear. Four out of nine of the flotilla's boats returned, one of them Ilett's, but Douglas had spent the money.

Although he hoped somehow to get into action, at the same time Douglas had come increasingly to see Milena as a true successor to Yingcheng. He later described her attraction: an odd face with 'delicate bones and nobility of line'; a 'twisted smile and curious sad dishonest eyes'; and a 'sinuous and cleanly made body, like a drawing made with an airbrush'. For six weeks Douglas spent nearly all his time with her. They had tea at the Cecil Hotel and dined and danced at the Monseigneur or drank cocktails at the Metropole, when they had money; when they were hard up, they enjoyed a slow, watered ouzo at a pavement café or ate bacon, egg, and chips at the café on the Boulevard Saad Zaghloul: a life more exotic perhaps than that with Yingcheng at Oxford, but Milena, with cosmopolitian assurance, cared little whether their pleasures were simple or grand.

With Milena Douglas renewed his talkative day-dreams and imaginative schemes for the future. After the war they would travel, even buy an island, and Milena remembers how hurt Douglas looked when on one occasion she asked him what they were to do for money. Douglas rarely revealed such schemes in letters; though sometimes he put them into a last page which he censored the following morning. But once in a letter to Olga, written when slightly drunk, the reading of *Valse des Fleurs*, set in Imperial Russia, set off his fancies in a page which he did not excise.

Whenever I read such fantastic descriptions it reminds me that England will never be my home country. I must make my life extend across at least half the world, to be happy. I love people, and I think my only real ambition apart from those ambitions connected with making my living, is to meet more and more people, each different and more fascinating than the last, and to love them all, and to be loved by them.

Milena's photograph of KD with their dog, Alexandria 1942

Douglas commented: 'You understand that I never say things like this unless I am drunk': but these were things he would probably have wished to say more often when sober, when he was happy. With Milena he was happy, and her warmth of character made it easy for him to share at least his playful romances.

To Milena Douglas's capacity for enjoyment made him attractive company. In addition he took her life seriously, writing, despite her protests, to abuse the British Vice-Consul in Alexandria after hearing that she had been casually treated on a visit to the Consulate. She also discovered his resolute sense of justice when Douglas ignored the convention that British officers should keep quiet, and gave evidence against the driver of an Egyptian army truck who had run over a boy. Their differences in temperament worried her, and she was convinced that she was not nearly intelligent enough for him, but when, in August, Douglas asked her to become engaged, he overruled such doubts, and with reservations she agreed. If they broke up, Milena recalls him saying, he would go off and get himself killed.

On 18 August he wrote to his mother of two possible moves towards the fighting. First he had heard that the Second Derbyshire Yeomanry might after all accept his return to them. Second he suggested that the Sherwood

Rangers at last looked like wanting him back. With his letter Douglas enclosed a poem which showed a composure very different from that of his two previous poems.

> My mind's silence is not that of a wood
> warm and full of the sun's patience,
> who peers through the leaves waiting
> perhaps the arrival of a god,
> silence I welcomed when I could:
> but this deceptive quiet is
> the fastening of a soundproof trap
> whose idiot crew must not escape.

The poem was called 'Devils' and the 'idiot crew' were devils inside the mind. Only because these were ignorant of the 'devils' outside, 'flying in the clouds . . . running on the earth . . . imperceptibly spinning / through the black air alive with evils', was the poet safe;

> Inside the unsubstantial wall
> these idiots of the mind can't hear
> the demons talking in the air
> who think my mind void. That's all;
> there'll be an alliance of devils if it fall.

Two days after this poem and letter, the Second Derbyshire Yeomanry joined battle without Douglas. Ten days after that, on 30 August, while Douglas still waited for notification of his move, the Sherwood Rangers took up battle positions without him: now, for the first time in the war, they possessed a full complement of tanks.

On the night of the 31st, the regiment tried to locate the enemy but failed. The next morning they met the experience which they had long awaited.

The Regiment advanced to within 2,000 yards of the enemy and opened fire. We shelled the German positions for five minutes. There was no reply—the very quietness of the enemy was ominous.

In front of us were black dots on the skyline, some moving, some stationary. It was our first view of enemy tanks.

C Squadron went ahead, and in open order in line sailed to within 150 yards of the enemy position. Then at last the German anti-tank gunners opened up. Two C Squadron tanks were hit immediately and went up in flames.

Now the whole Regiment advanced and came under intense enemy fire. Six C Squadron tanks and one from B were hit and blazed. Four more were disabled. The enemy had cunningly held his fire until we were right on top of him.

'The first of our Balaclava charges,' said John Semken, one of the participants, 'and not our last.'

155

John Masefield was killed in this engagement, along with another officer and five other ranks. Considering the nature of the battle these losses might have been trebled, and had not the reconnaissance troop under Lieutenant Garrett collected the wounded under heavy fire, they would certainly have been higher. On this, the regiment's first day of tank fighting, Garrett and Sweeney Todd won the M.C. and two troopers the M.M.

The following day it was apparent that the Germans had withdrawn, but they sent forward small parties of tanks trying to tempt the Sherwood Rangers on to their new defences. Proving their ability to learn rapidly, the regiment refused to be drawn, and spent the day watching bombers and artillery forcing the enemy to move from untenable positions. The next day, 3 September, the Sherwood Rangers examined the positions they had assaulted, finding twenty-one German tanks destroyed opposite their brigade's positions: how much had been due to their charge, however, could not be assessed. A party from Douglas's former A Squadron was used to help harry the enemy, but the regiment had finished its fighting for the present. General Montgomery, for whom this battle of Alam Halfa had also been a new experience—his first desert battle—gave the awards for gallantry, and on 14 September the Sherwood Rangers moved back to their training area at Wadi Natrun, having stayed on for a week to train on the battlefield, in the manner of a batsman practising his strokes after almost being bowled.

The battle of Alam Halfa had left Rommel's forces on the Egyptian border, but in their failure to break through the Allied defences they had lost the initiative. Now their long advance had not only been halted, it had left them waiting with stretched and harassed supply lines for what would clearly be a massive counterstroke. On 20 September Douglas wrote to his mother with the hope that he would be one of its participants: 'It appears to be arranged that at last I am to leave this ridiculous job and return to the Sherwood Rangers Yeomanry.'

Clearing the way for his departure he enclosed in his letter two poems, one of which wrote of war. Here, in 'Christodoulos', the old god of 'Encounter with a God' has become a fat businessman, a war profiteer and warmonger who 'moves, and shakes / his seven chins':

> . . . He is that freak
> a successful alchemist, and makes
> God knows how much a week.

From the 'smoke and smells' of his attic emerge the soldiers, who are the 'wastage from his alchemy', shouting for an enemy in the streets of the base town, 'weak as wounded, leaning in a knot'. Christodoulos, however, has other concerns. He is 'the original wise one':

from whose experiments they told
how War can be the famous stone
for turning rubbish into gold.

Douglas's other poem, 'Egypt', similarly made round a personification and
similarly satirical, concerned the world he hoped to leave behind: a country
of poverty embodied in a girl beggar who is diseased and blind in one eye
and who

> . . . in fifteen years of living
> found nothing different from death
> but the difference of moving
> and the nuisance of breath.

The passivity which Douglas had found room to celebrate in his poem on the Egyptian sentry is replaced by a diseased 'listlessness' and a criminal 'apathy': he concludes, 'My God, the king of this country must be proud.'

By the end of the month Douglas was at Wadi Natrun, meeting the Sherwood Rangers after their first tank battle, and surrounded by the preparations for the offensive. For the moment he was to stay with them, but not as a tank commander. Still officially attached to Division head-quarters, he was to become part of the headquarters supply group.

Afer two weeks in the desert, having left Alexandria for an indefinite stay, Douglas returned to the city by chance. In a letter of 7 October to Olga, he explained what happened:

I came back by accident, having broken down with a lorry outside Alex. I towed it in, in the dark, and went to [Milena's] house for the night. She was out with Norman. That seemed pretty natural, and I sat down to wait. They came in soon afterwards, and immediately a sort of strain settled on the room. Everything anyone said was forced out. Milena went up to find some blankets for me and I went after her and asked her what was the matter. She told me, partly, but not about Norman—she hadn't even told Norman.

Milena had said that she felt the same towards him as ever but it was not the love he wanted. While he was away, she had discovered she loved someone else. There was a brief scene as Douglas tried to get Milena to tell him more, the sounds of which brought Norman upstairs. The two men then went for a walk, in the course of which the situation between Milena and Norman became clear to Douglas. Milena recalls that when they returned half an hour later Douglas, who had earlier seemed explosive, now talked with wry resignation. To Olga, however, Douglas wrote:

That is the worst night I've ever spent, bar one. I'm still feeling somehow like a man might feel who has to walk miles and miles home with a bad wound, drag-ging his feet, trying to hold himself so as not to feel the wound too much. It has opened the old wound as well.

Earlier in his letter Douglas had explained the 'old wound', his loss of Yingcheng; he thought he had told Olga about it, but did not know whether he had made it clear that all his life since then 'had been a time of recovery from that episode. I had recovered, anyway, as far as anyone ever does. Now I have done exactly the same thing again.'

Douglas was writing from David Hicks's flat in Cairo, where he was spending a few days' leave. For two months he had lost contact with Olga; and it was a letter from her, at last reaching him after going to several wrong addresses, which had given him occasion to reply: 'I'm afraid I'm not much worth finding, though.' Having explained the events at Milena's house, he told Olga that if she thought they made him no use to her, she should write at once and say so; but it made no difference to his feelings about her:

ours is an understanding, and I think we love each other. One can't stop loving. But there are these women in the world who send me mad. I suppose I shall meet others, and if none of them will marry me, I shall never marry. Perhaps it is better than marriage to have friends like you. Please Olga, never think that anything that happens to me would alter that. Even if I had married a woman I was mad about, I should keep my friendships, and if it broke my marriage and ruined my greatest happiness, I would still keep them—I can't help myself.

Douglas did not think that he would get to Palestine 'for years, literally' but he would sooner or later, or Olga would leave it.

I don't like, almost I hate and fear many Jews—yet I feel more and more that in the end it will be a Jewess I marry. Probably from constantly suffering real or fancied injustice, I have acquired something of a Jewish mentality myself.[1]

For the present, he could do nothing except 'sweat it out': but Olga could help him a good deal, he felt, so long as she did not feel he was coming back to her 'as a sort of second best—I'm not, you are where you always were.'

Douglas stayed with Hicks for two more days:

Oct. 6 Keith Douglas arrived; took him and Bill Allen to dinner
   7 met KD Luckies 9.30
   8 lunch with MK and Douglas
   9 with Douglas Low and Douglas in Groppi's garden; Douglas left this evening.

Nine days later, back at Division headquarters at Wadi Natrun, Douglas wrote his first poem to Milena, 'The Knife'. If it drew on the poet Douglas had read to Mary Benson on board ship, it was his own love poem to Yingcheng, 'Stranger', which it most clearly echoed.

---

[1] Writing a poem of the Sabbath's busy atmosphere, 'Saturday Evening in Jerusalem', Douglas had concluded:

> But among these Jews I am the Jew
> the outcast, wandering down the steep road
> into the hostile dark square:
> and standing in the unlit corner here
> know I am alone and cursed by God
> as if lost on my first morning at school.

Keith Douglas

Can I explain this to you? Your eyes
are entrances the mouths of caves—
I issue from wonderful interiors
upon a blessed sea and a fine day,
from inside these caves I look and dream. . . .

Yes, to touch two fingers made us worlds,
stars, waters, promontories, chaos,
swooning in elements without form or time
come down through long seas among sea marvels
embracing like survivors on our islands.

This I think happened to us together
though now no shadow of it flickers in your hands,
your eyes look down on banal streets.
If I talk to you I might be a bird
with a message, a dead man, a photograph.

Within a couple of days Douglas had completed another poem, with the
title 'Milena',[1] and sent it to Hicks with a note asking him to 'print this if
you can, and soon—because it will all help my getting accustomed to the
situation.' It was the dirge of a lover who finds the desert wind, stars, moon,
and sands as 'wonderful and hard' as his lost love, leaving him with a new
mistress, pain.

[1] Published in *Collected Poems* with its first line for title: 'I listen to the desert wind'.

KD's drawing of Milena

6

The Western Desert

October 1942 - January 1943

> . . . the Germans undoubtedly fought as long
> and as well as they could. But when they broke
> they broke properly, and the pursuit was very
> like hunting in England, except that instead of
> killing the fox when we found him, we gave
> him a tin of bully beef and searched him for
> souvenirs.
>
> (November 1942 to Olga)

I

At the Divisional training area Douglas was surrounded by the preparations
for an offensive clearly intended to push Rommel back for once and all.
From the scale of the supplies and reserves which poured into the area, this
was to be no repetition of the limited 'Brevity' and 'Crusader' attacks, and
from the morale of those who were to take part, victory looked certain. Even
the Sherwood Rangers now appeared an impressive fighting force. They
had thirteen Crusaders, low-lined tanks which were fast if mechanically
unreliable, and although generally used for locating the enemy rather
than for assault, with their new six-pounder guns well able to account for
themselves. Nine of these were the main equipment of Douglas's former
A Squadron. The regiment's real strength lay in B and C Squadrons,
which between them had twenty Grants—powerfully armed and heavily
armoured tanks which had already helped give the Imperial forces superiority despite the fact that to fire the big gun in the sub-turret effectively,
three-quarters of the tank had to be exposed, and that they bore the nickname 'Ronsons', for their fuel 'lit first time' they were hit—and eleven of
the new Shermans, compact, heavy tanks which were mechanically sound
and well armed and were to become the Allies' standard tank throughout
the war. C Squadron had the Shermans as reward for their part at Alam
Halfa.

Douglas, having renewed his efforts to return to the regiment, had finally
learnt that his role in the battle was to be in charge of a two-ton truck at

161

headquarters. When the huge barrage announced the start of the El Alamein offensive on 23 October, he heard it twenty miles behind the lines. Three days earlier, along with his dirge to love, he had written an anticipation of the attack; but 'The Offensive' was an outsider's poem. The 'martial sun' is the moon's 'lord'; the stars are once more heroes in the sky, though they are now dead; 'devils' are to be loosed by the action; and Time again comes round eating. Before this catalogue of earlier images, however, Douglas had found the sinister ambiguity of his 'Christodoulos' poem, in an image which momentarily made contact with the occasion.

> So in conjecture stands
> my starlit body; the mind
> mobile as a fox sneaks round
> the sleepers waiting for their wounds.

Do they wait with soldierly cynicism for their 'Blighty', or as a doomed race?

An hour before daylight on 24 October, the Sherwood Rangers emerged from a lane through the enemy's minefield and advanced slowly for about a mile. As they prepared to move south, anti-tank guns opened up all round them with heavy fire, some at a range of only fifty yards. 'The whole scene', writes the regiment's historian, 'was criss-crossed with yellow tracer fire from enemy machine guns, and armour-piercing fire from the anti-tank guns came screaming through the darkness like devilish red-hot cricket balls.' With a stream of tanks and other vehicles bunched together in the lanes of the minefield, Christopherson's A Squadron could only move forward. Five of their nine Crusaders were immediately hit, though in the first five minutes two German tanks were set on fire. Then B Squadron's heavy Grants lumbered from the minefield into the appalling fire. Within minutes four were hit.

Kellett, realizing that if the rest of the regiment were trapped in the minefield's lanes daylight would make them a perfect target, ordered the remainder of B Squadron to line up beside his command tank, 'Robin Hood', and engage the enemy. Under cover of their fire, those in the minefield should turn round and escape. Four more Grants were lost and three of Christopherson's four remaining Crusaders, including his own. But the regiment had turned in the minefield, and the survivors from A and B Squadrons joined them behind Miteiriya Ridge.

The intensity of the fire had been such that when the Crusader of one troop leader received a hit which halted it, a second hit killed its commander and wireless operator, and a third its gunner. As the driver baled out he was machine-gunned before he could reach the cover of a slit trench. Trapped there until darkness, he was taken prisoner in the night by a patrol of very young Germans who gave him chocolate and water. Later, the tanks of another regiment rescued him.

In the evening, the regiment repelled two German counter-attacks, in the first destroying seven enemy tanks. Then, after another abortive attempt to break through the minefield, they were withdrawn for a brief rest. In these two days' fighting, twelve of the regiment had been killed; and along with Christopherson, wounded from a shell which burst just above his tank, and Garrett, wounded when bombs fell by the command tank, there were fifty-six wounded. All the officers of A Squadron had been either killed, wounded, or lost their tanks.

Anything Douglas knew of this was only through rumour; but four days after hearing the opening barrage, he decided he had had enough. Putting on a freshly laundered uniform, he loaded his kit on to his two-ton Ford truck and drove west, towards the fighting. He had decided to put into action his long-delayed plan. He would report to Kellett for duty, glossing over the fact that his orders were directly to the contrary: they had come from Division and he assumed Kellett would be too busy to check. If his story was not accepted by the colonel, Douglas planned to drive back past Alexandria and on to Palestine, where he would enjoy himself until he was caught and court-martialled.

With him Douglas took a fitter from Division, who would return the truck if Kellett accepted him; and his batman, who would stay with the technical stores lorry during the battle. The batman was delighted by Douglas's scheme: ' "I like you, sir," he said. "You're shit or bust, you are." '[1] Douglas felt that the plan was part of his 'little-boy' mentality which earlier might have 'wanted to run away and be a pirate'.

Through the huge backstage to the offensive, Douglas drove the fifteen miles to the regiment's supply echelon. There he tested his story and it seemed to be believed; Kellett would be glad to see him, he was told, for A Squadron had hardly an officer left. Four miles further on, Douglas found the rest of the regiment and reported to Kellett who was in the 15 cwt. truck used as an office. The colonel's welcome was as potentially ironic as Douglas's story had been evasive: ' "We're *most* glad to see you— er—as always." ' He sent Douglas to A Squadron to fix up a troop of tanks with its temporary leader Andrew;[2] and having prepared them for the move back into action the next morning, Douglas's mood was one of immense relief. Having a poem ready-made for the occasion, he sent back a copy of 'The Offensive' with a letter to David Hicks. Then, having writ-

---

[1] This, and subsequent quotations from direct speech, are taken from Douglas's war narrative, *Alamein to Zem Zem*, to which detailed references are given in the notes.

[2] Andrew, like 'Sweeney Todd', and 'Evan' below, are the names used by Douglas in *Alamein to Zem Zem*.

KD in the desert, 1942

ten to his mother,[1] with thoughts of the dangers which faced him and his likely response to them he went to sleep.

The next day Douglas, with the regiment, made towards the fighting; but apart from the bombs of a single plane, they came no closer to the battle than a view of the customary German counter-attack in the sunset. This was probably as well for Douglas, for he had never before seen a Crusader of the kind he now commanded, and had only once been inside its predecessor, the Mark II. His new model, the Mark III, had a crew of

[1] Both letters were lost.

three: driver, gunner, and commander, the automatic breech mechanism of its six-pounder gun having made redundant the fourth crewman of the Mark II, the loader. That night, however, the regiment came under fire heavy enough for Douglas to wonder whether his imagination had done justice to the reality of fighting. He felt loathe to leave the comparative security of his tank and found himself talking as excitedly and obscenely as everyone else.

In the mist of the following morning, they again moved towards the front, the Crusaders of A Squadron as usual at the head of the column, in order to locate the enemy and then lie low while the heavy tanks took over the fighting. Douglas's task was to follow the vague shape of Andrew's tank ahead of him in the mist; but seeing a British truck in what he had assumed to be no-man's-land, he went off to ask its business, and lost the regiment. After wandering through another regiment, and in his anxious search running over the body of a dead Libyan, he found the Sherwood Rangers and joined them to drink tea and read, while shells passed intermittently. In the afternoon they were still awaiting further orders when an infantry patrol came up to Douglas's tank and asked his help in dislodging a party of snipers. The ground all round was indented with weapon pits and slit trenches left by the enemy and it was the infantry's job to clear these of real or potential snipers and collect the prisoners. As there seemed nothing else to do, Douglas gained Andrew's half-hearted permission and moved into his first engagement with the enemy.

First his gunner, Evan, sprayed the area with fire from the tank's machine-gun, but after a few shots its firing stopped. Then, after a furious argument over what was wrong, Douglas ordered the driver to advance, and Evan, having discovered a fault in the remote control, mounted the gun on a biscuit tin on the tank's turret and fired aimlessly. Two Germans emerged from a pit, and when Evan clambered from the tank waving the revolver which he had snatched from Douglas, several more rose up from the ground. Douglas joined his gunner and taking from one of the pits a rifle, which was in fact jammed, he helped collect a party of forty prisoners. To Kellett's dissatisfaction, the prisoners were returned to Brigade as a prize of the infantry, while Douglas retired with his tank to tidy up its disorder and share the loot of clothing and weapons which they had won.

Fifteen minutes after they had returned to the regiment someone reported enemy tanks advancing. Messages over the tank's wireless made it clear that the advanced part of the regiment had begun a disorderly retreat, and as an intense barrage began falling where Douglas was stationed, his own feelings of fear explained their action. With as much understanding of psychology as of tactics, Kellett ordered the whole regiment to open fire at a range of a thousand yards. Douglas could see nothing of the enemy but in the din of explosions and gunfire and the feverish haste of loading and firing as often as possible, fear was replaced by exhilaration. With darkness, the action ended as suddenly as it had begun and at two o'clock the next morning the regiment was withdrawn for four days' rest.

A night or two later Colonel Kellett explained that they had withdrawn so that others could complete the crumbling process of El Alamein, leaving the regiment fresh to administer the *coup de grâce* to the enemy's armour. Then they could go home, leaving 'the other buggers' to do the chasing. Douglas found the speech impressive, and although he was not deceived, it gave him a chance to pass cheering news to his mother. 'A chance we might be home soon I believe at last.' His letter mentioned that Milena had decided to marry Norman and explained the circumstances of his return to the regiment; and although for reasons of censorship he could not say where he was, he left no room for doubt:

anything you read in the papers around the end of Oct., the date of this letter, may concern me. . . . I'm back with the regiment, which has done and is doing very well indeed. I am still supposed to be with Div. HQ, but they forgot about me, and I trotted off when no one was looking. They haven't noticed yet, although they told me they couldn't spare me to return to the regt.!

This news he repeated in a letter to Jean Turner: he was back and 'thank heaven for it . . . and life is pretty mobile and interesting.' Douglas also told her of losing Milena to Norman, 'in two heart-rending scenes'. Confirming that he bore no grudge, however, Douglas suggested that Jean, now in the W.R.N.S., should contact Milena or Norman if ever she were posted to the Middle East.

On 2 November the Sherwood Rangers moved back to battle. Many of the officers wounded in the first days' fighting, including Christopherson, had returned, and with Bethell-Fox back with A Squadron from a gunnery course, Douglas was now in more familiar company. Emerging at first light from a minefield, their re-entry was less smooth than expected. With enemy fire growing in intensity they were forced to deploy for action at once, though experience restrained any wish for a charge. Firing from hull-down positions, with the bulk of their tanks concealed from the enemy —in the case of the Shermans and Crusaders, if not the Grants—they held their ground and even pressed cautiously forward.

The landscape of Douglas's first two days of action had been littered with derelicts and the signs of earlier fighting. Now, with the added results of the 'crumbling process' which had gone on during their four days' rest, he passed through a strange new world. Everywhere there were unburied dead, Germans, Italians, Libyans, New Zealanders, Highlanders, and English, some in unbelievable postures, covered with flies, others reclining

Crusaders in the desert

A line of Shermans

Italian tank and Breda gun

Derelict German 50 mm. anti-tank gun

in trenches as if asleep. Moving, except under heavy fire, with head and shoulders above the turret top for better view, it was necessary to scan each trench and weapon pit for possible snipers and it was there the dead lay. With them were the wounded of the most recent fighting; but coming across a New Zealander whose leg was hit in several places, Douglas was told by the man that he had been lying for two days in his trench. The explosion which caused his wounds had damaged his water bottle so he had been without water. Douglas gained permission to take this man to safety, and having left him at the first-aid post, he recrossed this landscape to return to the regiment. A little later, he was crossing this ground again to refuel and take two tanks with oil leaks to the workshops. There Douglas was given the only available tank in running order. It was covered in blood from the wounds of two of its crew, hit by a sniper. Beside the tank, seemingly unshaken, the driver stood eating meat and vegetables out of a tin. Douglas had already learnt that the long delays which interspersed periods of action were spent reading Westerns and nibbling tinned cheese or making tea, beside the dead.

By the time Douglas and his crew had cleared what blood they could from their new tank it was too late to return to the squadron. So passing the night where they were, they returned the next morning. Blood was still tacky in the tank, Douglas's boots slipping on the floor, and crowds of flies followed them everywhere.

The previous day, the regiment had seen no more action after Douglas's departure for the workshops, but before he arrived that morning, A Squadron had already carried out 'a magnificent fighting reconnaissance'. Enemy machine-guns and snipers' nests had been pinpointed and then destroyed, and as they advanced, the squadron had hammered away at the German anti-tank screen. It was the ideal fighting for a Crusader, and with the engagement Christopherson had won an M.C.

This day, 3 November, Rommel had received Hitler's order not to retreat one millimetre, but he was already skilfully doing so: putting up screens of defence by day, counter-attacking with the sunset behind his forces, and withdrawing to new positions by night. Far from the *coup de grâce* they had anticipated, the fine reconnaissance of the early morning led the Sherwood Rangers to a day pinned down by relentless fire from the enemy's guns. By evening, losses in A Squadron, largely from the accuracy and power of the 88 mm. anti-aircraft gun which Rommel deployed as an anti-tank weapon, and mechanical failures had left Douglas in command. Ordered over the wireless by Kellett to 'control your squadron and stop it wandering', Douglas was able to reply: 'The Squadron now consists of my own tank and one other.' It was his first really bad day of action, and in its course Bethell-Fox had been wounded, his driver killed.

That evening, with the regiment settled into leaguer, Jack Holman of
C Squadron arrived late from the heavy day's fighting, his tank on fire. He
was first dressed down for his tardiness and then ignored as though a
stranger lost from some other unit. Douglas had seen his Grant return and
observed this treatment, and Holman recalls that he went out of his way to
make up for such an ill welcome. Douglas got men to put out the fire and
clean up the tank, and blankets and coffee for Holman and his crew, and
had to be dissuaded by Holman from making an official complaint. It was a
small incident but characteristic of Douglas's thoughtful independence and
it cemented a friendship with Holman.

The action of the day was not ended, however. As a couple of mugs
full of rum were being distributed to each member of the regiment,
perhaps in recognition of the continuous fire which they had withstood,
shells from both sides began to land in their positions. Before the Allied
artillery could be told to alter their range, a fragment from one of their
shells hit the adjutant, Major Warwick. With the fragment lodged in his
forehead, visible to all, he calmly instructed his successor before the ambulance arrived. When later Sweeney Todd was similarly to be removed from
battle by a British shell, he insisted that the ambulance first drive him to
the artillery's position where he returned their missile.

The German positions which had given such trouble were empty before
the regiment reached them next morning; and apart from an encounter with
a screen of 88s, removed by the supporting artillery, they spent the day
advancing without opposition. Douglas, having broken a track of his
blood-covered tank by driving over a pit, moved to a cleaner vehicle, and at
one point in the day delightedly watched the enemy retreat before his out-
of-range fire. For a moment, perhaps, he was the foremost tank of the
Eighth Army. That night the Brigade tried to sustain their advance, but
manœuvres in darkness proved beyond them; so as early as possible the
next morning, 5 November, they pressed forward again.

In a few hours on that day, they covered more ground than in whole days
of earlier fighting. Instead of pockets of snipers and anti-tank screens they
met only lorries of Italians driving to surrender, gun crews trying too late
to remove their vehicles, and parties of infantry, left behind without transport. One such party, of twenty-eight German engineers under the command of a lieutenant, delayed Douglas and, unused to such open ground,
once again he lost the regiment. In his lone wanderings, he met a column of
Italian lorries, unaware of his presence until he drew alongside them. Then
there was panic, at least in the rear of the column: those at the front sailed
on, ignorant of the fate of the rest. Soldiers poured from the three vehicles
which had stopped, running for the safety of a railway embankment, and
lorries further back turned round and made off. Douglas felt rather foolish

at causing such a stir, but finding himself left with three empty lorries he collected a kitbag and what weapons he could find, and put the vehicles out of action as best he could. Then, having at last located his squadron, he set off to replenish the fuel consumed in his travels.

While they splashed petrol into their Crusader, the sounds of a battle came over the tank radio. Clearly it was a new kind of action, with boyish shouts of enthusiasm and hunting calls. Technically, commanders were supposed to leave the regimental network free for Kellett's commands unless they had essential information to report; but in the excitement of this battle, some mistakenly used their 'A' set as intercom, innocently giving the whole regiment the benefit of their backchat with driver or gunner.

By the time Douglas had returned, as rapidly as possible, the regiment had destroyed three German Mark III tanks, one Mark III special, twenty-two Italian M13 tanks, two 75-mm. guns, one 50-mm. gun, and one assault gun. The battle of Galal Station was over, and not one member of the regiment had been killed. Colonel Kellett produced the required tribute.

This day, the fifth of November, 1942, is a Red Letter Day in the history of the Sherwood Rangers Yeomanry who, having commenced the war as Cavalry, trained as a Motor Battalion, taking part in the campaigns of Crete and Tobruk as gunners, then after one year's training as an Armoured Regiment won one of the most classic victories standing to the credit of any armoured regiment.[1]

If this was the start of the *coup de grâce*, the regiment waited impatiently for the next day. Not only was there the excitement of the hunt, there was the delight of loot: searching in 'the glorious brantub of war' for the spoils of victory. Italians and Germans had wine and even brandy in the desert; they offered a new range of foods which, though still military rations, had a continental flavour; and there were the precision implements of the two enemy armies: binoculars, a few cameras, and above all Biretta pistols and Luger automatics. Towels and blankets could be acquired, and several items in the enemy's wardrobe carried a panache which particularly appealed to the cavalrymen. One army lived off another, and on this front of the war, the exchange had been conducted with little acrimony. Speed, however, was essential. Without it the enemy would not only have time to fight, they would have time to take their possessions with them and booby-trap what they left.

---

[1] Liddell Hart, in his *History of the Second World War* (p. 305), was to be less enthusiastic: 'The 10th [Armoured Division] had been directed on Galal, . . . and there caught the enemy's tail, capturing some forty tanks—most of these being Italian tanks that had run out of fuel.'

2

The 6th of November proved a disappointing day for the Sherwood Rangers. The enemy had moved quickly by night and although the regiment reached Fuka aerodrome before evening, they had found neither the enemy's armour nor their loot. At this point, their advance met new resistance. Torrential rain turned the road behind them into mud, bogging down the supply lorries of their B echelon, and without these they could not move far.

On the 7th, their progress still retarded although the rain eased, the regiment reached the extensive if antiquated defences of Mersa Matruh. Mines held up an assault by their supporting infantry from the Buffs and their own frontal attack failed to take them into the town. In this advance Colonel Kellett's command tank, Robin Hood, received two direct hits: the first penetrated the visor, killing driver and loader; the second came through the front of the turret, passing between Kellett and the other two crewmen and doing little damage. The following day Kellett was able to lead the regiment into the town whose defences had been deserted. They were the first armoured troops to enter.

Douglas had little part in these activities. On the 7th he had again broken a tank track and his next two days were spent trying to get help for his vehicle. A morning spent waiting at the roadside for transport, however, had brought him a closer look at the enemy. With a party of German prisoners he had enjoyed a shooting match, at tins, receiving instruction from them on the mechanism of the Luger. Douglas's crew, left with the tank, had meanwhile been entertained by a group of Italians who turned out to be members of a concert party.

When Douglas rejoined the regiment outside the captured town on the 9th, he found that instead of further action they were to rest and refit while other brigades did the chasing. A search for loot provided each squadron with a luxurious black tent 'like a sheikh's', enabling them to pass nights free of blackout regulations; and for their better enjoyment, they found Chianti, Liebfraumilch, champagne, brandy, cherries, cigars, and chocolate. The advance from the first day at Alamein had been hard fought, and only five of the regiment's twenty-two officers, besides Douglas, had not been casualties. Over the radio on 11 November, however, they heard the church bells of Britain proclaim their victory.

Writing from Mersa to Olga, Douglas assessed the effects of the experience he had long sought. He had acquired 'a camera, some excellent clothes, a new camp bed and air mattress, and an Italian automatic'; earlier he had possessed three Lugers but gave two away and lost the third. He had picked up some German novels and Nietzsche's *Also Sprach Zarathustra*, and with the prisoners he had found that his German was better than he had thought although 'pretty lousy on the whole'. Douglas did acknowledge that the first days had been 'undeniably sticky', with his worst that spent in the blood-covered tank: but as far as credit was concerned he felt, like Churchill, that it should go to the gunners. He made no comment on his personal responses but the mood of his letter suggested that he had come to take the whole experience in a matter-of-fact way, though he was stone deaf from the gunfire. Going on to affirm that he would visit Palestine, Douglas expressed an inability to remain in 'more or less undiluted English company for long', but the desolate and bitter tones of October had vanished.

During his two weeks in action Douglas had little time for letters; but he described his impression of 'Mersa' in a poem of remarkable poise.

> This blue half circle of sea
> moving transparently
> on sand as pale as salt
> was Cleopatra's hotel:
>
> here is a guest house built
> and broken utterly since.
> An amorous modern prince
> lived in this scoured shell.

While war's passing restored the town to its history, for the 'cherry-skinned soldiers' who strolled down to idle on the beach war remained in a distant future, present only in the 'immensely long road' which travelled to Tripoli. The ruins of the town, which could still 'deceive a passer-by', had retained the impact of battle, but the drama they revealed was as passive as sculpture:

> faces with sightless doors
> for eyes, with cracks like tears
> oozing at corners. A dead tank alone
> leans where the gossips stood.

It was a place out of war, but behind its 'skeletal' calm it carried the reality Douglas had recently witnessed, a logic which he suggests is emphatic enough for fish to understand:

> I see my feet like stones
> underwater. The logical little fish
> converge and nip the flesh
> imagining I am one of the dead.

After a week at Mersa, the world Douglas had left for El Alamein caught up with him. With the roads now safe and loot for encouragement, the Divisional Staff reached Mersa and Douglas was summoned to headquarters on the pretext of an unpaid mess bill. There he was told that provided he apologized to the G1, the officer in command of Intelligence, he could remain with the regiment.

Colonel Kellett had in fact interceded for him, for if Douglas's suspicions that he had not wanted him back were true, Kellett would not turn away someone who had fought successfully with them. If it had been Douglas's guts which he most hated, it was that particular organ which had brought him from desk to Crusader. Acting out this parody of the school episode over the rifle, Douglas found the General, the G1, G2, and the 'Ack and Quack' colonel playing cards in the Divisional mess tent. Perhaps the G1 grunted at him, but he received no other greeting from the players and was left to the attention of a young captain. After the card game finished, the G1 invited Douglas outside and expressed disappointment at not being told of his desire to leave. Douglas, who had asked several times and had been refused each time, kept quiet. They had a drink to bury the hatchet and he returned, officially, to his regiment.

To clear the air, Douglas was sent for new spectacles for himself and supplies for the regiment, to Alexandria. It meant freedom and mobility while the others waited around, so perhaps it was Kellett's reward. For Douglas it brought the dubious pleasure of a return to the city where he had left Milena. In Mersa harbour, however, he had met Norman Ilett: the flotilla had moved westward, to shorten the range for offensive patrols. After initial unease the meeting had developed into an enjoyable drinking session; to meet Milena, therefore, might not prove too painful. Arriving with his troop sergeant, Nelson, Douglas was still undecided whether or not to call on her. But he found himself walking along Rouchdy Pasha towards the Pegnas' house, without thinking.

It was strange to find how easy it was for me to cross the little strip of garden and open the old door with its peeling paint, without the thought much disturbing me, of all the times I had gone there before with an evening of dancing and moonlit strolling before me. The effect of battle had been admirably cathartic.

The sight of Milena 'beat my fortitude down', but taking refuge in conversation, and meeting her parents, he came through. That evening he and Sergeant Nelson and Milena went together to a film, and the two soldiers slept on the floor in the drawing-room.

Douglas did his shopping, helped by M. Pegna who accompanied him round the bazaars to make sure he was not swindled, and by Milena who watched his delight at smuggling drink and tobacco out of Saccone and Speed at duty-free prices. After a miserable evening with another girl friend, Titsa, he went again to the cinema with Milena, this time alone. Then, in the morning, with 3,000 newly baked loaves and 'Masha', a doll given him by Milena for good luck, he drove back with Sergeant Nelson.

173

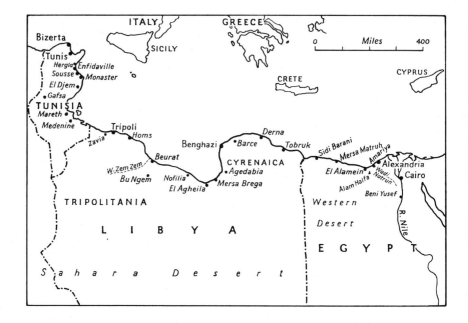

The trip had been simple and enjoyable, and Nelson recalled that Douglas had made a point of tacitly promoting him to commissioned officer for its duration so as to take him into his messes—where someone could well have caused trouble.[1] Douglas did not care.

On their return to the regiment, they heard that they were to move on. The tanks would go by transporter to hasten their progress and they expected to reach the battle, beyond Benghazi, in about ten days. During the regiment's two weeks at Mersa, the enemy forces had been chased across the Egyptian border, Tobruk had been recaptured, and on the 20th, Benghazi reached. The chasing seemed to be moving at a fair pace. To add to their optimism, on the day the regiment had entered Mersa, the Americans had landed in Algeria: by now, with the Free French and the British First Army, they were in Tunisia.

With some difficulty, the squadrons loaded their tanks on to transporters on 24 November. The Eighth Armoured Brigade, of which they were a part, was being moved as an independent unit, retaining their fox's mask insignia, to the Seventh Armoured Division. While the Tenth Divisional Staff returned to Cairo Douglas embarked on the seven-hundred-mile journey up the coast road towards the fighting, for the first time in an official capacity.

[1] Douglas achieved the change of rank by using the slip-on badges which most officers wore on their shirt epaulettes.

3

For compensation on their long and uncomfortable journey by transporter Douglas had the pleasure of seeing the places which at Wickwar had been only names in the news. From Libya they moved into the greener country of Cyrenaica, past villas declaring *'Ritorneremo'* or *'W il Duce W il Re'* and signboards announcing 'Under New Management', to see the green trees and red and white roofs of Barce. They missed Tobruk, but had a mirage-like glimpse of Benghazi, its square white houses, squat domes and minarets in the distance, seemingly untouched by war.

Early in December their ten days' journey ended at Agedabia, where once more surrounded by hard sand and camel tuft, they halted to learn that the enemy's retreat had ceased at Mersa Brega, the terminus of previous advances. There a system of formidable defences in a narrow, easily held gap between impassable marshes had awaited their return. For nearly two weeks, however, the Sherwood Rangers took no part in the fighting, though they were again up to strength in tanks. A Squadron was complete with Crusaders, B with eleven Shermans and two Grants (though they soon lost two Shermans to the Greys), and C with eight Shermans and six Grants.

On 13 December they moved into their first action, but with only a reduced force under Major Player. The plan was that A and C Squadrons, supported by a battery from the Fifth Royal Horse Artillery, should advance purposefully, in the hope of luring the enemy's tanks to a fight. No opposing armour appeared and although the squadrons were shelled the venture seemed to have failed. That night, however, the Italians facing their advance left their positions to await their arrival deeper in the defences at El Agheila.

Fog had lingered well into the morning as the regiment moved forward next day and fierce fire from anti-tank guns met them. A Squadron came under the worst of the fire and Garrett, for the present in its command, had his tank hit twice before running over the 50-mm. gun responsible for the damage. In the evening the Italian armour mounted a counter-attack. If the Italian gunners had bravely defended during the day, their tank men's advance was suicidal. Even the Crusaders could outfight their outdated M13 tanks, with some justice nicknamed 'sardine tins'. Thirteen were destroyed by the brigade, and of the six knocked out by the regiment, Sergeant Nelson accounted for three. That day they had also destroyed twelve anti-tank guns and taken fifty prisoners, with few losses to themselves.

Returning to leaguer that night, Bethell-Fox was wounded for the second time in a total of two days' fighting. He had been sitting on the turret of his tank, singing, he remembers, with his legs swinging inside:

Keith Douglas

That was stupid. For the shell went off on the back of the tank behind me; I remember turning round and watching it explode, green and yellow, and feeling my left arm, hit at the elbow, swinging up to my face.

Falling or jumping from his tank, he found time to curse some German prisoners sitting near by in the sand, before passing out. It was to be over a year before he rejoined the regiment.

The Italians vacated their positions during the night, but, delayed by a dispute over which regiment should claim El Agheila, the Sherwood Rangers found themselves behind other regiments in the advancing column and took no part in the heavy fighting of the next two days. Meeting up with the New Zealanders at Wadi Regel on the 19th, they learnt that the whole battle had been unsatisfactory. While the enemy had been dislodged from their first line of defence, the New Zealanders' left hook had lacked power to encircle them.

Although further advanced than at any earlier stage of the campaign, the Eighth Army's two months' chase had simply brought them to a point where Rommel had regrouped his forces in a powerful defensive position. To those who knew of events on the other side of the Axis armies in Tunisia, it was also clear that little help could be expected from the Allied invasion force there. In mid-December they too had been checked, by von Arnim outside Tunis. The plan of encircling Rommel with First and Eighth armies had given way to the reality of fighting two armies on separate fronts.

For a month the Sherwood Rangers waited. What loot remained in the surrounding countryside had been denied its appeal by the ingenious variety of booby traps bequeathed by the Italians; and travel, even when officially permitted, held no attraction in a landscape sown with mines. The regiment had exercises with their supporting artillery and with the anti-tank guns of the Norfolk Yeomanry; they had a sports competition, and an enjoyable Christmas, for despite the difficulties of the nine-hundred-mile supply line which delayed further advance, there was turkey, pork, Christmas pudding, iced cake, a bottle of beer, and fifty cigarettes for each man. Douglas, always impatient, found the experience of hanging around a strain.

Living with the squadron, he saw little of Kellett and nothing of the regiment's second-in-command, Player, who had joined the Long Range Desert Group for one of their adventures. Player, having walked up to a British armoured car which turned out to be the property of the Germans, was taken prisoner and brought to Rommel's headquarters where he was entertained by General Bayerlein and two German staff officers who had been at Oxford. Handed over to Italians, he escaped by getting his guards drunk, and made the two hundred miles back to his

176

regiment to report that the Germans, 'even in defeat, were disciplined, efficient and well turned out'. What they reported of him, in his wool-lined yellow suede waistcoat and brown suede boots, is not recorded. For if Kellett was known throughout the brigade for his fastidious dress, Player's panache was now known to more than the Eighth Army.

During their month of waiting, Douglas had plenty of opportunity to get to know his squadron's officers, and if he remained something of an outsider, the shared experience of battle had brought a level of mutual accept-

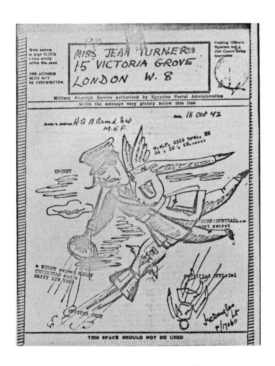

ance. No one really riled him in the squadron, and he had seen the value and something of the charm of Christopherson's diffidence. Now observed at leisure, Garrett's skilful handling of everyone and every situation possessed the appeal of a new kind of art, and one unknown to Douglas with his forthright and prickly ways. Garrett had been stable lad, jockey, dealer, and breeder of horses, enviably familiar with yeomanry's pre-war world. His fund of stories and familiarity with the affairs of the men provided a companionship especially valuable in their long nights in the black tent, while his skill on the battlefield had proved his value to the regiment.

Lieutenant Ian McKay, a taciturn devotee of fishing, provided a quieter, more benign audience than Douglas, and Lieutenant Stockton, recently risen from the ranks after some years as a regular, gradually contributed a good supply of stories under Christopherson's encouragement. For a while Douglas found such a small world sufficient, and attempts to make their surroundings more habitable and their food more varied, left room for his boyish inventiveness. At Christmas, he wrote to his mother:

I have been trying cooking with flour and margarine, making sort of jam puffs, today, and of course in spite of all precautions have sat in the jam, and temporarily spoiled my new German trousers: but the puffs were a great success.

Five days before Christmas, three books had arrived from his mother, one of which was *The Faber Book of Modern Verse*. Douglas already had with him the odd books he had brought from Division headquarters, which included *Alice in Wonderland*, *The Quest For Corvo*, *The Story of an African Farm*, *National Velvet*, and David Gascoyne's *Short Survey of Surrealism*. From deserted German positions he had picked up copies of Goethe and numerous German novels; and in the tent there was generally the Eighth Army *News Sheet*, *Punch*, *Country Life*, the desert army's two-page magazine *Crusader*, and newspapers from Egypt and England. But it was not easy to concentrate on reading under their conditions, and conversation took most of the time.

After Christmas mail started coming through: a real luxury to them now, 'only less valuable than sleep, which is, as ever, the most satisfying thing of all.' Making this comment in a letter to Margaret Stanley-Wrench on 8 January, Douglas tried to respond to her 'green pictures' of England. They had moved to Nofilia where the desert was more fertile.

There are indeed flowers of various indeterminate sorts and colours even on these bits of desert, mostly they are mauve and yellow. Occasional and quite veritable daisies and dandelions. Birds come and go, wagtails, geese, quail and a curious sand coloured lark.

But he confessed: 'I have not a naturalist's eye or memory'. From Milena Douglas heard that she was officially engaged to Norman and he sent three pounds for a present. 'It wasn't as generous as it sounds', for the sum repaid that which Norman had left in his keeping before the Tobruk raid. From his mother he learnt that Kristin was married. Replying to this letter, he asked whether John Hall's collection of their poems had appeared, for he had received another number in the Modern Reading Library series; and he looked forward to evidence of his first appearance in one of the war's main literary magazines, *Poetry* (*London*). Its editor, M. J. Tambimuttu, had been so impressed by Douglas's poems in *Fords and Bridges* that he had sought his address from John Hall. Although Douglas had heard nothing from him, Tambimuttu had printed 'Stars' and '*Pas de Trois*' while Douglas was in Mersa, and in December 'The Prisoner' had appeared. In January he published the first of Douglas's Middle East poems to appear in England, 'The Offensive'. That it was this pre-Alamein poem which Douglas sent back to his mother on 10 January suggests that he had written nothing since Mersa: but possibly Douglas chose this poem as an uncensorable way of announcing his position, for the regiment's period of waiting was clearly about to end.

4

At a conference on 10 January, Montgomery announced his plans for the 'final phase of the North African campaign'. The enemy were in a well-defended position at Beurat, a hundred and forty miles to the west. This was to be assaulted by the Fifty-first Division with armoured support, advancing along the coast road. At the same time the New Zealanders and the Seventh Armoured Division were to make another left hook through the desert.[1] This time, however, there were to be no preliminary probings of the defences which could give the enemy time to retreat. The long approach was to lead straight to a full-scale engagement.

By night the regiment successfully accomplished the two final approaches, placing them within two miles of the Bu Ngem road, and the enemy, on the 14th. At daybreak on the 15th the whole brigade advanced, the Sherwood Rangers in the lead, followed by the Third Royal Tanks and the Staffordshire Yeomanry. Major Christopherson, illegally keeping a diary at the time, recorded what met them.

We drew fire almost immediately we had crossed the road. The Germans had 88-mm. guns, and other anti-tank guns very cleverly concealed in this very long wadi, which gave them a magnificent field of fire, as we came over the horizon. They also had heavy machine-gun posts in many of the sub wadis, which were most difficult to locate and most unpleasant for crew commanders.

The Crusaders of his squadron made for sub wadis on the forward slope in the cover of which they could spot for the heavier tanks and direct their fire.

Douglas had set out from Nofilia with a troop of four tanks. One had broken down on the way; a second, his own, developed a water leak as soon as they arrived at the wadi; and as they raced for cover, a third was hit, its commander, Sergeant Nelson, being wounded. Douglas took over the only remaining tank of his troop, retaining its corporal commander as gunner, and moved into battle alone.

[1] The regimental history places their brigade in the centre group rather than the left hook.

179

The ground on his flank was particularly undulating, but nosing from slope to slope, he located what looked like a gun emplacement, so he called for supporting fire. This was turned down until he could provide more exact information, however, and as he waited for the next move, Douglas watched first one heavy tank and then four infantry carriers being hit on the ground from which he had warned them; so he decided to look closer.

Moving his tank along the shallow groove which had protected him, Douglas made across three hundred yards of open ground to reach another

Christopherson

cleft, apparently unnoticed. To his right, a hundred and fifty yards away, he saw on the side of a spur an erection of sandbags which he took to be a vacated enemy position. As he looked, however, a head and shoulders appeared, and raised two flaps which unmistakably belonged to the turret of a German Mark III tank. At two thousand yards this tank's 75-mm. gun could send armour-piercing shot clean through a Crusader; but the person in its turret had clearly not yet noticed his presence. Douglas ordered his gunner to fire at the target, and radioed Kellett; ' "Give the bugger hell" ', came the reply. There was a long silence, and then Douglas's corporal reported that the gun would not elevate.

Douglas ordered the driver to move and informed the colonel of his plight. Then, when he looked out again, he discovered that they were heading directly for the Mark III. Having already heard one report from its gun, Douglas shouted instructions to the driver to turn, but using his 'A' set instead of his intercom, so the whole regiment heard his directions while the driver moved steadily forward. The German, assuming that

Douglas must be manœuvring to ram him, slid out of sight behind the spur.[1]

Not to be defeated, Douglas lined up his tank so that its gun could be directed, without need for elevation, towards the outline he saw on the ridge. When he arrived at his firing position, he found that his new target was not the Mark III but an abandoned 50-mm. gun. Such a metamorphosis gave him time to realize that he had no idea where he was, whether ahead of his regiment and the first to meet the enemy, or left behind in a desperate retreat; so as soon as he saw a stream of Allied traffic he joined it, making with them for the cover of a bowl in the sand dunes.

There the engine of Douglas's tank, already capable of no more than second gear, ceased altogether, and the good fortune of this breakdown was immediately demonstrated when the Grant beside him, moving up to the tip of the bowl, was hit. The area then came under fire, and having waited while his driver found what was wrong with the engine of his tank, and helped John Semken put out a fire in his Sherman, Douglas edged forward to see what was doing the damage.

As soon as he neared the brink of the bowl, armour-piercing shot from a 50-mm. gun came right through his turret. The corporal shouted to him to get out and they both did so, noticing that the Grant beside them was ablaze. His driver, however, was still in the tank, so with the help of a couple of men, Douglas hauled him out and into a nearby weapon pit, where they found that he was badly wounded in the neck. As Douglas moved back to his tank the blazing Grant blew up not ten yards from him. Some bedding wrapped round him and hurled him against the side of his Crusader. Hardly bruised, he fetched morphia for the driver and returned to his tank once more to move it from the area of the shelling. Revving up the engine, which was still running, he rolled the tank forward till its engine failed and then got out. Facing him on the edge of the bowl, about fifty yards away, was a German tank. Thinking with irrational clarity only of capture, Douglas started to run, and ran until he could run no more, then walked. The Germans made no attempt to shoot him.

Douglas was now in a landscape populated largely by those who, like himself, had lost their tanks. Crews hid safely in deserted German gun pits, or nursed their wounded in trenches dug for lorries. Others still crawled towards cover, brutally wounded or burned beyond recognition. One of these, a C Squadron corporal, Douglas carried to a weapon pit already taken over by wounded from the regiment. He could not stop thinking of capture, and suspecting his own motives, he offered to bring help and set off to get it.

Joined on the way by a new lieutenant, Douglas at last saw a vehicle: one

---

[1] This engagement was later to be described in the regimental history as Douglas's 'cunning stalking' of the enemy.

of their infantry's scout cars. It was buried over its differential in sand. Behind it, however, was the car of the technical adjutant, just moving off. As Douglas shouted, a Sherman fired and before he could shout again his companion said, 'Look out. There's a trip wire.'

I knew already; I had just tripped it. I should have thrown myself down at once, but a sort of resignation prevented me, and I walked on a few steps before the mine exploded.

S mines were normally laid in series, and this one set off a second and a third mine, each sending a cannister into the air which then exploded, releasing hundreds of tiny ball bearings. Douglas was hit in the right foot, right calf, left thigh, the small of his back, under his left arm, and in his left shoulder.[1] His companion was more severely wounded.

Hearing the explosions, people from the nearest scout car ran to help. The technical adjutant turned his car round, and the two officers were loaded on to it and driven to the regimental ambulance. Douglas told the adjutant about those he had left in the weapon pit but the adjutant seemed preoccupied with driving over the rough and potentially mined ground. At the ambulance, the M.O. cut off Douglas's clothes and his shoes and covered him in bandages. Then, after morphia and brandy, they were driven back to the forward dressing station.

That night, the technical adjutant, Captain Churchman, was to join Sweeney Todd and Major Christopherson as volunteers to look for the wounded. Tanks were still burning in the darkness, but they could see no movement.

After a time they stopped, and Captain Churchman shouted into the night. A feeble voice answered, and they discovered Corporal Levy and another wounded man lying beside him, and Corporal Slater who had been badly wounded in the back. The Germans had left that spot only a few minutes ago, and their leaguer was just over the hill. With difficulty they loaded the bodies on to the dingo. On the way back they passed a small 'Honey' tank and saw a body moving beside it. It was Captain Burrows, our observation officer. . . . He was taken back to the leaguer, where our new Medical Officer, Captain 'Hilda' Young, amputated his foot.

Nine troopers, three corporals, a sergeant, and two lieutenants had died in the day's fighting.

In the regimental history the day's experiences gave no cause for enthusiasm:

We had taken more punishment, perhaps, than we had been able to inflict. But the vital thing was that the Regiment, by standing and fighting on until nightfall, enabled the whole army to advance on the following morning.

[1] A horoscope written for him at the age of thirteen had warned: 'The spine, legs, calves and ankles are sensitive to hurt.'

In the main New Zealand dressing station Douglas's wounds were cleaned, and he was relieved to find that the wounded he had last seen in the Zem Zem wadi, including his driver, all arrived safely. Douglas's wounds were not serious but promised a return to the Delta, and the next day, while the regiment pursued the Germans, who had retreated in the night, he was moved to a casualty clearing station; then, from another clearing station, he passed on to an airfield to start his eastward journey.

In these two days' fighting the Allied troops had lost fifty tanks: fourteen more than the total with which the enemy had started the battle.[1] On 23 January the Eleventh Hussars entered Tripoli, but the enemy had gone; and the following day the Sherwood Rangers continued their chase, Christopherson's A Squadron possessing only three tanks in running order. That day, 24 January, was Douglas's twenty-third birthday, and he spent it on a hospital train, passing through Alexandria. On 25 January he was comfortably settled at No. 1 General Hospital at El Ballah, in Palestine.

---

[1] The Centauro Division also provided fifty-seven obsolete tanks, making a total strength of ninety-three tanks. Montgomery had started with four hundred and fifty.

7

El Ballah to Enfidaville

January - May 1943

You do not gradually appreciate such qualities
but your mind will extend new hands.
('Cairo Jag')

I

Douglas spent six weeks at El Ballah, much longer than he at first expected, for although his train journey had been painful he had been able to
walk on his first day in hospital. The wound in his foot became infected,
however, and healed slowly. Otherwise he was fit enough to wander round
the hospital and even to dance, with his foot in a bulbous bandage. So while
the Sherwood Rangers fought past Tripoli to cross the Tunisian border and
assault the Mareth lines Douglas enjoyed without conscience the respite
his wounds had earned. Living conditions at El Ballah were good, and until
early March, when he learnt from the officer in charge of his wing of
the hospital that as a surgical case he would not be entitled to leave, and
once more the frustrations of a fight with authority consumed him, Douglas
led a leisurely and trouble-free life.

Such circumstances had always favoured his poetry, and his three months
in the world of battle which he had so long anticipated had left him with no
lack of material. In March, the first of the poems which resulted appeared
in *Citadel*, 'Dead Men'.

> Tonight the moon inveigles them
> to love: they infer from her gaze
> her tacit encouragement.
> Tonight the white dresses and the jasmin scent
> in the streets. I in another place
> see the white dresses glimmer like moths. Come
>
> to the west, out of that trance, my heart—
> here the same hours have illumined

El Ballah to Enfidaville

sleepers who are condemned or reprieved
and those whom their ambitions have deceived;
the dead men whom the wind
powders till they are like dolls: they tonight

rest in the sanitary earth perhaps
or where they died, no one has found them
or in their shallow graves the wild dog
discovered and exhumed a face or a leg
for food: the human virtue round them
is a vapour tasteless to a dog's chops.

All that is good of them, the dog consumes.
You would not know now the mind's flame is gone
more than the dog knows: you would forget
but that you see your own mind burning yet
and till you stifle in the ground will go on
burning the economical coal of your dreams.

Dead Man.

Ever since, as a poet of fifteen, he had looked through the machine-gun sights of '·303' and imagined war, he had seen it as a denial of the positive, lyrical impulses of his work. Similarly the dead, who had entered his work at school, had been as threatening as they were attractive. Attempting to complete his poem 'I love the dead', he had written:

Keith Douglas

> My gods the dead possess my soul.
> On sands and seas they laze
> their satiate sockets ridicule
> my visionary gaze . . .

Now, placing the poet in the landscape of the dead men he had seen round him at El Alamein, he retraces this old conflict. The 'white dresses' which now embody the romantic world of Cairo or Alexandria are out of the imaginary ballroom of 'Haydn—Clock Symphony', where 'dresses, white dresses, sweep and dip / to the high notes as distant as the moon.' That ballroom had been a manifestation of the dreams which are now derided by the dead men; entering it had given 'the carriage of a god' to the man who, in his sleep,

> Walks in the corridors and in the deep
> Recesses of your mind; where you have trod
> The polished ground of dreaming every year.

And it had been the fact that he was 'Death's servant' which denied him permanent residence.

If the terms are the same, the battlefield has redefined the argument. Now the dead men are an undeniable reality and the romance at best an attractive day-dream. Yet Douglas writes from the battlefield, in a mood which is not only meditative but romantic: 'Come / to the west, out of that trance, my heart'.

Earlier, the transition to a brutal reality would have destroyed the credibility of diction and form as it had destroyed that of 'Russians'. Now, though intrusive rhymes, uneven rhythms, heavy ironies, and forced metaphor reduce the lyricism, it maintains a subsistence level; and as Douglas searches for an over-all pattern, his own capacity for irony can be used to put the nihilism of the dead in its place:

> Then leave the dead in the earth, an organism
> not capable of resurrection, like mines,
> less durable than the metal of a gun,
> a casual meal for a dog, nothing but the bone
> so soon. But tonight no lovers see the lines
> of the moon's face as the lines of cynicism.
>
> And the wise man is the lover
> who in his planetary love resolves
> without the traction of reason or time's control
> and the wild dog finding meat in a hole
> is a philosopher. The prudent mind resolves
> on the lover's or the dog's attitude forever.

186

Keeping wholly within the terms of the argument defined by the dead men, in his final sentence Douglas releases the poem from their hold. He offers no mitigating evidence beyond the impulse which had sustained the contemplative framework and ironic detachment of the whole poem. Prudence is a just response to the simple nihilism of the dead, but it is not a point of rest for the poet.

In 'Cairo Jag' Douglas re-explores the relationship between the battlefield's dead and the base town's pleasures. Now he writes from the base town, and instead of seeking a connection he points an absolute contrast. Cairo has a surface variety: beside the exotic Turkish girl 'who says she is a princess—she dances / apparently by levitation', and Marcelle who is 'always preoccupied with her dull dead lover', his letters 'tied in a bundle and stamped *Décédé* in mauve ink', there are 'the streets dedicated to sleep / stenches and sour smells', women offering their children 'brown-paper breasts / dry and twisted'.

> . . . But this stained white town
> is something in accordance with mundane conventions—
> Marcelle drops her Gallic airs and tragedy
> suddenly shrieks in Arabic about the fare
> with the cabman, links herself so
> with the somnambulists and legless beggars:
> it is all one, all as you have heard.

By one day's travelling, 'you reach a new world' where the vegetation is of iron, with 'gun barrels split like celery', and 'metal brambles'. At its centre there is a man whose possessions link him with another base town, Tripoli, but in making this connection they only accentuate the transformation which the battlefield has achieved:

> . . . you can imagine
> the dead themselves, their boots, clothes and possessions
> clinging to the ground, a man with no head
> has a packet of chocolate and a souvenir of Tripoli.

Cairo could be comprehended, its variety reduced to an essential sameness, but the battlefield denies such control, offering sights which can easily be imagined but which express an irreducible strangeness. In two more sections Douglas defined its peculiar nature and its effect upon the participant.

The battlefield parodies the world outside it and yet offers a recognizably human society, with 'new ethics' and 'fresh virtues', 'new arts' and possibly 'new religions', philosophers, lawyers, artists, and rulers. Its impact on those who enter it is dramatic and absolute:

Keith Douglas

You do not gradually appreciate such qualities
but your mind will extend new hands. In a moment
will fall down like St. Paul in a blinding light
the soul suffers a miraculous change
you become a true inheritor of this altered planet.

I know, I see these men return
wandering like lost sounds in our dirty streets.

Reversing the ethics of the revelation brought to St. Paul on the road to Damascus, these men are made killers; but the battlefield offers a revelation nonetheless. The mind 'will extend new hands', and if the 'blinding light' which brings this discovery, at first suggests that the 'true inheritor' is the man killed in a shell-burst, Douglas places his final emphasis upon those who survive.

It was the desire to reach the battlefield's vision which Douglas celebrated in another poem:[1]

DESERT FLOWERS

Living in a wide landscape are the flowers—
Rosenberg I only repeat what you were saying—
the shell and the hawk every hour
are slaying men and jerboas, slaying

the mind: but the body can fill
the hungry flowers and the dogs who cry words
at nights, the most hostile things of all.
But that is not new. Each time the night discards

draperies on the eyes and leaves the mind awake
I look each side of the door of sleep
for the little coin it will take
to buy the secret I shall not keep.

I see men as trees suffering
or confound the detail and the horizon.
Lay the coin on my tongue and I will sing
of what the others never set eyes on

What had seemed, by the end of the second stanza, a statement of failure Douglas gradually turns into an announcement of promise. He calls for help in his quest, his sight is blurred; but not only was the man who told Jesus, 'I see men, as it were trees walking' miraculously cured of blindness,

[1] In the last period of waiting before the advance to Wadi Zem Zem, Douglas had written to Margaret Stanley-Wrench: 'I have an idea it's somewhere round here St. Paul made one of his journeys.' It was the same letter which described the flowers around Nofilia.

his words were an indication that he was already partially healed.[1] Again linking his vision with death, through his allusion to the coin placed on the dead man's tongue to pay for his passage to the underworld, Douglas has no doubt that he will sing of what the others have not seen.

Each of these poems grew from a different kind of impulse: in 'Dead Men' Douglas returned to his lyrical dreams to convey the message of those killed on the battlefield; in 'Cairo Jag' he recorded the intractable contrast between the base town and the 'new world' only a day's travelling away; and in 'Desert Flowers' he affirmed a new and ambiguous vision. In a sequence of three poems, 'Landscape with Figures', Douglas took up a new theme, that of his own relationship to the battlefield. He starts by contrasting two views: from a great height, 'a pilot or angel looking down', sees, as Wilfred Owen had seen in 'The Show', an insect world. Vehicles, 'squashed dead or still entire', are 'stunned / like beetles'; 'when the haze settles', 'scattered wingcases and / legs, heads, show'. In contrast there is the intimate searcher:

> But you who like Thomas come
> to poke fingers in the wounds
> find monuments, and metal posies:
> on each disordered tomb
> the steel is torn into fronds
> by the lunatic explosive.

The dishonest poetry of 'monuments, and metal posies' may easily be dismissed but poetry cannot, for the battlefield parodies art as thoroughly as it parodies 'ethics' and 'virtues'. At Oxford Douglas had described poetry as

like a man, whom thinking you know all his movements and appearance you will presently come upon in such a posture that for a moment you can hardly believe it a position of the limbs you know.

Death on the battlefield has mastered such art:

> On scrub and sand the dead men wriggle
> in their dowdy clothes. They are mimes
> who express silence and futile aims
> enacting this prone and motionless struggle
> at a queer angle to the scenery
> crawling on the boards of the stage like walls,
> deaf to the one who opens his mouth and calls
> silently. The décor is terrible tracery
> of iron. The eye and mouth of each figure
> bear the cosmetic blood and hectic
> colours death has the only list of.

[1] Mark VIII, 22–6.

The battlefield has reversed the relationship between art and life by peopling this deeply expressive tableau with actors whom we know cannot get up and move after a curtain has fallen. Douglas who had safely witnessed ballet dancers who appeared to defeat the laws of nature, now looks on a scene where such security is denied.

> A yard more, and my little finger
> could trace the maquillage of these stony actors;
> I am the figure writhing on the backcloth.

This doubting Thomas seeks only to prove the unreality of what he sees, but the yard which separates him from it is an infinite distance.

It is the anguish of the last of these lines that Douglas takes up in the third poem of the set. He is 'the figure burning in hell' and that of the grave, priestly observer; the lover, 'all / the aimless pilgrims, the pedants and courtiers', and the brutal soldier. It is this last role in which he expects to be most clearly recognized:

> more easily you believe me a pioneer
> and a murdering villain without fear
> without remorse hacking at the throat. Yes,
> I am all these and I am the craven
> the remorseful the distressed
> penitent: not passing from life to life
> but all these angels and devils are driven
> into my mind like beasts. I am possessed,
> the house whose wall contains the dark strife
> the arguments of hell with heaven.

If Douglas's experience of the battlefield had offered him a vision, it had also given to his theme of multiple personality a new and painful intensity.

2

In the middle of March Douglas moved to a convalescent depot at Port Said, where he was to stay for a few weeks. His spirits had been lowered by the conflict over leave and when, on 2 April, he wrote to Olga, his dejection remained:

It's evident you're in as bad a state as I am; neither of us can suffer fools gladly, and we are both hemmed in by them. . . . I suppose the war will eventually end, but the trouble is that all these idiots live on when one would have thought there was a golden opportunity to liquidate them.

As you see, I am as bitter and sickened as you are, not by the war, but by the bloody fools who are surviving it in every country of the world. When we meet it'll be good for us both if we do more kissing than talking.

With his letter Douglas included 'Gallantry', a simple, satirical piece as striking in what it did not attack as in its efficient demolition of sentimentality. On the top of his copy Douglas explained its origin:

I was discussing Rupert Brooke with someone the other day, who has a book which a very sentimental hospital sister has lent him. I wrote a poem to slip into the book when he gives it back (unsigned, of course) which I hope will shock her sentimentality a bit.

> The colonel in a casual voice
> spoke into the microphone a joke
> which through a hundred earphones broke
> into the ears of a doomed race.
>
> Into the ears of the doomed boy, the fool
> whose perfectly mannered flesh fell
> in opening the door for a shell
> as he had learnt to do at school.
>
> Conrad luckily survived the winter:
> he wrote a letter to welcome
> the auspicious spring: only his silken
> intentions severed with a single splinter. . . .

After introducing a third victim, whose suspected fondness for little boys is not mentioned now he is dead, Douglas returns to the colonel. 'It was a brave thing', he said; but the 'three heroes never heard what / it was, gone deaf with steel and lead.'

> But the bullets cried with laughter,
> the shells were overcome with mirth,
> plunging their heads in steel and earth—
> (the air commented in a whisper).

In hospital Douglas had made no attempt to take up the protests of the Great War poets: his impulse had been consistently to explore and comprehend, not to attack. Now, giving the 'brave speech' to a colonel and not a staff officer, he makes no suggestion that its sentiments are callous or at all responsible for such deaths. His account of the victims' deaths disposes of their nobility of character without describing the horror of war, and the final personifications of heartless weaponry are a show of literary strength and not an indictment. Another poem, 'The Trumpet', considered the false attraction of notions of heroism through his own response and that of other fighting soldiers. For two stanzas he endorses the historic attraction of the trumpet's cry 'that war is sweet', and only then turns to those who hear the trumpet sounding in the desert.

Tonight we heard it
who for weeks have only listened
to the howls of inhuman voices.
But as the apprehensive ear rejoiced
breathing the notes in, the sky glistened
with a flight of bullets. We must be up early

tomorrow, to forget the cry and the crier
as we forgot the conversation
of our friends killed last month, last week
and hear, crouching, the air shriek
the crescendo, expectancy to elation
violently arriving. The trumpet is a liar.

Douglas is not protesting, he is making the facts clear; and the force of his discovery grows from its personal nature. He was not like Owen 'a pacifist with a very seared conscience'. Had his war been less mobile and had it seemed as ideologically pointless as Owen's, he might have become one.

Early in May Douglas wrote an essay to explain why, 'In the fourth year of this war we have not a single poet who seems likely to be an impressive commentator on it.' Starting from an acknowledgement of the achievements of the Great War poets, he made it clear that the poet of this war could not duplicate their success:

hell cannot be let loose twice: it was let loose in the Great War and it is the same old hell now. The hardships, pain and boredom; the behaviour of the living and the appearance of the dead, were so accurately described by the poets of the Great War that every day on the battlefields of the western desert—and no doubt on the Russian battlefields as well—their poems are illustrated. Almost all that a modern poet on active service is inspired to write, would be tautological.

Behind his negative emphasis, however, there was another, more positively related to his own immediate position as a poet: an affirmation that war poetry could only be written by those with substantial experience of war. 'Poetic pioneers and land girls', 'desperately intelligent' conscientious objectors, R.A.M.C. orderlies, students, and 'occupants of British barrack rooms' could not be expected to produce it. Even the bombing of England had not been sufficiently heavy or long 'for that alone to produce a body of "war" poetry'.

Douglas's emphasis was unremittingly placed on such poets' lack of sustained first-hand experience of warfare. For those who had this experience, his emphasis was upon the need for time. The soldiers had not found anything new to say, but 'Their experiences they will not forget easily, and it seems to me that the whole body of English war poetry of this war, civil and military, will be created after war is over.' Douglas, perhaps encouraged by an erroneous notion that Owen had written his major work while engaged in battle, demanded a long time scale. It was in any case an appropriately dampening demand on the patience of the editors his essay rebuked. But while he had written no more than a handful of poems at El Ballah and Port Said, Douglas had been little daunted by the 'tautology' of his experience.

3

Before leaving El Ballah at the end of March Douglas wrote two poems on subjects other than war. One, 'Snakeskin and Stone', defined the relationship which he desired between simplicity and complexity; the other, 'Words', asserted a new confidence in his art. The snakeskin stands for complexity, its 'lozenges are a calligraphy' which teaches truth through its 'cryptograms': the pebble, though 'smooth, utterly cruel and old', is 'truth alone'. Having established these 'two pillars' in two stanzas, and in a third explained that between them 'stand all the buildings truth can make', Douglas turns his attention upon their enemy, symbolized as the bald head of oratory:

> The bald head is a desert
> between country of life and country of death;
> between the desolate projecting ears
> move the wicked explorers, the flies
> who know the dead bone is beneath
> and from the skin the life half out . . .

The mouth of this speaker 'sucks and spews' out words, 'with insult to their bodies'; they are dead and yet effective within the debased standards of the world, for those who 'think the desert hidden' or the dead words living

> are fit to profit from the world.
> God help the lover of snakeskin and stone.

The second poem, 'Words', ignores the false standards of the world, celebrating a new assurance which needs neither the magic of 'The House' nor the squad drill of 'The Hand'. Now the poet is presented as a lepidopterist, confidently informing the uninitiated of the skills of his craft:

> The catch and the ways of catching are diverse.
> For instance this stooping man, the bones of whose face are
> like the hollow birds' bones, is a trap for words.
> And the pockmarked house bleached by the glare
> whose insides war has dried out like gourds
> attracts words. There are those who capture them

in hundreds, keep them prisoners in black
bottles, release them at exercise and clap them back.
But I keep words only a breath of time
turning in the lightest of cages—uncover
and let them go: sometimes they escape for ever.

Even the final acknowledgement of occasional failure is the departing
flourish of the expert indicating the elusiveness of any art worth pursuing.

When Douglas set off for his leave with Olga in the middle of April, he
had been away from the battlefield for three months. On the first morning
of his holiday, sitting at a pavement table of a Tel Aviv café, the desert
fighting was suddenly brought back to him. In the newspaper he read an
announcement of Colonel Kellett's death. On 22 March the Sherwood
Rangers had moved into a full-scale assault on the prepared defences at

Kellett and Player in Palestine, 1940

Mareth. Kellett, promoted to full colonel as second in command of the brigade a couple of weeks earlier, was not with them, but as they passed through the Allied minefield at dawn, they had seen him beside his tank, watching their advance. Later that day, standing up in his tank, shaving under fire, he was killed.

Reading of Kellett's death Douglas felt both incredulity and loss, writing later:

It was impossible to realize it. The whole moment and everything in it—the coloured tables, the sunglare on the pavements, the white houses and the morning pedestrians—seemed suddenly part of a dream.

Drafting a poem on his week with Olga in Tel Aviv Douglas took up this sense of unreality:

> Imposed like a face in a dream
> upon the dark pattern of dancers
> your face draws down my lips
> our hands like strangers in a city
> meet on the metalling of the table
> the talk mills round us like a crowd,
> when we speak it is like children
> who speak quietly who are watching
> a wonderful scene, in that moment I
> feel myself fainting with a wound
> and feel

Here Douglas's fragment broke off, but from it he shaped 'Tel Aviv'. Echoing the casual comment of his letter to Olga from Port Said that they should do 'more kissing than talking', it is written after the event it describes:

> Do not laugh because I made a poem;
> it is to use what then we could not handle
> words too dangerous then, knowing their explosive
> or incendiary tendencies when we are so close—
> if I said this to you then, BANG will
> have gone our walls of indifference in flame.

It was not the bitterness expressed in Douglas's letter which the poem's lovers kept at bay, but the whole world of experience outside their moment. They had followed the philosophy of 'Dead Men', and Douglas proves their defeat of war by turning its violence into harmless metaphor. Unlike the lovers of 'Dead Men', however, these are consciously escaping, using their comprehension of war's reality to achieve a triumph over circumstance.

195

In your locked mind your news from Russia is
and if I think, there is waiting Libya
Tripoli; the many heads of war
are watching us. We are not unaware
but are this evening finding heavier
than war the scents of youth, youth's subtleties.

We who cannot put out a single hand
to help our balance, who can never lean
on an old building in the past
or a new building in the future, must
balance tiptoe on a pin,
could teach an angel how to stand.

The far-reaching claims of the Oxford lovers of 'Invaders' have faded as completely as Douglas's earlier hopes that he could 'lean on' the old buildings of the city and its promised renaissance. With destructive pressures firmly identified with the battlefield, while he is away from it Douglas can defeat their hold.

After his week with Olga Douglas enjoyed another week of leave with Milena and her family in Alexandria. He seemed thoroughly to have been cured of his 'old wound'. His simple enthusiasms had returned. During his stay Milena's father had a birthday, and having got him a blue and white check shirt for a present, Douglas spent a whole day searching the shops and stalls for a red scarf to go with it. In the evening he returned, delighted with his prize. There was no unease to his friendship with Milena and she recalls that he had gained not only his old vitality but a new assurance.

4

From Alexandria Douglas returned to the R.A.C. base depot near Cairo to await a posting back to the regiment. There, a letter from Christopherson brought news of another death. The direct assault on Mareth having proved unsuccessful, the regiment had moved into a 'left hook', their 'second Balaclava charge' and 'the most spectacular and frightening battle we had taken part in'. In its course, Captain Garrett, whose stories of horses and regimental life had enlivened the long delays from Mersa onwards, had been hit by shrapnel, and died the next day.

Douglas felt little relish for his return to the regiment. From the news he had heard, rumours and accounts circulating at the base depot, and the dejection of Christopherson's letter, it seemed to him that the regiment 'could never recover from the punishment it had taken'. El Alamein had been anticipated as a decisive counter-stroke and the race towards Mersa a hunt for a defeated enemy; but these were part of almost another war. Dozens of battles had been fought since Wadi Zem Zem and still the enemy armies remained intact and unified on defensive ground.

On 6 May he set out by air from Cairo, to arrive by evening at the regiment's 'left out of battle camp', a few miles behind the front. There Douglas learnt of another crucial loss to the regiment. On a reconnaissance on 24 April, Colonel Player, who had been in command since Kellett's promotion, had been wounded when shells fell all round his jeep, and that night he had died. Douglas, joining the regiment outside Enfidaville where they faced the encircled Axis armies, found them at one hour's notice to move in support of an infantry attack. For commander they now had an officer from another Yeomanry regiment, Viscount Cranley, M.C., who possessed the reputation of having had more tanks 'shot away under him' than any other officer in the desert. His score looked like having every chance of increasing.

Meeting officers he had not seen for four months Douglas learnt of a new scale of fighting. At Mareth they had advanced under a 'creeping barrage' from the combined guns of two R.H.A. regiments, six field regiments, and three medium regiments, with bombers and 'tank-buster' planes making sorties overhead. The barrage had moved forward at a hundred yards per minute for the first thousand yards, then fifty yards per minute for the next two thousand, the regiment's tanks following a hundred yards behind the guns' target area.

Douglas spent long enough waiting for the attack to have good reason to feel relieved when it was temporarily called off: the infantry advance had not gone well. So instead of moving straight into battle, he found himself sent, with a three-ton lorry, in the direction of Gafsa, to look for wine and sheep (officially to get jeep spares). He returned a couple of days later without the jeep spares and the wine, though he had found the sheep, and plenty of peaches. At once he was dispatched in a renewed search for spares and wine, this time in the direction of the First Army.

Staying with a Free French unit on his first night away Douglas was able to help five Frenchmen celebrate the news that Tunis and Bizerta had fallen. Another night out, and he returned to find the Sherwood Rangers, whose battle had not materialized, celebrating with a cocktail party and variety concert. That day, the German Ninetieth Light Regiment, which had fought them right across the desert, had surrendered, removing the Sherwood Rangers' last prospect of battle; and the next day, 14 May, the surrender of the Italian army officially completed the campaign. The Ninetieth Light marched to the prisoner-of-war compound accompanied by their regimental brass band, and treated their captors to a concert which opened with 'We're Gonna Hang Out the Washing on the Siegfried Line'. A day or two later they played the British at football and beat them.

In search of loot, Douglas visited the positions last held by the enemy, but returned to camp having collected only a large number of fleas. The loot had been taken by those last in action or collected to await the arrival of the 'back-end' people who were making their way towards Tunisia. He also visited Enfidaville; and where in 'Mersa' he had seen a town taken over by soldiers, Enfidaville awaited its recovery by civilians.

> In the church fallen like dancers
> lie the Virgin and St. Thérèse
> on little pillows of dust.
> The detonations of the last few days
> tore down the ornamental plasters
> shivered the hands of Christ.

> ('Enfidaville')

Instead of men and women only the daylight comes in from the fields, 'like a labourer, tired and sad'; and Douglas uses this personification to move towards a sympathy which he had never before expressed so openly. For this sunlight, 'peering about among the wreckage', passing corners 'as though with averted head' and 'seeing no one move behind the windows', anticipates the return of Enfidaville's inhabitants:

> But already they are coming back; to search
> like ants, poking in the débris, finding in it
> a bed or a piano and carrying it out.
> Who would not love them at this minute?
> I seem again to meet
> the blue eyes of the images in the church.

Offering his compassion as a question, and as the response of a particular moment, Douglas gives edge to an emotion which he did not approach easily. He was reaching pity from the far side, but this impulse towards it was not an isolated one.

At the same time as his first drafts of 'Tel Aviv', in a poem which never became more than a fragment,[1] Douglas had viewed a dying breed of nobles with similar tenderness. At first he had presented them as 'lunatics' who suffered the 'attractive pitiful delusion' that they were living. In his final attempt, however, their devotion to the past surprises him into emotion.

> As I watch each closely—for they are ghosts
> and grow invisible before our eyes
> I feel the hand of pity on my heart
> shaken by their fealty to the past. Look,
> their gestures. These in their rich lifetime bore
> the mark of their nobility and pride.

[1] The poem is untitled; *Collected Poems* prints it under its first line, 'I watch with interest, for they are ghosts'. Its date is uncertain.

These are descendants of his 'Famous Men'. Before, Douglas had always spoken of such creatures as an initiate would, one who proclaimed their return or announced his possession of their secret. Now he writes as an outsider who has learnt respect, and wishes to record their nature, uncertain of success:

> Can you apparel in their proper gear
> these skeletons of conversation falling
> from the lips of a dead nobleman or king
> while still we know what nobles and kings were.

If the experience of battle had brought Douglas to compassion for the civilians of Enfidaville, it is likely that his response to the deaths of Kellett, Garrett, and Player lies behind this fragment.[1] Later he was to describe Player as 'a figure straight out of the nineteenth century', with ideas which were 'feudal in the best sense' and Douglas believed that everyone not only loved him but 'pitied him a little'. Reading of Kellett's death, Douglas explained, 'I was amazed to find . . . that I felt like a member of the old régime who looks on at a bloody revolution.' Garrett was too much a man of horses to attain the grace of the two colonels but his death had given him an inextricable link with the regiment of which Player and Kellett were the embodiment. Douglas's months with the regiment, fixed in the hierarchical cavalry ways it had brought to Palestine in 1940, had taught him how alien he was to the world of 'noble lunatics'. Their deaths, in the campaign in which he had for the first time shared their experience, had also taught him pity. Now, with the fighting over, Douglas set about writing their elegy, 'Aristocrats'.

At the foot of one of this poem's manuscripts Douglas made a note on Colonel Player, whose grave he could have seen on his visit to Enfidaville, for Player had been buried in the churchyard there.

Lt.-Col. J. D. Player, killed in Tunisia, Enfidaville, February, 1943, left £3,000 to the Beaufort Hunt,[2] and directed that the incumbent of the living in his gift should be a 'man who approves of hunting, shooting, and all manly sports, which are the backbone of the nation'.

Several members of the Sherwood Rangers have seen in the poem's first stanza a sly portrait of Player; in its second, Douglas describes an encounter during the fighting at Wadi Zem Zem; and at the poem's close he draws on the sporting language of the yeomen's radio code. Offering his tribute, however, Douglas not only places his new compassion in the context of war's brutality, he builds it out of a sharply evaluative irony.

[1] In one draft, Time 'behind their backs turned them [the gentlemen] to smoke'.
[2] The same hunt which provided a centre for the social life of the Second Derbyshire Yeomanry at Wickwar. Player was in fact killed in April.

~~[crossed out]~~

Among these obsolescent gentle heroes

~~The gentle horse with~~ terror in his eye
clear in the bone, looks up at a shell-burst
away, fly the images of the shires
he puts his pipe back in his mouth
Peter was unfortunately killed by an 88

It took his leg away in ragged shreds
and when I saw him crawling he said
~~I say~~ it's most unfair, they've shot my leg off
Peter, have you got a tourniquet on
No I suppose I ought to have really,
How can I live among this ~~gentle~~ ~~I ask~~ ~~wept~~
obsolescent breed of heroes ~~becoming almost~~
for they are fading into true legends
in which their ~~chivalry it and~~ chivalry ~~are~~
are celebrated, each fool & hero is immortal

~~[crossed out lines]~~

~~[crossed out]~~

~~The mountains were their cricket pitch~~
~~their in the valley, the~~
~~accounted for several of the field.~~
~~Under the stones and earth they dispose themselves~~
~~with their habitual famous unconcern.~~

If I come here again I shall never hear
the scream and the arrival of explosives
~~but somewhere beyond the~~ ~~[crossed out]~~
~~but somewhere beyond the~~ ~~[crossed out]~~
stony marshes
~~[crossed out]~~
a man waggling a hunting horn at his lip

El Ballah to Enfidaville

ARISTOCRATS

'I think I am becoming a God'
The noble horse with courage in his eye
clean in the bone, looks up at a shellburst:
away fly the images of the shires
but he puts the pipe back in his mouth.

Peter was unfortunately killed by an 88:
it took his leg away, he died in the ambulance.
I saw him crawling on the sand; he said
It's most unfair, they've shot my foot off.

How can I live among this gentle
obsolescent breed of heroes, and not weep?
Unicorns, almost,
for they are fading into two legends
in which their stupidity and chivalry
are celebrated. Each, fool and hero, will be an immortal.

The plains were their cricket pitch
and in the mountains the tremendous drop fences
brought down some of the runners. Here then
under the stones and earth they dispose themselves,
I think with their famous unconcern.
It is not gunfire I hear but a hunting horn.

To make possible a celebration of heroism Douglas had to give its true context: not only the gently humorous nonchalance of the first stanza's hero, but the incredible stupidity of the second's. Douglas worked hard at this second stanza, revising it more thoroughly than any other part of the poem except for the conclusion. He had at first included two further lines pointing up Peter's foolishness by revealing that he had not bothered to use a tourniquet: this Douglas compressed by substituting 'foot' for 'leg' in the last line of the stanza, making Peter describe even his own wound euphemistically. Similarly, Douglas removed an additional physical detail: he had first written 'it took his leg away in ragged shreds'; but he wanted only as much description as would supply the documentary evidence on which the aristocrats' stupidity would be understood.

Douglas in the third stanza pivots his own reaction on the ambivalent expression, 'and not weep', blending exasperation and pity. There is no doubt of the dual nature of their heroism and his response, and even after the first lines of his final stanza have transformed the sporting clichés of their radio code into a language of true elegy, Douglas returns to his irony to make way for the final gesture with its echo of Roncesvalles. The dead aristocrats 'dispose themselves', the verb blending graceful disposition and the disposal of their bodies; and, allowing just enough uncertainty with 'I think', Douglas hesitates wryly over their 'famous unconcern'.

In the Preface which Douglas had quoted in his school notebook, Wilfred Owen had written:

This book is not about heroes. English Poetry is not yet fit to speak of them.

Douglas was not writing of the heroes Owen had in mind, the tortured victims of war. These aristocrats are the traditional heroes of the English schoolboy of the period, diffident and pacific and also stupid. But they can be celebrated because their virtue does not lie in a natural capacity for fighting, though the 'noble horse' manages it successfully: it lies in their refusal, like that of John Anderson, to be contaminated by war. Where the poet of 'John Anderson' had been a manipulator of his audience, however, Douglas has now become an intermediary.

5

Awaiting his return to the regiment, in Cairo at the beginning of May, Douglas had bought a desk diary from Boileau and Caloghiris' bookshop. It was not to be used for a diary, for as he had written to his mother on his voyage to the Middle East, 'keeping a diary or making a sort of diary letter —while I admit it's an excellent idea—is something I could never do.' The small book was to contain a narrative of his battle experience. Eventually to be published as *Alamein to Zem Zem*, though Douglas himself could not decide upon a title, it was not a private record but an account addressed to an audience.[1] Beginning at the base depot, Douglas wrote in the book at intervals, tracing events until he had a complete account, from his departure for El Alamein to the end of the campaign outside Enfidaville. At the base depot Douglas's battle experience was already nearly four months behind him, and beside the first page of his account he noted: 'I look back as to a period spent on the moon, almost to a short life in a new dimension.'

If the passage of time and the return to life in a civilian world clarified and defined the strangeness of the battlefield, it could only heighten qualities already present in Douglas's vision of it. For he had approached this life 'in a new dimension' with curious detachment. In his first paragraph he casts himself as a country visitor who has been to the 'great show' of the battlefield; or a child, fascinated by the machinery of a factory, 'without caring or knowing what it is all there for'. Even when he could order his thoughts, he looked for 'something decorative, poetic or dramatic': the concerns of the artist.

---

[1] Writing to Douglas at Weedon on 15 October 1940, Blunden had commented: 'I hope that you will write presently new "Memoirs of a Cavalier" in a spirit of great cheerfulness, though also a farewell to the neighing steed.'

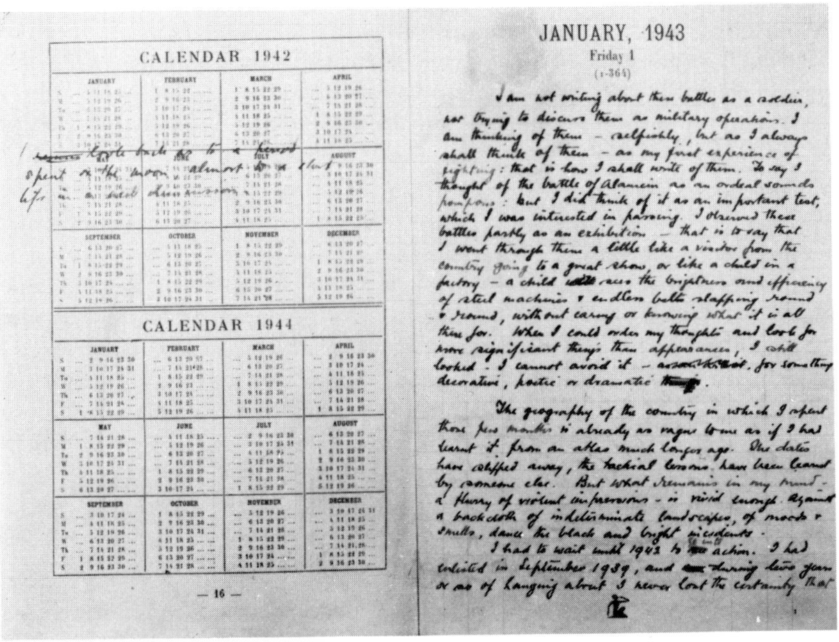

CALENDAR 1942

JANUARY, 1943
Friday 1
(1-364)

CALENDAR 1944

— 16 —

[handwritten diary entry]

I am not writing about these battles as a soldier, nor trying to discuss them as military operations. I am thinking of them – selfishly, but as I always shall think of them – as my first experience of fighting: that is how I shall write of them. To say I thought of the battle of Alamein as an ordeal sounds pompous: but I did think of it as an important test, which I was interested in passing. I observed these battles partly as an exhibition – that is to say that I went through them a little like a visitor from the country going to a great show, or like a child in a factory – a child who sees the brightness and efficiency of actual machines and endless belts slapping round and round, without caring or knowing what it is all there for. When I could order my thoughts and look for more significant things than appearances, I still looked – I cannot avoid it – associations, for something decorative, poetic or dramatic.

The geography of the country in which I spent these few months is already as vague to me as if I had learnt it from an atlas much longer ago. The dates have slipped away, the tactical lessons have been learnt by someone else. But what remains in my mind – a flurry of violent impressions – is vivid enough against a backcloth of indeterminate landscapes, of moods and smells, dance the black and bright incidents.

I had to wait until 1943 to see action. I had enlisted in September 1939, and during those years or so of hanging about I never lost the certainty that ...

An outsider through this detachment, Douglas was also an outsider to most of his regiment. Shared action might have brought him closer to his fellow-officers, providing the common ground lacking during his training with the regiment in Palestine: but on the battlefield he had lost none of his independence of spirit. Two small incidents not recorded in his narrative but recalled by Jack Holman, give some indication of his relations with the senior officers. Although Douglas had found the affectations of the radio code curious enough to write a piece of doggerel called 'Code Words: An Ode in Code', in action its endless permutations of wickets falling, field changes, and dropped catches had annoyed him. Once, having waited some time for a pause in the repartee, Douglas announced: 'Since there appears to be a tea break at Lord's perhaps I can butt in with some very important information . . .' Although he had been waiting to report the sighting of a gun position, he was reprimanded for the speech. The second incident occurred while the regiment rested outside Mersa Matruh, the battles of El Alamein over. A few bottles of vintage port specially ordered by one of the senior officers had arrived and the mess was honoured with the chance of sharing them over dinner. Player sampled the port and, through the ritual hush, declared its excellence. Douglas, lower down the table, knocked

203

back his glassful, picked up the empty bottle and handed it to the orderly with the words: 'Fill it up again, my good man!'

If such iconoclasm distressed his senior officers it provided frequent amusement to his fellows, and they were equally impressed by Douglas's determined opposition to injustices in regimental life. Sometimes he could pursue a point too long or too far, sometimes he seemed intolerant of minor foibles or to be wasting his energy, but his value in a world in which the junior officers' main desire was to keep out of trouble was generally recognized.

In military situations Douglas acted with similar lack of orthodoxy. Neither senior nor junior officers had any love for the professional army, and even the pre-war yeomen who were determined to make a name for the regiment saw themselves as fighting soldiers from necessity rather than choice. To both groups, however, Douglas appeared strikingly unmilitary. Bethell-Fox, who shared Douglas's independence but had been a professional soldier before the war, commented:

he always seemed to me somewhat wasted in the Army. Regimental life with its discipline, its thoughtless automatic routine, its conventions . . . must have been terribly difficult to accept.

And Sergeant Nelson, who had stayed with Douglas at Milena's, was later to write:

In battle he was only moderate as a tactician, and I feel would have been hopeless commanding a force larger than a troop, but he was brave and set an example to his men.

Douglas's bravery, humour, and sense of justice drew affection from almost all his comrades, and his behaviour from El Alamein to Wadi Zem Zem had not only led his squadron leader to recommend him for an M.C.,[1] unknown to Douglas it had brought the respect of Colonel Kellett.

To his fellows, however, Douglas approached battle with too cavalier a sense of individual freedom. Instead of moving strictly according to the plans of the colonel and the squadron leader, Douglas had a tendency to regard his job as a roving commission. If he saw something which interested him, he would take his Crusader across for a closer look. If a battle was on, instead of remaining hull-down while the heavy tanks fought it out, Douglas would join in. If nothing was happening, he would get down from his tank and wander around, while his gunner and driver replied to urgent radio commands that they did not know where he was. Jack Holman recalls that

---

[1] Christopherson's recommendation after the battle at Zem Zem was not forwarded: 'This is not particularly mortifying except that I think it's a pretty ribbon' (Douglas, 25 May 1943, to his mother).

Douglas enjoyed jumping from his tank to throw hand grenades, a practice which always earned him an order to leave 'the cowboys and Indians stuff' to the infantry.

In his narrative Douglas recorded his place in the regiment and his own unorthodox behaviour with fine candour and judgement. Of the regiment, he writes with insistent justice as well as amusement and sympathy. Of himself, he writes of what his comrades considered to be waywardness as, first, the result of inexperience, second, a justifiable independence, and third, an inability to stop dreaming. Douglas is as critical of himself as of others but his position is more than that of the over-seeing author who is able to be wise after the event: it is one of authority. For if he closely defines his own absent-minded or impulsive behaviour, he does so as an experienced soldier; and to the detachment which runs through the account he adds a keen sense of identification. Drawing on the areas of his character which had long attracted him to the military life, Douglas is able to use the first-person plural pronoun, not as the assumption of a role but as an admission of full participation.

To see these tanks crossing country at speed was a thrill which seemed inexhaustible—many times it encouraged us, and we were very proud of our Crusaders; though we often had cause to curse them. . . .

We shared out the plunder with the immemorial glee of conquerors, and beneath the old star-eaten blanket of the sky
lay down to dream of victory.

The discovery that Douglas's quotation is from T. E. Hulme is surprising: his context has so caught the open-air mood of the soldier that the line reads like Kipling.

In the course of his narrative, Douglas enjoys having the mechanism of a Luger explained by German prisoners; he is pleased by the varieties of food created from limited supplies; and his anger at discovering a booby-trap fixed by Italians to a dead body leads to the expression of soldierly prejudices about those who do not fight openly. Still the soldier, he praises the bravery of Italian gunners at El Agheila and feels more murderous towards lazy N.A.A.F.I. officials and callous medical orderlies than towards the enemy. The enjoyment of simple pleasures, the momentary display of prejudice or impetuous anger, and the sense of justice, are all traits of his character which identify him with the ordinary soldier. Douglas makes such an identification when he writes that his sense of the ridiculous prevents him from shooting the fleeing Italians whose lorries he had met: 'like a few other fighting soldiers I lack the true ferocity of Battle School Instructors and armchair critics.' When a German cowers to the ground, fearing that

Douglas will shoot him, Douglas, like Player, Christopherson, or perhaps the German tank commander who allowed him to stagger fifty yards at Wadi Zem Zem without firing, 'felt very embarrassed' and lowered his rifle.

In a campaign which affected few civilians; which for tank men at least remained mobile; which brought both armies a number of local successes and on several occasions a real sense of progress; which brought the opposing armies together on the set stage of the desert and gave them the shared experiences of drought, sandstorms, long supply lines, and difficult terrain; which had been entered upon, at least by the Imperial forces, with a sense of honest purpose if not patriotism; which involved neither partisans nor many civilians of the armies' nationalities; and which included comparatively few atrocities—in such a campaign, the 'new ethics', 'fresh virtues', and arts of the fighting soldier flourished as nowhere else in either this war or the last.

To this campaign, however, Douglas brought the curiosity of an artist. The causes of war, he writes, are unexciting for 'a poet or a painter or a doctor':

> But it is exciting and amazing to see thousands of men, very few of whom have much idea why they are fighting, all enduring hardships, living in an unnatural, dangerous, but not wholly terrible world, having to kill and be killed, and yet at intervals moved by a feeling of comradeship with the men who kill them and whom they kill, because they are enduring and experiencing the same things. It is tremendously illogical—to read about it cannot convey the impression of having walked through the looking-glass which touches a man entering a battle.

If this is a poet's response it none the less articulates that of his unpoetic companions as well. For the sharpness of the language Douglas uses to define moods, scenes, and responses releases what was there for all to see. His wit strives more for justness than extravagance; and the 'decorative, poetic or dramatic' elements which he seeks are not the preserve of the poet but a means of communicating a strange experience to others. So he offers a constant stream of analogies drawn from the world outside the battlefield, as a shifting gauge on which to measure the import of what is seen.

Surrendering Germans rise up from weapon pits, grinning sheepishly, as though 'caught out in a game of hide and seek'; in the darkness, bullets sing past 'like innocuous insects'; the crew of a tank which is hit tumble out of the turret and huddle together, 'supporting each other like revellers going home'; Douglas looks for his squadron, dashing from tank to tank in the mist, 'like a short-sighted little dog who has got lost on the beach'; at dawn, tanks seem to crouch, 'still, but alive, like toads'. Through the familiarity of such points of reference Douglas maintains that the battlefield's inhabitants are people who normally live in a civilian world. As these similes and metaphors accumulate, their varying degrees of significance and seriousness gradually establish an over-all interpretation of the battle-field. It is a world which demands such a sliding scale, for neither the cynical expectations of the experienced participant nor the innocence of the out-sider can thoroughly master its deceitful logic. A tempting Chianti bottle can be attached to a mine; a German who appears to be doing physical exercises can be a man propelled into movement by a spinal wound. Not being 'wholly terrible', the horribly deformed body which the soldier imagines his hand has touched at the bottom of a slit trench can turn out to be a comfortably sleeping companion; from a Sherman tank advancing with smoke and flame as though commanded by a ghostly crew, can emerge Major Semken, smiling, his face 'black as a Christy Minstrel's'. This world is not even consistently deceptive: a haversack taken from a deserted vehicle can truly be full of useful loot; or a man whose 'grotesque huge mouth dribbled and moaned like a child exhausted with crying' can truly have been burned beyond recognition.

In his poems Douglas had extracted different elements from this varied material and concentrated intently upon them, attempting to gain a hold over the complexity of the battlefield through the mastery of each element. In his narrative it is the variety of the whole which concerns him, its sur-prises and revelations which often depend for their significance upon a subsequent, unforeseen event. As in other physical adventures, events on the battlefield are intensified and confused in their sequence. The sudden arrival of a shell, a breakdown in equipment, or a new move by the enemy can produce a completely new set of circumstances; but each of these changes has an importance which is potentially absolute. For unlike any other area of experience, battle has at its centre a single purpose: to kill. Its strange sights may turn out to be harmless, its sudden shifts of circumstance life-saving: but such benevolence is remarkable because the participant knows what normally he must expect.

Describing his first morning at El Alamein, revealing his innocence as a newcomer, Douglas offers a paradigm for the definition of his new world:

Up above in the clear sky a solitary aeroplane moved, bright silver in the sunlight, a pale line of exhaust marking its unhurried course. The Bofors gunners on either side of us were running to their guns and soon opened a rapid, thumping fire, like a titanic workman hammering. The silver body of the aeroplane was surrounded by hundreds of little grey smudges, through which it sailed on serenely. From it there fell away, slowly and gracefully, an isolated shower of rain, a succession of glittering drops.

Douglas's visual sensitivity and the poise of his syntax presents a description which could be laid out in free verse to make a fine Imagist poem. And like a good Imagist, Douglas follows his sustained moment of aesthetic response with a definition of its triumph over reality:

I watched them descend a hundred feet before it occurred to me to consider their significance and forget their beauty.

For the soldier, this ability to suspend reality carries an irony which mocks the aestheticism, for 'significance' on the battlefield is not the elusive truth sought by the poet but a simple matter of fact, rarely withheld for long:

The column of tanks trundled forward imperturbably, but the heads of their crews no longer showed. I dropped down in the turret and shouted to Evan who was dozing in the gunner's seat: 'Someone's dropping some stuff.' He shouted back a question and adjusted his earphones. 'Bombs!' I said into the microphone.

The experienced soldier would not have suspended the truth for more than a moment (nor would he have bothered to waken the gunner): each strange experience of the battlefield comes fully equipped with its own simple and generally threatening meaning.

Only the dead, who peopled the landscape through which Douglas travelled from El Alamein to Mersa, defied this pragmatic logic. They both finally defined the purposes of battle and resisted comprehension. Time and again Douglas describes their appearance, registering their presence as honestly as possible before passing on: for they are the climax of war's artistry and the focus for Douglas's most persistent curiosity. One dead Libyan gives the impression of a man resting, until a fly crawls across his cheek. The clothes of another group have been wrapped round their mutilated bodies by explosive, 'as though with an instinct for decency'. Dead Italians 'lay about like trippers taken ill', the débris which surrounds them looking like the litter of a picnic. A crew killed inside their tank lay 'in a clumsy embrace', their bodies 'so to speak, distributed round the turret'. A dead Highlander has his legs bent double under him, for the corpse has been used as a booby-trap.

Focusing with varying degrees of intensity upon this succession of dead men Douglas never allows more than a momentary pause in his narrative. His metaphors convey moments of fascination or horror, surprise at the variety of appearances offered by death or its capacity for deceit, but they are not shaped into the kind of pattern which he sought in a poem like 'Landscape with Figures'. He is a witness, present in the landscape and engaged in activities which move him on, past the dead men; he is not an artist shaping conclusive patterns. In a short story, 'The Little Red Mouth', Douglas placed a description of a dead New Zealander as an emotional climax, a fact of war which broke in upon his day-dreaming amid the delays of tank warfare and overwhelmed him. At the end he is 'trembling with horror' and stunned into the repetition of a line from the poem he had been reading at the story's opening. It is a dramatic and clearly pointed conclusion. In the narrative Douglas encounters the same dead man and describes him in similar terms, but there is neither drama nor over-all meaning in his response: 'This picture, as they say, told a story. It filled me with useless pity.' What had been an isolated incident selected

for its point in a short story is one event in a narrative, its impact reduced by the movement through a wider experience. As Douglas watches this dead man his tank moves past and the head of a living man is raised from the next pit. He is wounded, needing assistance, and Douglas's attention becomes thoroughly engaged in asking of his wounds, gaining permission to leave the battle, loading the man on to his tank and taking him back to a regimental aid post as a mortar starts shelling them. Having delivered the man he cannot stay to enjoy the pleasures of active sympathy but must return to his squadron. Even the encounters with dead men must take their place in the pattern of continuing action.

Douglas most fully projects the essential continuity of battle experience in the longest chapter of his narrative, which concerns the fighting at Wadi

209

Zem Zem. Previously he had described the constant fluctuations in the pace of tank warfare: the halts of uncertain duration which might barely give time for a mug of tea, or which might leave the tank crew free to read half a Western; the days or weeks of inaction and the intense half-hour of a bombardment; or the whole day of fighting tanks and guns, followed by a night under fire. At Zem Zem, however, Douglas presents in detail a few hours of sustained battle; and here the fortuitous logic of the battlefield is fully revealed.

The protagonist is in the position of a picaresque hero at the mercy of a plot which he has no hope of comprehending, but which is primarily designed to kill him. Thus subject to the flow of events, he is at the same time thoroughly active. At each turn he faces decisions on which his own life and those of others may depend. Having made one decision, a new set of circumstances may reverse its import and demand another decision. It is a kind of blind-man's buff in which the mind tries to make sense of each moment as physical sensations continually persuade and deceive.

In the middle of a battle which either side could be winning, Douglas climbs from his broken-down Crusader to find himself facing a German tank:

'Capture,' I thought suddenly. 'I shall be captured.' There was no sign of the regiment. Only the shells of tanks, and the enemy, coolly surveying the landscape. If I ran to the hole they would find us all. I think I was as near panic as I have ever been. My thoughts flickered with my glance over all possible refuges. I began to run, keeping my tank between me and the enemy: I was bound to come into the open and to make an easy mark for their machine-gun, and I thought of this and accepted the thought. I did not care if they shot me but I was unnerved by the thought of capture. I ran about two hundred yards. After that the headache of the early morning reasserted itself, the sore in my leg throbbed insistently under its dirty bandages, the scorched places on my face and the scratches on my leg made themselves felt, and I had no more breath to run; I was quite exhausted. I began walking, too tired to care any more even about escape, until I should have a breathing space.

I walked forward blindly and almost tripped over a man on the ground. He was a 'C' Squadron corporal, and his right foot was not there; the leg ended in a sort of tattered brush of bone and flesh. . . . 'Kneel down,' he said. 'I can get on your back.' I got on my knees and he fastened a grip on me like the old man of the sea. I tried to stand up, and at last achieved it, swaying and sweating, with the man on my back; his good leg and his stump tucked under my arms, his hands locked at my throat.

Douglas makes from the action at Wadi Zem Zem a natural climax for his narrative. He does not end with his tripping the S mine, however, but carefully describes his being moved further and further from the battlefield, through field aid posts and dressing stations to El Ballah, distancing the previous events and diminishing the force of their climax. Having settled into El Ballah, he takes up his story again at Enfidaville, recounting the news of the regiment's deaths, and moving on to narrate briefly his trips for supplies and the ending of the campaign. It is an epilogue, draining away the violence and excitement of his actions from Alamein to Zem Zem in the trivial pleasures of his travels outside the perimeter of the last days' fighting.

In the narrative as a whole, Douglas makes no attempt to impose an order on the actual course of events; but he does order his account so as to release an inherent dramatic movement: first the fluctuations of the fighting up to Mersa; second the inaction of the 'Silly Season' before Zem Zem; third the fighting there, followed by its anti-climax; finally the inaction of the end of the campaign. Rough edges and loose ends prevent the narrative from taking on the full pattern either of fiction or of a formal history, but through emphasis and omission, Douglas gives enough shape to his account to enforce a view of a whole campaign. In the last section, while the common-place expeditions for supplies deny drama to the ending of the campaign, through their distance, the scale of fighting beyond the narrator's observation is established. Finally the living, like those who survive a Shakespearean tragedy, on the book's last page honour the dead and think enthusiastically of the loot they shall find.

Within such a structure Douglas was prepared to cover in detail his own conflicts with others, to write an amusing set-piece on their radio code, and to dwell on trivia which mattered at the time; for his aim was to present his own experience of war as truthfully as possible. His mother's criticisms, some months later, of his descriptions of his comrades, he countered by saying that they represented his views during the campaign: some of his opinions he had subsequently altered but to put them right would require another book. At the same time a friend of his mother's raised objections to the narrative's treatment of his visit to Milena from Mersa and its emphasis upon loot. Douglas replied in a letter which defended the integrity of his whole enterprise: 'You want "selectivity" again—a suppression of something ugly but true. . . . I'm not sure that the instinct for selectivity isn't based on sentimentality anyhow.'

8

Tunisia and Egypt

June - November 1943

> To write on the themes which have been concerning me lately in lyric and abstract form would be immense bullshitting.
>
> (10 August 1943 to J. C. Hall)

I

Although the Sherwood Rangers had assumed that promises of a return home after the campaign's end were an unnecessary carrot intended to encourage the donkey across North Africa, they had at least expected a good rest.

We were soon disabused and offered as consolation prize four whole days of leave, some in the Tripoli area, where there is nothing whatever to do, and some in a leave camp here, where the men are inspected and 'disciplined' as much as ever. You can imagine what effect this has had. I hope someone will ask a question or two in Parliament, although of course they'll get no satisfactory answer.

The arrival of the 'back-end' forces, sporting the Eighth Army badge and receiving a heroes' welcome, further infuriated Douglas: it was they who posed as battle-torn heroes, 'dirty and half naked', for press photographs, while the fighting troops, 'even on a half-pint of water', kept themselves smart. Writing thus to his mother on 28 May, Douglas added that he had never seen a dead Highlander 'who had not got his stockings pulled up and clean red hackles'.

For all his discontent with the treatment given the regiment after action, within two weeks he was writing differently:

The country here is marvellous, we bathe morning noon and night in deep blue translucent sea, I am browner than ever in my life and hope to spend my leave at Monaster, a peacetime resort where I can go to a dance every night.

The change was brought about partly because of the departure of the rest of the brigade, in whose presence more official activities had been maintained.

212

On its own, by the sea at Hergla, the regiment was able to organize its own freedom, and Douglas, made officer in charge of their entertainments, was able to travel and meet civilians as often as he wished. On one of his earlier trips in search of spare parts he had already befriended a French family in Sousse, the Barbaras, and now he saw more of them. On each of his visits they welcomed him like a long-lost son, though they had a son of their own who also wrote poetry. For the regiment he organized parties and dances, at least one of which, for a hundred members of the regiment and a hundred girls, was held at Monaster. There were bands to be found and hospitals to be visited in search of dancing partners, and after his travels there was the sea and wine at sixpence a bottle. To complete his contentment, on 9 June he wrote to his mother as a captain.[1]

Douglas mentioned in the same letter a chance meeting with a friend of John Hall's, Geoffrey Wagner, whom he too had known slightly at Edgeborough and Oxford,[2] and wrote to Hall the next day. From his mother he had received copies of a review of their *Selected Poems*, and a description of Stephen Spender's remarks on it in the *New Statesman*, but he had not yet seen the book itself, which had been published in February. Having described the 'hell of a good time' he was having, it was of Hall's work that he first wrote. Though one of Douglas's first and most loyal admirers, Hall had been disappointed by the work Douglas had sent him in the months before action. Writing to Mrs. Douglas in October 1942 that he was sending 'Christodoulos' and 'Devils' on to Tambimuttu, Hall had commented that they worked 'too remotely, cleverly but not movingly', and that he did not like them; and on 2 February he had written that he was still unhappy about Douglas's recent poems. Now Douglas counter-attacked:

You have been making cutting remarks about my poems for so long I ought to retaliate but I haven't seen any of yours for a long time except here and there. The nastiest and truest thing I can say is that you are getting too involved and precious, chiefly because you now find yourself in a backwater and have nothing to write about that is relevant.[3]

The argument is that of his essay on 'Poets in This War'.

Turning to his own work, however, Douglas wrote with new conviction,

---

[1] Douglas drew attention to his new rank, saying: 'I hope the new form of address will please you, although it will be a long time before I get the pay through.' In letters of May he had still given his rank as lieutenant though his military record notes: 'P/A/Capt. 27.4.43; T/Capt. 27.7.43'.

[2] Wagner later wrote, 'Douglas, while detesting all war stood for, seemed to me in brief meetings in Tunisia, mentally and emotionally invigorated by the life of action. . . .'

[3] Ironically, praising Douglas's poems for their 'perfection' in a letter to Mrs. Douglas on 30 October 1941, Hall's only reservation had been that they were 'perhaps rather far removed from reality'.

explaining the kind of poetry which must be written now, and drawing a line between his writing before and after action:

The same applied to me in pre-Alamein days and I reacted differently but if anything produced worse. With regard to your criticism of my stuff, I think you are beginning to condemn all that is not your own favourite brand, and are particularly anti reportage and extro-spective (if the word exists) poetry—which seems to me the sort that has to be written just now, even if it is not attractive.

On 14 June the regiment moved southward towards Tripolitania. At El Djem they were able to examine the ruins of a colosseum larger than that of Rome, and at Medenine, an Arab fortress. At Zavia, the King arrived for an inspection to which the Sherwood Rangers contributed three hundred and fifty men, and an E.N.S.A. concert party brought them entertainment from Beatrice Lillie, Vivien Leigh, Dorothy Dickson, and Leslie Henson. By the end of the month, under a new Colonel, Ian Spence, they had leaguered in a large palm grove on dunes beside the sea at Homs.

From there, on 26 June, Douglas wrote again to Hall. He had by then received a copy of their *Selected Poems* and warmly thanked Hall for all he had done towards keeping him in print in England. He considered Hall's choice of his poems 'surprisingly near what I'd have made myself'. However,

The squadron area at Homs

Douglas clearly did not imply by this an agreement with Hall's present preference for his earlier work, for he went on:

On the selection, Norman Nicholson appears the best of us—which perhaps he is, being the eldest. I think a few more biographical details might have been given in front . . . I am glad you put in 'Caravan', although I don't think 'Famous Men' *and* 'Images' were *both* necessary. I wish the dates of all these poems could have been put on them, as it would have made it easier for reviewers not to talk cock about them.

Selected Poems, although it appeared early in 1943, in fact represented Douglas's work up to September 1941; thirteen of the poems included had been written at school and Oxford, five during army training in England, and only one, 'Negative Information', in the Middle East. There was no indication in the selection that this work represented the Keith Douglas of eighteen months before.[1] It was therefore not altogether unjust that a couple of the reviewers wrote of Douglas as one of the *Eight Oxford Poets*, and that Spender turned his review into a general commentary on 'The Maturity of the Poet'.

Having pointed to the poems of Hall's he liked best, and suggested that Hall was not fair to himself in his selection, Douglas observed:

I think you need a little more cynicism, or should I say indifference to emotion once felt, in your poetic make-up. . . . You are too much affected. I don't want that you should lose the sensitiveness, or even some of it. But that you should be deeply affected, and yet not show it so much—a little more of the traditional Englishman—however much you deplore him—would make your poetry much stronger and more impressive.

To make sure that Hall received his thanks for the volume, Douglas accompanied his air letter with an airgraph. There, having stated his gratitude: 'Thank you very much for all you have done towards keeping me in print in England. I'm sorry Sheila Shannon didn't agree with you that it was worth it. Anyway, she gave you and Norman a write-up',[2] Douglas turned to his own work, again identifying creative impulses with the availability of experience, but this time placing a negative emphasis:

Did you ever receive the poems I wrote in hospital? I am not likely to produce anything but virtual repetitions of these, until the war is cleared up now, because I doubt if I shall be confronted with any new horrors or any worse pain, short of being burnt up, which I am not likely to survive.

---

[1] Despite the brevity of most of its reviews, the book gave Douglas his first share in the wartime poetry boom, selling almost all the two thousand copies printed in its first six months.

[2] Geoffrey Wagner had given him a copy of Miss Shannon's *Spectator* review.

With this 'cheerful thought' Douglas reached the bottom of his page.

At Homs, however, Douglas completed a new war poem which had little to do with those he had written in hospital. In 'Aristocrats' he had mediated between his awareness of the aristocrats' foolishness and their heroism: now, in '*Vergissmeinnicht*', he mediates between the participant in war and the outside world whose humane laws he violates. Douglas writes as a combatant, voicing the casual irony and honest satisfaction of the soldier.

Revisiting the 'nightmare ground' where earlier he had engaged a gun emplacement, Douglas, with his soldierly companions, sees a dead gunner 'sprawling in the sun', like a sunbather. The sight reminds them of the drama of the battle, the gunner's successful shot at their tank:

> . . . As we came on
> that day, he hit my tank with one
> like the entry of a demon.

The scene excites their curiosity:

> Look. Here in the gunpit spoil
> the dishonoured picture of his girl
> who has put: *Steffi. Vergissmeinnicht*
> in a copybook gothic script.

Such a sight barely modifies the tankmen's sense of satisfaction. They see him

> . . . almost with content
> abased, and seeming to have paid
> and mocked at by his own equipment
> that's hard and good when he's decayed.

Their sense of justice is almost beyond reproach, but the photograph had introduced the world outside war, denying the immunity to feeling claimed by their professional response.

> But she would weep to see today
> how on his skin the swart flies move;
> the dust upon the paper eye
> and the burst stomach like a cave.

Douglas, as poet, has intervened; holding true to the visual facts observed by the soldiers, his diction distances and softens their force. Neither soldier nor lover would see the dead man like this, but it is a view which blends their frank observation with a sensitivity brought from outside the battlefield. Through such a fusion Douglas can draw from a sensitive comprehension of the scene's significance, the humane poise which the event itself would deny:

Tunisia and Egypt

> For here the lover and killer are mingled
> who had one body and one heart.
> And death who had the soldier singled
> has done the lover mortal hurt.

Douglas had travelled far from his El Ballah poems of dead men and their denial of lyricism; at Homs, early in July, however, it was of these poems which he heard good news. On 1 June he had sent Tambimuttu copies of 'Gallantry', 'Words', 'Desert Flowers', and 'Landscape with Figures'. Now Tambimuttu wrote that he wanted to print these poems in *Poetry (London)* and to include them in two anthologies he was going to edit: *Poems From the Services*, for Nicholson and Watson, and *Poetry in Wartime II* for Faber and Faber,[1] who had published its predecessor. Tambimuttu added:

Also would you care to make a selection of your poems for possible publication by Poetry London (Nicholson and Watson) in book form. I think a book by you would be interesting. I hope you will include as many Middle East poems as possible.

Douglas had gained an unpromising impression of Tambimuttu as an editor from Geoffrey Wagner, and in the biographical note which had accompanied his first appearance in *Poetry (London)* Douglas had found himself placed in 'the Tank Corps', an organization which did not exist. Undaunted, he sent his acceptance from Homs on 11 July. He would be glad to make a selection, though someone would have to send him a list of the titles of poems he had sent his mother and Blunden because he could not remember all of them. 'As to including a lot of Middle East stuff,' he said,

there isn't as yet a very great deal to include; because I like to write in comfort or not at all and the nearest to comfort available most of the time is not near enough. A few flies are enough to destroy inspiration, if they keep on the job the way Egyptian, Tripolitanian and Tunisian flies do. What I have written has been written in hospitals, con. depots, Base depots etc.—emotion recollected in tranquillity. . . .

As he was now living in 'a hole in the sand with a piece of canvas over it, in the inadequate shade of a palm tree', Douglas did not expect to be very creative. While they were 'sitting around', however, he was 'angling for' the job of Brigade Entertainment Officer, which would enable him to live in a house with his own room and a vehicle at his disposal: 'If I get the job I'll send you bags of literature, in all forms and on all subjects.'

Besides his living conditions, Douglas had regimental activities with

---

[1] Neither of the proposed anthologies appeared.

which to contend. For at Homs they were no longer on their own, and stationed with the rest of the brigade, an appearance of useful training had to be maintained. Swimming classes were given to non-swimmers and new tradesmen were trained; for the education of the officers, squadrons fought battles over the telephone, the opposing sides tracing out the conflict on sand tables; and at the Roman theatre in Leptis Magna they were told of the successful invasion of Sicily. Off duty, there were few compensating pleasures, for Tripoli, despite its pink and white oleanders and its mimosa, had little food and drink to offer and the only things to be bought were shoddy souvenirs.[1]

At the end of July, however, his hopes of the post of Entertainment Officer having remained unfulfilled, Douglas was posted away from the regiment to attend a course in Palestine. From there, on 10 August, he wrote to John Hall a final and full-scale defence of his recent poetry. Again his remarks were provoked by Hall's comments, for where Hall had written in October 1941 that he would be interested to see any poems which showed Douglas's reaction to the war, now that he had received these war poems he was not very keen on them.[2] 'Incidentally', wrote Douglas, 'you say I fail as a poet, when you mean I fail as a lyricist', and lyricism Douglas now related to his previous inexperience.

In my early poems I wrote lyrically, as an innocent, because I was an innocent: I have (not surprisingly) fallen from that particular grace since then. I had begun to change during my second year at Oxford. . . . Well, I am still changing. . . .

Douglas acknowledged that he might be 'awkward and not used to the new paces yet', but he showed no uncertainty about the nature of what he must do:

my object (and I don't give a damn about my duty as poet) is to write true things, significant things in words each of which works for its place in a line. My rhythms, which you find enervated, are carefully chosen to enable the poems to be *read* as significant speech: I see no reason to be either musical or sonorous about things at present. When I do, I shall be so again, and glad to. I suppose I

---

[1] Hamo Sassoon remembers another chance meeting with Douglas at Homs. As Sassoon was making for Egypt, Douglas urged him to call on a Greek girl in Alexandria. It was Titsa, whom Douglas had found unwell from her family's fasting when he met her on his visit from Mersa Matruh.

[2] Blunden was also to express reservations. Having found 'The Offensive' 'a very keen impression of that silent crisis', on 16 August 1943 he wrote of 'Aristocrats' that it was excellent in a 'dry ironic' way, but lacked that 'fullness of music and broadness of understanding' which would bring in all readers, the acute and the general. Blunden, with his own experience of the Great War to draw on, none the less echoed the emphasis which Douglas had insisted upon ever since he had seen action: 'The fighting man in this as in other wars is at least the only man whom truth really cares to meet.'

reflect the cynicism and careful absence of expectation (it is not quite the same as apathy) with which I view the world.

Hall had written of 'regrouping' the poem's components. This struck Douglas as a confession of defeat: 'There is never much need to regroup. Let your impulses drive you forward; never lose contact with life or you will lose the impulses as well.'

Underlying his whole argument is the theme which had pervaded his essay on 'Poets in This War' and his earlier letters to Hall. Without the impetus of first-hand experience, the poet could not write significantly at all. Now Douglas had this experience, his technique demanded refinement to match it. The experience was war.

I never tried to write about war (that is battles and things, not London can Take it), with the exception of a satiric picture of some soldiers frozen to death, until I had experienced it. Now I will write of it, and perhaps one day cynic and lyric will meet and make me a balanced style.

Two days after this letter, as if to drive home his case, Douglas sent Hall another new poem. He had started it in Tunisia, and the fourteen sheets of drafts and revisions which went into its making confirm the rigours of technique which he still demanded. The poem started from an image for his own move to death:

> As a weightless mosquito who
> meets her shadow on the stone
> a puffball, enclosed in my own silence
> as in a glass sphere, I am gliding
> towards the minute when shadow and self are one
> meeting unnoticeably as insects do.

While working on this, Douglas developed a separate analogy, between the trajectory of a shell and a ball thrown into the air by a child. Seeing that this, too, could express the ease of his move from life to death, he merged the fragments. A complete poem had not resulted, however, and he turned to another field of imagery, sorcery.

Beginning with a sorcery which echoed his first theme, of an easy passage to death, Douglas moved through several attempts to one in which he was not victim but killer:

> . . . I have committed sorcery
> sorcerers are of the angels cursed,
> for by sorcery the focus of love is diffused
> so the waves of love travel into vacancy
> it is sad to be a ghost.

Next he transformed this loosely expository mood into one of more dramatic and intense self-discovery:

> . . . leaps out and turns to dust
> a man of flesh. I have committed sorcery,
> see how my hand turns black. I am accursed
> who have the focal point of love diffused
> the waves of love travel into vacancy.

As Douglas allows ideas to accumulate around this image, he sharpens his focus on the nature of his crime. The victim of his magic moves 'in ways / his mother would have recognized', and the sorcerer is 'amused' by his achievement in killing him. After what must have been several hours of work, Douglas brought his two themes together in a poem of four stanzas: first his own movement to death, then his discovery of the force of gravity, then his killing the other man, and finally his own death.

> My hand has made a man of dust
> of a man of flesh: a sorcery
> achieved by fragile mechanism.
> Now, my face smiling in the prism
> of another, he erases me.
> It is easy to be a ghost.

On 12 August Douglas sent a completed poem to John Hall in which the original theme of his own death had disappeared.

> How to Kill[1]
> Under the parabola of a ball,
> a child turning into a man,
> I looked into the air too long.
> The ball fell in my hand, it sang
> in the closed fist: *Open Open*
> *Behold a gift designed to kill.*
>
> Now in my dial of glass appears
> the soldier who is going to die.
> He smiles, and moves about in ways
> his mother knows, habits of his.
> The wires touch his face: I cry
> NOW. Death, like a familiar, hears
>
> and look, has made a man of dust
> of a man of flesh. This sorcery
> I do. Being damned, I am amused

---

[1] The copy sent to Hall was called 'The Sniper'.

Suddenly he makes a man of dust
from a man of flesh.

Under the parabola of his ball
the child turned into a man
looking in the air at the bright thing.
The ball fell in his hand; it sang
in the closed fist Open, Open.
for the gift you hold is lethal

+ Suddenly there is a man of dust
the live man gone as if by sorcery;
look down, some demon, and be amused
to see the focus of women's love diffused
the waves of love will travel into vacancy
~~I am the creator of a ghost~~
it is sad to be a ghost.

Under the parabola of his ball went
the child turning into a man
looking upwards at the thing
in the air. The ball fell: it sang
in the closed fist: Open Open
behold a gift, a lethal instrument.

The weightless mosquito touches
her tiny shadow on the stone
like a balloonist
am borne along to die

Under the parabola of a ball
a child turning into a man
I ~~stared~~ stared into the air at the bright thing.
The ball fell into my hand: it sang
in the closed fist: Open Open
behold a lethal instrument.

The weightless mosquito touches
her shadow on the stone
~~Brightening like to breath~~
~~vacant indeed~~

with such an infinite
lightness, in a brief minute
my shadow + I will join
for the mosquito death approaches

In my dial of glass appears
the young man I have come to kill.
He smiles, and moves about in ways
his mother knows, habits of his.
The wires touch his face. I call
NOW. Death, like a familiar, hears.

to see the centre of love diffused
and the waves of love travel into vacancy.
How easy it is to make a ghost.

The weightless mosquito touches
her tiny shadow on the stone,
and with how like, how infinite
a lightness, man and shadow meet.
They fuse. A shadow is a man
when the mosquito death approaches.

The emphasis of the poem has rested on the corruption of the soldier, so powerful now that the signs of humanity which had limited his satisfaction in '*Vergissmeinnicht*' add to his pleasure in killing. Even while the physical details of the second stanza reveal the humanity of the victim, they assert the sensuous force of the killer's imagination. The abstractions of the third stanza, which define the extent of his crime, reinforce the sense of fantasy which has made such murder possible; and even the lucid metaphysical language of this second half of the poem is potentially damning. For as he responds to the sensitivity of his image of death in the final stanza, the poet does not rule out the possibility that this is the musing of a connoisseur of death.

2

Apart from his three weeks at Homs Douglas had lived independent of his regiment ever since Wadi Zem Zem. Even in Tunisia he had spent as much time as possible with civilians. A month on his own in Palestine, officially attending a course, offered a more attractive way of passing the time than brigade sports and training with three broken-down Shermans with rusted guns, at Homs; and largely through the hospitality of a family from Hamburg, the Hofsteins, Douglas had an enjoyable month. Mrs. Hofstein mended and ironed his clothes and fed him from family rations, as Mrs. Pegna had done; and there was an attractive and 'vaguely intellectual' daughter, Eve: though Douglas was unable to do more than arouse the jealousy of her fiancé, a policeman, also from Germany.[1]

On his way to Palestine, Douglas had called on Milena, and on his first week-end on the course he had stayed with Olga, whom he found anxious and depressed. Within a week, however, her life had been transformed: she found a new job with half the hours and the same pay, and met a man she had thought to be dead, who proposed to her and whom she decided to

---

[1] Douglas was pleased by a gift from Eve, a copy of Rilke's poems in German. He had had with him at Homs a volume of Rilke's *Selected Poems* in translations by Ruth Speirs, published in Cairo.

marry after the war. Douglas was delighted, writing to his mother that Olga certainly deserved her good fortune.

Having stayed at the Hofsteins' for the latter part of the course, and had a friend of Olga's, Vera Nova, for company, he was sorry to leave Palestine at the end of August. Only Tunisia had attracted him more as a place to settle, and he made inquiries at the British Council about the prospect of a lecturing post in either of these countries, or in Egypt, after the war: the 'Great Men', he said, seemed 'tolerably favourable'. Ever since El Ballah, Douglas had been thinking intermittently of his long-term future. From hospital he had asked his mother to keep open his few literary contacts; from Tunisia he had indulged the prospect of one day marrying and living there after the war; and from Palestine he had written of the British Council opportunity, or of taking courses in 'Costume design, Décor and Interior decoration'.

But returning to Cairo at the start of September, to wait at the R.A.C. base depot for the arrival of his regiment, Douglas was overcome by the frustrations of the present. The 'innumerable' women he met were either 'too stupid to take out more than once' or failed to keep their first date with him. The dentist who set about extracting two wisdom teeth took them out in several pieces and 'completely wrecked the inside of my mouth'. He had 'blood poisoning, desert sores etc.'; no one would do anything for anyone except at exorbitant prices; and Egypt was a 'sink':

the king is the biggest shit of the lot. He is the biggest landowner and exploits more fellahin working all day for next to nothing and living in mud huts, than any of his great fat oily subjects. He also keeps storerooms in which he amasses such things as potatoes, prior to 'arranging' a shortage of these commodities, so that he can sell them at four or five times the proper price.

For consolation Douglas had the satisfaction of smashing the taxi of a driver who had demanded an exorbitant fare.

As Titsa and I knew the fare, we refused to pay it, so he got out and opened the bonnet and said 'Very sorry. Taxi broken.' It obviously wasn't so Titsa and I said 'Where?' and pushed him out of the way to look at the engine. I yanked all the distributor leads out and mixed them up and split the vulcanite top of the distributor. Then we said: 'Yes, you're quite right. It's broken. Goodnight' and went off and took a tram before he realised what we'd done.

It was a return of his bloody-mindedness, which always came over him in periods of frustration and uncertainty. By the twentieth of the month, however, he heard of a chance to break free of his empty existence.

In March 1942, describing his plan to see action unofficially, Douglas had written that once he had done so he would be able to return to a 'cushy job' on the staff without conscience. Now the possibility of such a job arose.

Keith Douglas

John Waller, a staff captain engaged in military journalism, having heard of Douglas's return to Egypt, had written some weeks earlier offering him a job on his staff. Addressed to the base depot, his letter had followed Douglas to Palestine and back, and on 20 September Douglas replied with thanks, and the suggestion that they should talk about the offer if it was still open. The main snag was that it was a lieutenant's post, but Douglas had other reservations:

As you see I am a Captain—by the skin of my teeth. If there seems to be any chance of going into action again I should probably want to go—not that I like action that much, but I don't see why my friends should get blown up while I drop out. On the other hand, if we're going to hang about, I shall be wanting a job, and if I am already out of it when the regiment departs I shall just try to get back. And if I don't get back I shan't worry, much. A conscience is a nuisance. I find most of the people in the regiment extremely stupid and boring. I hate fighting but if I stay behind I feel much worse. I have already been blown up once, but it didn't larn me, unfortunately.

Saying that he would telephone Waller, though 'the phone here is a bad one, and I'm bad on phones', Douglas suggested they meet the next Sunday at the Bar Petit Coin de France 'at 6.30. I'll wait till 6.45.' When they met Waller agreed to see if the staff could be reconstituted to make room for a captain.

Later in the month the regiment returned, having left Homs on 14 September. Douglas joined them at their tented camp at Beni Yusef near Cairo, to share their duties of guarding residences, ministries, and hospital stores in the city. 'After two days in this camp', he was writing to Waller of another possible job: 'I have no hesitation in saying please go right ahead to get me an interview re the P.R. East Africa job.' For six weeks he awaited an outcome to Waller's efforts, his tedious duties broken only by ten days, 18 to 28 October, attending a course on the 'Observation and Correction of Fire', at the R.A.C. Schools, and a final visit to Milena, returning Masha to her 'as I'm not going to war for a bit'. Hardly surprisingly, when he wrote his first poem for a couple of months, 'I Experiment', he reiterated his pre-Alamein theme of experience as a cyclical process. His manner, however, was appropriate to the poem's title, experimenting with form by the omission of punctuation, and with substance by the use of phantasmagoria:

> The shadows of leaves falling like minutes
> seascapes discoveries of sea creatures
> and voices out of the extreme distance reach us
> like conjured sounds Faces cruising like spirits
>
> across the backward glance of the brain
> In the bowl of the mind a pot pourri . . .

224

Tunisia and Egypt

David Hicks, with whom Douglas had stayed on earlier visits to Cairo, had moved to Teheran, and although he visited Hicks's old flat to meet Bernard Spencer again, Douglas found no replacement for him. Through Spencer, however, Douglas now made his first contact with the writers who contributed to *Personal Landscape*. Twice he met Terence Tiller and Lawrence Durrell, and although he saw them only in a group, he left a strong impression on both of them. Durrell was later to write that Douglas seemed 'delighted with his war' and 'glad to have tested his courage':[1] and another writer in Cairo at this time, G. S. Fraser, reported a couple of meetings with Douglas in similar terms:

his talk was all of burning tanks and roasting bodies. About fighting he said it was an experience he'd been glad to have but that he'd seen everything that was necessary. Everything else would be repetition; waste.

Having baffled Oxford's literati with his persona of reactionary horseman and rugby player, Douglas must have enjoyed playing the role of hardened soldier among Cairo's exiles.

It was a role he was not to play for long. Before Waller had been able to conclude his efforts to make the job on his staff a captaincy, the regiment learnt that at last they were to leave the Middle East. On 29 October they were issued with battle dress and put on forty-eight hours' notice to move. Although their destination was not officially known, it was guessed that they were to return to Britain to prepare for the opening of a second front in Europe. Douglas made no last-minute attempt to get away. If they were to be caught up once more in the course of the war, he would go with them, for in this situation he saw no reason why he should be excluded.

With the editors of *Personal Landscape* Douglas left copies of most of his war poems, for future publication in the magazine.[2] Among them was a last poem on Cairo life, which he had sent earlier to Tambimuttu, 'Behaviour of Fish in an Egyptian Tea Garden'. If Douglas had warned Hall he would produce no more 'galleries of images', he had clearly not implied a repudiation of metaphor:

> As a white stone draws down the fish
> she in the seafloor of the afternoon
> draws down men's glances and their cruel wish
> for love. Slyly red lip on the spoon

[1] Despite the brevity of their contact, Durrell is said to have modelled Johnny Keats in his *Alexandria Quartet* upon Douglas.
[2] 'Desert Flowers' had possibly been published there before his departure; the number in which it appeared is not dated.

225

TAMBIMUTTU
Poetry (London)   9C5173
Craven House
LONDON   GB.

Military Airgraph Service authorized by Egyptian Postal Administration

Write the message very plainly below this line

170611 CAPT. K.C. DOUGLAS. NOTTS S.R. YEO. MEF. OCT. 3RD.

Behaviour of fish in an Egyptian teagarden.

TEAGARDEN

Sender's Address

As a white stone draws down the fish
she on the seafloor of the afternoon   **SEAFLOOR**
Draws down men's glances and their cruel wish
for love. Slyly, her red lip on the spoon

Slips in a morsel of ice-cream; her hands   **MORSEL**
white as a shell, submarine
fronds, sinking with spread fingers, lean
along the table, carmined at the ends.

A cotton magnate, an important fish
with great eyepouches and a golden mouth   **EYEPOUCHES**
through the frail reefs of furniture swims out
and idling, suspended, stays to watch.

Crustacean, an old man clamped to his chair
FISSURES sits near her, and may coldly see
her charms through fissures where the eyes should be;
or else his teeth are parted in a stare.

Now a young man, a lean dark mackerel
lies in the offing; as through water looks
through currents of sound. The flat-eyed flatfish sucks
on a straw, staring from its repose, lazily

CIRCLING And gallants in shoals swim up and lag,
circling and passing near the white attraction;
sometimes pausing, opening a conversation;
fish pause so to nibble or tug.

↓
PAUSE Dear Tambimuttu — I hope you can read this: I've
repeated doubtful words in block letters.   keD.

But now the ice-cream is finished, so
hard for the fish shown off to this swimino
and she sits down at the table, a whistle stone,
nucleus except to a collector, a dead man.

KD's snapshot of a Cairo teagarden

> slips in a morsel of ice-cream; her hands
> white as a milky stone, white submarine
> fronds, sink with spread fingers, lean
> along the table, carmined at the ends.

For five more stanzas Douglas sustains the underwater image. Watching or moving towards the woman, the men are fish. A cotton magnate 'with great eyepouches and a golden mouth' swims through 'reefs of furniture' and stays to watch. A 'crustacean old man', clamped to his chair, might see her 'through fissures where the eyes should be'. A captain on leave, 'a lean dark mackerel, / lies in the offing; turns himself and looks / through currents of sound'. A flatfish sucks on a straw, and gallants 'in shoals swim up and lag', pausing and conversing as fish pause 'to nibble or tug'. Through this succession of delicately timed metaphors, Douglas not only conveys a variety of sexual awareness, he establishes the duration of the woman's attraction.

> Now the ice-cream is finished, is
> paid for. The fish swim off on business
> and she sits alone at the table, a white stone
> useless except to a collector, a rich man.

On 5 November, assuring Olga that she would always be welcome in England and that he would 'very likely' be back, with the British Council in Greece or Palestine after the war, Douglas sent her this poem. Two days later, the Sherwood Rangers were ordered to remove their cap badges and flashes for a move to a supposedly secret destination. With such security, they knew it was home; and on 17 November, with the regiment, Douglas embarked for England.

9

England

December 1943 - June 1944

For the heart is a coal, growing colder
when jewelled cerulean seas change
into grey rocks, grey water-fringe . . .
cold is an opiate of the soldier.
('On a Return from Egypt')

I

The voyage to Britain on a ship well supplied with nurses and other female passengers was almost as pleasant as that from Durban to Port Said two and a half years earlier, though the officiousness of the officer in charge of troops on board brought some annoyance to the Sherwood Rangers and to Douglas in particular. As the Straits of Gibraltar were now clear, they were able to spend a week in Augusta harbour, Sicily, and still arrive off the Scottish coast on 9 December, only three weeks after leaving Egypt. After two frustrating days offshore, waiting for a berth, the regiment had the consolation of the most cursory customs inspection—no one declared anything and no questions were asked—and at once the Sherwood Rangers travelled south to a camp at Chippenham, arriving on 12 December. It was a curious homecoming, for many their first sight of Britain since 1940; but the pleasure of return was conditioned by the knowledge that they had come back to prepare for another campaign. For the present, however, at least three weeks leave was granted to all those who had served in the Middle East, and Douglas set off to see his mother at East Grinstead where she had kept house for the Babers since December 1942.

It was a more secure and pleasant situation than Mrs. Douglas had known for many years. Much of the time she had the house to herself as Colonel Baber and his wife Jocelyn were both engaged in war work in London, and when they were staying at East Grinstead she was accepted as a member of the family. Finding his mother well settled, and having pleased her with the more mature and relaxed manner he seemed to have gained from his service abroad, Douglas set off for a few days in Oxford.

There he found Joan Appleton busily arranging the dance for a charity pantomime and running a club for Allied servicemen and women, the Charter Club. At Joan's invitation he gave a talk to the club on his

229

experience of the desert war. To his audience of servicemen, many of whom were also waiting for the invasion, Douglas spoke of the desert's landscapes and flowers, the variety of its scenes and noises and the moods of its day. Joan was pleased by the sensitivity of the talk but impressed above all by the fact that Douglas did not once mention the fighting. With such a subject and audience one might have expected soldierly panache and adventure; instead there was a thoughtful and pacific curiosity.

In the evenings he wandered round some of his old haunts in the city. He saw little of Joan, who worked till late each night, but he slept at her parents' house at Boars Hill. On departing for Christmas, Joan recalls, Douglas told her not to forget his birthday. She asked what he wanted. 'Cigarettes and Baudelaire' was his reply.[1]

Douglas and his mother had in fact been invited to spend the holiday in Cornwall with Jack Holman of C Squadron, who, learning during the voyage of the uncertainties of Douglas's family situation, had offered to put them up. The return of the Babers to East Grinstead, however, meant a postponement of the visit. If the prospect of staying in a household where his mother worked had aroused unhappy memories, they were dispelled by the Babers' welcome. By the end of the holiday Douglas was happy to accept the position of honorary son. Mrs. Baber's forthright manner, her fund of experience from the work she was doing with refugees, and her love of argument made her excellent company, and some months later Douglas was to comment affectionately in a letter to her, that she was someone he could have 'fallen heavily for' if they had been twenty at the same time.

With her husband he established an impressive understanding. A veteran of the Great War who had stayed on in the army, only to have his hopes of a military career frustrated by ill health, Colonel Baber now had to content himself with an army desk job. His values were traditional, but Douglas respected him for having known what fighting was like and having returned from it with a gentler and more conventional creed than his own. To Colonel Baber Douglas's cynicism was an echo of his own response to the experience of the trenches, and he felt confident that Douglas's evident honesty and manliness would lead him back to the values he now humor-ously disparaged. Douglas had once more been cast in the role of rebellious young man, but he assumed the part with a grace and sense of humour which delighted his mother.

The week in Cornwall after Christmas was equally successful, with Mrs. Douglas much enjoying the chance to talk to someone who had served with her son in the desert, and Jack Holman's mother making sure that they had a relaxed and leisurely time. But the return to Chippenham in particularly hard weather, early in January, to find there living conditions reminiscent of

---

[1] The copy of Baudelaire is in Mrs. Douglas's possession.

those at Lulworth Cove three years before, bitterly ended a good first month in England. A letter from Jean Turner, whom Douglas had not seen on his leave, gave him the chance to revert to an earlier tone:

At the moment it's no good writing you a letter as I feel so savage about this filthy country and the way it is run that I couldn't say anything entertaining or amusing. I now live in a tin hut and a sea of mud (which freezes every few days) and no laundry arrangements or showers, with about half as much food as civilians are eating.

Since leaving the Middle East the Sherwood Rangers had assumed that their eventual destination would be the mainland of Europe; and at the beginning of February they had their first training in ' "European " type of country', at a firing camp in Kirkudbright. Back in Chippenham, they learnt that they were indeed to open a second front, and when, in the middle of February, B and C Squadrons left Chippenham for training with amphibious tanks, it was evident that the regiment was to be in the leading wave of a sea-borne invasion. With the pace of training certain to quicken with the spring, leave was granted, and it was with this knowledge of the nature of his fate, and ignorance of its timing, that Douglas left Chippenham for eleven days in East Grinstead and Oxford.

In Oxford Douglas again stayed with the Appletons, visiting Tony Rudd's aunt, who was now in Oxford, and at the Appletons' meeting Joan's sister Betty, now married with a child. Betty recalls his seriously chiding her for marrying so soon when she could have had his pension: for he would not survive Europe.

The Charter Club had a spare room at the back, so while Joan served tea and sandwiches to Americans, Poles, Frenchmen, and Chinese, Douglas worked at his war narrative and prepared illustrations for it. For the rest of his leave he concentrated on arrangements for the publication of his work. The Babers lent him and his mother their London flat, from which Douglas paid daily visits to Tambimuttu at his *Poetry (London)* office in Manchester Square.[1] During his leave he signed a contract for a volume of his poems to appear in the Editions Poetry London series, published by Nicholson and Watson.

If the imprint carried less prestige than that of Faber and Faber, it none the less promised reasonably large distribution and more lavish production than was customary; Editions Poetry London despite wartime austerity published some of the most finely produced and expensively illustrated books of the time. Tambimuttu suggested that Douglas should do illustra-

---

[1] One evening Douglas and his mother walked through the blackout to call on John Hall in Notting Hill; he also took her to meet Tambimuttu. On another occasion Michael Meyer remembers waving to Douglas across the floor of the Café Royal.

tions to go with the poems, and Douglas, pleased at the prospect of present-ing his talents as both poet and artist, produced some two dozen line drawings. The war narrative he left for Tambimuttu's consideration.

During these eleven days Douglas had a first opportunity of participating in London's literary life. *Poetry* (*London*) and its editor provided a real point of focus for the younger poets of the period, and Tambimuttu spent much of his time with writers, not all of them unknown, in the pubs of Fitzrovia. He found Douglas as impressive as his poetry, and would have been glad to take him along to meet some of his literary circle. But Douglas had little taste for the fellowship of London pubs. Instead he talked to Tambimuttu in his office, trying to get as much business as possible done, for it was unlikely that he would be able to watch over the publication of his work. Moreover, while Douglas responded to the charm of the editor on whose efficiency his reputation was likely to depend for some time, the fact that an issue of the bi-monthly *Poetry* (*London*) had not appeared for twelve months gave cause for apprehension.

At Nicholson and Watsons, however, Douglas had found in Tambi-muttu's assistant, Betty Jesse, a potential ally for his work and a companion more attractive to him than those of the Wheatsheaf and Soho. Intelligent, sophisticated, and although only a little older than he, in the midst of a crumbling marriage, Betty was well used to the attentions of young writers who hoped she would put in a good word for them with Tambimuttu. She had been impressed by the poems Douglas had sent back from Africa and curious to find out what their author was like. In the Manchester Square office she and Douglas talked often, and hearing of his love of riding, Betty, who rode each week in Hyde Park, arranged horses for them on the last day of his leave. Although when the day came Betty seemed not to enjoy her ride, Douglas invited her for the evening to the Piccadilly. An evening's dancing with a woman whose company he enjoyed was the perfect climax to a successful leave. Towards its end, however, as Douglas wrote to Betty on his return to Chippenham, he had 'rather bitched the evening up'.

When he was telling her about his mother, Betty had suddenly said: 'It must be nice to have a mother who wants you all the time.' Douglas could not believe that she would make such a 'Little Nell' remark without some reason; he could only guess that she wanted to tell him a story. He wanted to hear it, and knowing how an exchange of stories could turn an acquain-tance into a friendship, he wanted to tell his own. What followed he described in his letter.

When I was very small I climbed up some scaffolding once, and a workman underneath told me to jump off and he would catch me. After he said it three times I jumped and he did catch me. On Thursday night I repeated this per-formance, only you stepped out from underneath and grinned like a cat while you watched me 'working it out', as though anyone has to work it out when he's dived onto his neck. Then you lectured me like a Mother Superior while I was down and couldn't kick. No wonder I spilt your beer.

Of course it doesn't matter but I think you decided I was a bit dotty; so that's the explanation. I could provide a plot for Dickens myself (possibly in collaboration with Freud, now that they're both in Limbo) so you see you kind of set me off. Never mind, skip it; I'll behave quite properly and cattily again next time. I don't know (nor care) if you've commented on my erratic behaviour to Tambi or your husband or anyone; but anyway this letter is for you and the nearest waste paper basket. The Bête Noire style will begin again in our next issue.

The 'Bête Noire style' took up a comment Betty had made without being particularly serious: chiding Douglas for his arrogant, cynical manner with her, she had called him her *bête noire*. She meant little by it, but her comment had struck home. Before the close of his letter Douglas wrote, 'Now (and all your fault), I have to think of and write a poem called Bête Noire!'; and on the back flap of the envelope he sketched the creature, a bulbous little demon with stringy legs and forked tail, 'on Squander Bug lines'. Douglas had written to Betty as soon as he got back to camp—'writing

Betty Jesse

letters at once, like one does after getting back to school'—and using the same notepaper as his letter, he embarked confidently on his poem.

> This is my particular monster, I know him;
> he walks about inside me: I'm his house
> and his landlord. He's my evacuee
> taking a respite from hell in me
> he decorates his room of course
> to remind him of home. He often talks of going

> Such a persuasive gentleman he is
> I believe him, I go out quite sure
> that I'll come back and find him gone
> but does he go? Not him. No, he's a one
> who likes his joke, he won't sit waiting for
> me to come home, but comes

Here Douglas broke off. He had embarked on what he described the next day as five hours of writing which left all his muscles tired, in which, 'sitting down to try and describe' the beast he had 'sensations of physical combat'.

His first attempt at the poem having stopped short, Douglas presented the beast as 'a toad or a worm curled in the belly', but within three lines he had turned from the beast to himself. He is the thing

> . . . I can admit only once to
> anyone, never to those who have not their own.

> Never to those who are happy, whose easy language
> I speak well, though with a stranger's accent.

Douglas had come too quickly to an understanding for the poem to need to be continued.

Next he gave up form and rhythm, listing the beast's features in the hope of finding his poem later. It is 'a jailer', allowing him out on 'parole' then bringing him back. Inside his mind, it breaks into his conversation, using Douglas's own words. It can overthrow him 'in a moment', and can be overthrown, 'if I have help'. But again the poem moved from the beast to a statement of personal fact:

> I have been trying to get help for about eleven years
> If this is the game it's past half time and the beast's winning

Douglas's own voice breaks through the procedure of his poem. A little less than eleven years earlier, he had written of the need for a companion, seeking her at Eastbourne Baths, trusting that if she were found she could put out the '*ignis fatuus*' of his discontent. His first letter to Kristin had proposed such a role for her; in his first year at Oxford his poems had celebrated Yingcheng's assumption of it, and in his second, Antoinette had been told of it; again, for a few months with Milena, he had been able to elude the devils outside him. Betty's words had given him an image for something which he had known about himself for a long time; but the attempt to write '*Bête Noire*' had become a struggle to master destructive feeling through poetic control.

Twice more he approached the poem, no longer trying to establish metaphors for the beast's behaviour, but to place it as a counter-current to a mood.

> The trumpet man to take it away
> blows a hot break in a beautiful way
> ought to snap my fingers and tap my toes
> but I sit at my table and nobody knows
> I've got a beast on my back.
>
> A medieval animal with a dog's face
> Notre Dame or Chartres is his proper place
> but here he is in the Piccadilly
> sneering at the hot musicians' skill. He
> is the beast on my back.
>
> Suppose we dance, suppose we run away
> into the street, or the underground
> he'd come with us. It's his day.
> Don't kiss me. Don't put your arm round
> and touch the beast on my back.

Setting the beast in the world where Betty had first conjured its presence, Douglas holds it in the safety of his syncopated rhythms for two stanzas. Then the poetic impulse, which had depended upon the detachment of his wit, is lost. Again he had started to care too much about the experience itself for it to remain poetically viable; and again the poem had stopped.

His fifth attempt returned to the unconcealed lyrical intimacy on which his second version had foundered. Now the creative activity of his fragment is devoted to an affirmation of the imaginative powers which the creature cannot destroy, but having encompassed a perfect gesture, he leaves the beast with all its power at the foot of the poem.

> If at times my eyes are lenses
> through which the brain explores
> constellations of feeling
> my ears yielding like swinging doors
> admit princes to the corridors
> into the mind, do not envy me.
> I have a beast on my back.

235

If at times my eyes are lenses
through which the brain explores
~~huge dim~~ ~~~~ small stars of feeling
my ears the yielding doors
through which come noble visitors to the mind

If at times my eyes are lenses
through which the brain explores
Constellations of feeling
and ~~the yielding doors~~ my ears the yielding doors
through

If at times my eyes are lenses
through which the brain explores
constellations of feeling
my ears yielding like swinging doors
admit ~~the princes of thought~~
        princes to the corridors ~~leading~~
into the mind, do not envy me.
I have a beast on my back

senses
frances

Douglas's efforts to locate the beast had drawn him back through almost an anthology of his earlier work, which started with 'The House' and ended with that poem's corridors and princes. In his 'stranger's accent' he had echoed the 'separative glass cloak / of strangeness' which clothed the visitor to 'Syria', and the language of the girl from Monte Nero, which he found hard to speak in 'Forgotten the Red Leaves'. The 'medieval animal with a dog's face' had first been seen in 'Soissons', to return as the 'Devils' inside and outside his mind in 1942; and the exploring mind of the final attempt was that which had created 'The Hand'. In another effort to find the poem he wanted Douglas had even revised the loneliness of his poem on 'Saturday Evening in Jerusalem' to contain his new discovery, incorporating into his revised draft the line 'I have a beast on my back'.

When, a week or so later, Douglas wrote again to Betty, he admitted defeat: 'I'm sending up an excuse (to be used as a preface) for not writing a poem called Bête Noire.' In his 'excuse', he gave *'Bête Noire'* as the name of the poem 'I can't write', offering two of his attempts and a couple of lines from a third, as quotations from his failures to write the poem. If his quest for the poem had been a failure, Douglas's 'excuse' none the less acknowledged a paradox within his defeat. The poem was also 'a protracted success I suppose':

Because it is the poem I begin to write in a lot of other poems . . . if he [the beast] is not caught, at least I can see his tracks (anyone may see them), in some of the other poems.

The tracks are clear and the poems in which he had begun to write *'Bête Noire'* readily identifiable. Along with those echoed in his fragments, 'Menippus in Sussex', 'Triton', 'Russians', 'A Ballet', 'The Creator', and the first half of 'John Anderson' are only the beginning of a list. The beast had ridiculed his early lyricism, introduced Time and Death and the skull of 'The Prisoner', and driven poem after poem towards an awareness of loss.

In providing these tensions, which established the dialectic on which virtually all Douglas's work was based, the beast could be seen in poetic terms as a richly creative presence. Having dislodged Douglas from his early romanticism and taught him the themes of mortality and loss, the beast had equipped him ideally to write of the experience of war. Douglas had gained access to the nihilism of the dead, the insensitivity of the killer and his calm damnation, because these were external manifestations of the creature he well knew. In the context of war, he had in fact already written his *'Bête Noire'* poem, in 'Landscape with Figures'. There a demon had offered him the delights of war's destruction and the fascination of the dead, before revealing that Douglas himself was the centre of 'the dark strife / the arguments of hell with heaven'.

In his 'excuse' Douglas had written that he knew 'nothing about the beast' beyond the 'infinite patience and extent of his malignity'.

My failure is that I know so little about him . . . he is so amorphous and powerful that he could be a deity—only he is implacable; no use sacrificing to him, he takes what he wants.

The battlefield had been similarly immune, but its very implacability had enabled Douglas to reveal that its world was 'not wholly terrible'. Its defiance of his expectations released the participant from commitment to its horrors as the whole truth. Here, perhaps, in the knowledge that he could do nothing certain to placate his beast, was a similar release. Douglas had come to understand its creative effect on his poetry even if he could not write its poem, and in the assurance of his final comment, 'no use sacrificing to him, he takes what he wants', he placed the beast at a distance from which its personal hold on him could perhaps also be withstood.

2

At Chippenham in early March, the regiment was not particularly busy. Apart from training, Douglas had to attend to the personal problems of a hundred and nineteen men, but this still left him a fair amount of time if not freedom. When the invasion was to take place, he still did not know, so these weeks provided what looked like a good chance to complete arrangements for his work. For the war narrative he completed a series of illustrations: wash drawings of tanks advancing across the desert, derelicts, a Cairo street scene, and a man in a burning tank, this last picture carrying words: 'a good many casualties in tanks are burnt to death', 'cannot get out of the turret', 'small arms ammunition explodes'. There were also line drawings showing dead men, dogs at a grave, men brewing up, and other desert scenes, among them a drawing titled 'Pietà', of a dead man lying in the midst of a group of comrades. In the manner of his school picture of soldiers at bayonet practice, Douglas had based its design on an early French painting of the School of Touraine, a postcard reproduction of which he had on the wall of his hut.

Douglas awaited Tambimuttu's decision on the narrative's publication, with some impatience. Learning from Betty's first letter that there was not yet any decision, he had replied despondently:

But I suppose you'll get someone to read it sometime: after all, I suppose they do read everything that's submitted sooner or later. Anyway it's sweet of you to try. If you finally come to the conclusion that it's no use trying, please send it back, and I'll scrap it.

On 10 March, he wrote in a different tone:

About Tambi, is it any good my saying will he either make up his mind or send it
back because someone else wants it? I am writing a letter to this effect and I'll
put it in this one. If you think it's a good thing, give it him. If not, tear it up.
Needless to say I don't want it back and no one else wants it, though I dare say
I could persuade Faber's, who view me with a kindly eye (Uncle Eliot's) or
Gollancz.

With the first of these letters, however, Douglas had been able to announce that the narrative had passed an important hurdle. His colonel, to
whom he had submitted a copy of the book, had returned it with a 'masterpiece' of a letter: a response which Douglas found delightful enough to
deserve paraphrase in his letter to Betty:

I have read and enjoyed the MS. Now I am not quite sure what is expected of me.
I assume I don't have anything to do with the security angle, which seems O.K.
   From the Regimental angle, it seems a pity to go for 'Sweeney Todd' to such a
tune, if in the final form he is to be easily identifiable.
   Some of your remarks about Flash [Kellett] will raise a storm, but I suppose it's
a free country and you can write what you like within the limits of the law.

239

Douglas considered that a person who could write like this was someone 'whose orders I don't mind obeying'. All the same, he hoped it 'shook him'.

On 13 March Betty was able to write that Tambimuttu had decided to publish, and on the 18th Douglas was given a contract, promising advance royalties of £20 with a further £20 if the manuscript was delivered within a month. He had already received an advance of £10 for the volume of poems which now had not only a title, *Bête Noire*, but a drawing for its cover. If Douglas had been unable to write the beast's poem he had drawn its picture. His final design showed a desert landscape with the square blocks of Arab houses on the horizon, in the foreground a rearing red horse. On its back was a rider, neither huntsman nor cavalryman, but a hunched, naked figure worthy of Bosch. On the man's back was a dog-faced devil, clinging so tightly to the rider that it seemed to grow into him.

Douglas had also heard that *Lilliput* were to pay six guineas for the publication of his story of the horse's dissection. He then submitted two other stories, 'Giuseppe' and 'The Little Red Mouth', but on the 27th they were returned as being too similar to the horse story.[1] Douglas then tried them with *Horizon*, but although they found the stories 'well and vigorously written and certainly very interesting' they considered them 'not suitable for this magazine'.

At the same time as '*Bête Noire*' Douglas had written a poem describing the feelings of those who were 'Actors waiting in the wings of Europe'. In 'Sandhurst' he had similarly anticipated experience of battle, but now he could write at first hand. For those 'entering at the height of the din' it would be hard to hear their thoughts and hard to gauge 'how much our conduct owes to fear or fury': but it was the present period of waiting which preoccupied him.

> Everyone, I suppose, will use these minutes
> to look back, to hear music and recall
> what we were doing and saying that year
> during our last few months as people, near
> the sucking mouth of the day that swallowed us all
> into the stomach of a war . . .

Now they were no more people, but food for war, 'swirling in an uncomfortable digestive journey'. What they said and did had a 'slightly / fairy-tale quality', but there was an excitement in 'seeing our ghosts wandering'.

With the same equanimity Douglas made his farewell to 'Women of four countries'. To reach this poem he moved through six successive drafts, but as if to demonstrate that the intractability of '*Bête Noire*' had been a

---

[1] 'Giuseppe', a story of war, remains unpublished. With unusual kindness, *Lilliput* had set a typist to type up a copy of one of his stories before returning it.

One of KD's sketches for the cover of *Bête Noire*

problem unique to that poem, this time he arrived at a perfected artefact. The poem was dedicated 'To Kristin Yingcheng Olga Milena'.

> Women of four countries
> the four phials full of essences
> of green England, legendary China,
> cold Europe, Arabic Spain, a finer
> four poisons for the subtle senses
> than any in medieval inventories.
>
> Here I give back perforce
> the sweet wine to the grape
> give the dark plant its juices
> what every creature uses
> by natural law will seep
> back to the natural source.

These first days of March had proved remarkably creative; unfortunately, that month Douglas not only lost the colonel whom he had grown to respect ('[he] was too good for us and has gone, militarily speaking, to a Better Place'), he and the regiment gained a colonel who felt they needed stiffening up. The regiment's historian recorded:

He was appalled by our Middle East habits, and introduced us to early-rising, P.T. in the morning, and 'Inglese' clothes with boots and gaiters. It was trying for all, but by now we had learnt to suffer.

With Headquarters and A Squadron still at Chippenham and B and C Squadrons engaged elsewhere with their swimming tanks, it was difficult for Colonel J. D'A. Anderson to settle into command, and rumour did not help: Colonel Anderson was said to have been Brigade Major of a brigade which at the start of the war in France had gone into action with practice ammunition.

Even before the rigours of Colonel Anderson's command began, life at Chippenham had severe limitations for Douglas. There was little social life. Occasionally he got into Cambridge, but even there he found 'not much wine, one very indifferent woman and no song'. There was a dance or two, once accompanied by five Chinamen: 'I didn't dance once with the Chinamen, though at a later dance I had one loopy foxtrot with a Chinese girl (national costume complete)'; and a party, with some 'incredibly stupid young students (can it be that I behaved like that only four years ago?).' Even another chance meeting with Joe Arsenault, in a Cambridge book-shop, led to nothing, for Arsenault was too busy training for the invasion to have free time. They did, however, agree to meet in Europe.

In such a situation, Betty Jesse provided a natural focus for Douglas's necessitous imaginative scheming. He awaited her letters impatiently, and although when they came their main subject was the publication of his work, Betty's evening out with him had been curious enough to sustain some personal comment. Douglas had been 'delighted' to learn that his behaviour on their day together had been 'excellent in many ways'; and presumably Betty had suggested that he had been too sensitive, for in a postscript to his second letter he suggested that 'raw' was the word she wanted, 'only it doesn't sound so nice'.

You're a strange person if you don't want any sympathy—possibly you mean pity. Personally I can always do with any amount of sympathy, although I don't often get it, ask for it, or feel it for anyone else. (Sometimes I do all three.)

Such brusque confessions run through the few letters he wrote her from Chippenham, offering the same defensive intimacy as his earliest letters to Kristin and Olga: hoping to deepen a brief relationship while leaving his defences intact.

If I may say it without committing a breach of security (*my* security) it has seemed a long time between the letters, although I know you wrote as soon as you'd any reason to. I find it hard not to write to you sometimes, though I certainly shan't allow myself to do it too often: and I enjoy getting your letters more than most things (that's not saying much, au moment).

Drawing attention to his defences was of course a way of writing personally.

At the end of his second letter, however, Douglas explained the importance of this new acquaintance: 'My relationship with you has a lot of unknowns and I hope I never quite get the equation to come out, because it's fascinating and I need something to keep me from becoming mud.' Douglas had always needed such an interest, to give him a sense of purpose beyond his present, mundane preoccupations. It was not just a matter of providing material for his day-dreaming; he needed someone to whom he could communicate the substance of his daily life. The intimacy he desired could extend to seemingly simple things.

With his letter of 10 March he had enclosed 'a daffy letter' which was 'letting down my shield a bit'. The enclosure was a letter provoked by Bethell-Fox's return to the squadron at Chippenham.

Dear Betty,
Do you remember Johnny in the diary? . . . Well, he's come back—to see *me*. And he's pleased to see me, too: not just ordinary polite pleased, but like a puppy who's been left alone in a house. This amazes me, but it's nice, I suppose. Why should I write and tell, when I've already written you one letter which no-one has posted, and anyway, as you say, we don't know each other? The only thing to

do is not to post it, or to pretend I'm not going to post it for a day or two (and then tear it up or post it). Really I feel quite happy and I didn't realise what a rare sensation this is. Nothing worries you, you say, so you wouldn't know what my state of mind has been like. Anyway I'm being terrifically unemotional with Johnny. . . .

Douglas then confessed that he did know why he was writing to Betty, drawing himself deeper into the feelings he desperately wished to express and equally wanted to hide.

I do know why I'm writing to you, as a matter of fact: because this evening is a little like the day I got your letter saying you'd got a horse and you were coming dancing. Gosh, this is drivel, isn't it. Betty I hope this isn't a mirage, this little golden age, even if it's only for a week or two. Please forgive this outburst, if I'm weak enough to send it you.

Douglas sent the letter because he felt that if Betty could understand it, 'it might do some good': if she could not, then he must be mistaken in her.

The part of Betty's letter about himself and the 'very small pieces, no more than a hint' about herself had reminded Douglas of his letters from Olga, 'who thinks she knows all about me, and herself, and life—presumably because the first two have made the same sort of mess of the third.' But Olga's letters, and now Betty's, were 'the most interesting' he received. As someone who had long professed a mistrust of introspection, a dialogue about himself, under cover of his correspondent's sophistication, fascinated him and answered a need. At Chippenham, waiting for the invasion, Douglas's emotions were once again acting out the conflict between too much and too little feeling. If he was afraid of becoming 'mud', his letter about his friend's return had really been a plea for help in the face of potentially overwhelming emotions. Trying to arrange a meeting with Betty, in March, he had suggested the source of such feelings:

If I can manage that day, it'll be the last, I fear, because awful things happen after that, nameless and unnecessary, but not at first, perilous. Later on of course, I shall have to engage someone to pray hard: I don't suppose you'd be any better at that than I am.

By the end of March it was clear that they were shortly to leave Chippenham, already partly equipped and trained with the new Sherman Fireflies which they were to take into Europe. These, the 'most formidable tanks in the Allied armies' at that time, were fitted with seventeen-pounder guns, powerful enough in their first test at Chippenham to blow over a hut with their blast and produce a flash which made observation impossible and singed off the gunner's eyebrows.

On 2 April, Douglas managed a Sunday visit to Betty in London.

Sunday was a wonderful day. These haywire occasions are what make people friends—and lovers, sometimes. In a sense everything couldn't have gone wronger, but in hundreds of other ways that was made up. If I never see you again, it's not a bad time to remember as the last day of a short and peculiar friendship, which has made me happier—and of course unhappier—than I have been for a long time. But, before you start bawling me out for being gloomy, I'll hasten to say I'm sure it's not the end, although the flap is definitely on, now.

Betty had at last told him of her 'cat's cradle of a life', and he was left feeling that his 'fair comprehension of what's happening' and a desire to help 'which quite shakes me up' were not enough. Trying to find a way of helping he turned to one of his own perennial problems, money, urging Betty to take seriously an offer of help from his salary once he was in action. It was a wild idea and Douglas recognized that it sounded pretentious 'when I'm notorious for being permanently broke and over borrowing', but just as at Oxford he had offered Jean part of his grant if it would facilitate her return to university, he desperately wanted to help others out of difficulties he knew so well. It was part of his long frustration at being dependent himself, a frustration which led to his passionate determination that someone should get his pension.

Don't dismiss this idea at once, or be contemptuous of it or amused at it—and don't think it would make the least difference to either of us, as friends, or change our situation at all. It's simply that I'm mad about being free and about other people being free, and if you decide to take your courage in both hands, I would do anything in the world—short of completely sabotaging myself, which wouldn't help either of us—to help you.

Douglas was writing on Tuesday the 4th of April, two days before they left Chippenham. Their destination was to be an area prohibited to civilians, and in the first half of his letter Douglas had made a bid for a last meeting with Betty. It seemed unlikely that he would get leave, and at the end of the letter he suggested a plan for that contingency: 'If all else fails, come out of town one Sunday and meet me at the borders of the prohibited belt, and we'll really go for a walk.' There was a chance, however, that he would be able to escape for a day or two and he was determined not to miss it.

I'm going to ask you in a letter—because so many things in conversation embarrass you—if you will stay a whole week-end with me, before the second (so-called) front opens—and if I get a week-end, which isn't likely. This isn't because I want, as your favourite phrase is, 'to climb into bed with you.' As you must know, of course, I am quite enough in love with you from a sex point of view, to want that. But what I do want is not to have to fight against the whole of London (or the clientèle of the Southern Railway) for every moment I spend with you. It would be marvellous to be in a room with you and shut the door on all the problems and perils of both of us. You will probably feel that actually sleeping together will only make you another complication, and I don't suppose you want to sleep with me, anyway. But I hope you can see that it needn't happen just because we shut ourselves up together. I'm afraid this is very pompous, but I always get pompous when I'm having a job to express myself (like an M.P.).

Douglas suggested the Grosvenor as a possible place, for although the idea of it revolted him, one could be anonymous there, and complete anonymity was 'almost as good as solitude'.

If Douglas did not not know whether Betty would agree, at least he now had confidence enough to know that she would understand his request and not feel that it was 'an ordinary pass thinly wrapped up'. If she had nothing to say about it, he suggested that she could ignore it in her next letter and not be afraid of hurting his 'ridiculous' feelings. Having made clear his intentions, however, he now wanted to make clear these feelings.

. . . as you see, references to being in love with you seem to creep into conversations and letters of mine from time to time. Actually, I know no more certainly what's happening to me than you know what *will* happen to you. But you can be quite sure whatever it is, it isn't another problem for you; I am not dependent on you, you have absolutely no responsibility for me or need to worry about hurting *me* as little as possible, etc. etc. You can skip me, unless I happen to open up a way of escape for you. If so use me as much as you like—you can be sure I'll use you just as much, if you do. What I asked at the beginning of this letter is something which means a hell of a lot to me, and so does everything else I have to do with you; I think about you a great deal, having an amorphous rather than complicated life otherwise. But it's all duty-free as far as you're concerned: I'm an extra piece of furniture, if you like you can use it, but you can leave it behind in any of a hundred cloak rooms. You'll be glad to hear from now on is just news, and you can read it when you like.

The news was unimportant: a trip to a tank range on the coast, a visit to a bad film, and a near-disastrous attempt to trick some fellow-officers out on a spree.

The next day Douglas received a letter from Betty which had crossed his in the post: 'Comparison of your letter . . . and mine . . . is rather amusing. I like yours better—probably if I'd been in a hurry mine would have been improved.' Having had tea in Cambridge that afternoon, with a Frenchman 'in a red velvet képi', at 'sparrowfart' the next morning, 6 April, the Chippenham squadrons moved south.

3

The regiment's living conditions within their 'prohibited area' at Sway were as comfortable as those of Chippenham had been uncomfortable. The weather became more benevolent, and surrounded by a New Forest spring, 'flowers and sunshine' attended them, 'however oily and mechanical' their duties. Tanks had to be water-proofed and drivers instructed in the art of driving them ashore in five foot of water. Douglas, however, remained preoccupied with thoughts of a final meeting with Betty, impatiently awaiting her reply to his letter. On Monday, 10 April, he wrote to her:

Dear Betty,

I have been feeling very depressed waiting for your letter—which shows I am not so conceited—or at least that there are bounds to my conceit. Now it (in two parts) has arrived, I feel very much encouraged and for some reason much less frightened of the future. I can understand your not wanting to sneak about in and out of hotels; I don't myself. In any case I don't think London will see me again for some time: I don't think they'll let us far out of here. But I am going to find out how near here you are allowed to come from London, and I'll try and slip across the border and join you on a Sunday or on a Saturday, staying overnight. So stand by for a telegram .... If we don't meet, DON'T consider it an 'unfinished story'; go on writing to me, and you know unless I'm killed or crippled I shall feel about you as I do now: so try not to be too impatient and rush off with someone else, my sweet.

Having explained that being crippled would not alter his feelings but could change his chance of expressing them, Douglas turned to the spring weather, which was 'going like a symphonic accompaniment to one of Sam Goldwyn's hits':

just too sugary and sentimental for words, sun and olde worlde cottages and lovers everywhere—and I, like any other dope in the film audience, am taken in (I hope you'll come and hold my hand and watch the show with me). Will it happen? We must at least worry about it and get in a hell of a flap and then it *may*.

'So overcome' with spring, Douglas sent four men under a lance corporal to pick primroses to put in the rooms and huts: 'much raucous laughter from the remaining soldiery, and they (the four chosen) slunk away blushing.'

On the 17th the whole regiment gathered for the first time since February, to take part in a landing exercise in the Southampton area. None of them knew the date for the invasion, though Montgomery had announced the plans to a select group at St. Paul's School on 7 April. On the 28th Douglas was writing to Jocelyn Baber: 'We suspect the worst whenever anything arrives in an O.H.M.S. envelope—but of course it may be weeks.' Four days previously, however, he had managed his meeting with Betty. Douglas and Bethell-Fox left the camp on Saturday night without leave. Dining locally, they caught the overnight train to London, arriving at 4.20 a.m., and Douglas, having made his way to Nuffield House, first fell asleep on a sofa and then in the bath. The rest of the day until the midnight train was Betty's. After a busy journey back, Douglas and Bethell-Fox were in camp by 3.30 on Monday morning.

On the train from London they had first treated an American armed with a gin bottle to a lecture on the nature of poetry, with special reference to Gascoyne, Verlaine, and Louis Aragon. Then Douglas had informed a 'truculent civilian' that if his four-year-old daughter's drawings really were as good as Graham Sutherland's, he should try and retard the girl's growth, 'she was obviously at her best age and might grow like Daddy.' Their two-hour harangue ended by provoking the man to recite fourteen lines of *Richard II*, 'quite well'. Despite losing a belt, razor, shaving bag, flannel, and khaki sweater on his travels, Douglas had managed to keep safe the silk handkerchief which Betty had given him.

There was the customary two-mile run before a breakfast at which Douglas greeted the colonel as though he had never been away, and in the evening, a cocktail party at brigade headquarters. There Douglas met an aristocratic Land Girl who wrote short stories and poems, and after about four gins, he took her into the garden:

After a bit I took her glasses off, to see if she looked better without them, but she didn't. I didn't want to be nasty so I said: 'You want to keep your face moving, then you'll be all right.' Thinking this over I didn't think it sounded so nice after all, so I tried to improve it by saying she had a nice dress anyway: but unfortunately about then I spilt a pint of gin down the front of her so I had to walk her round the garden to get her dry.

Still 'frightfully canned', Douglas was writing to Betty. Where previously he had apologized for the sentimentality brought on by such a state, however, he now welcomed the effect of his mood.

I only hope being drunk will enable me to escape the various sorts of shyness that prevent me sounding sincere when I say nice things to you. But I want to say that I couldn't love you or anyone else more than I did at moments yesterday—not if I know you for years. You were so kind (in the sense that a girl is kind to her lover, not in the YMCA sense) and sweet (I am resuscitating old words that have been slaughtered but I am giving them back their virtue), and I blundered about and ended up annoying you with remarks about your face which were only prompted by a fear that you couldn't be as happy as you were making me. Dear Betty. Thank you for telling me your story: go on trusting me and perhaps I can do something to make you happier. . . . Never believe a single catty remark I make; you are a difficult person to address, and I am as shy as you.

Acknowledging that his next letter would 'no doubt be saner', Douglas urged Betty not to say 'Thank you for your incredibly sentimental letter': 'because now I've said it for you, and anyway I should come to London leave or no leave and spit in your eye.'

For two months Douglas's energies had mainly been given to his visits to Betty. He made no practical proposals: the fact that they were not ruled out by her was enough. What mattered was that during his time of waiting she had been there, and the continuance of their relationship would allow its imaginative development in his mind when the war once again took over. Against thoughts of death and negation, Douglas could pit thoughts of love and its positive feelings, acting out in his imagination a conflict which lay behind virtually all his poetry. Before leaving the Middle East, in 'I Experiment', he had brought this conflict into the open: the poet's cycle of roles ended with a shell-burst, 'the apathetic buzz buzz / pirouetting to a crescendo BANG'.

> The finale if it should come is
> the moment my love and I meet
> our hands move out across a room of strangers
> certain they hold the rose of love

Drafting his valediction to 'Women of four countries', he had seen their love 'as treasure for my grave / if I should die tomorrow'. Under the influence of the brigade cocktail party, Douglas had written:

I don't need anything to fight for now, but at least there is you to look at beyond the fighting, and I can get through any amount of fighting, however little I care for it, if I can think about you and have your letters.

If the tone of his remarks was, as he suggested, sentimental, he was writing no less than the truth.

Early in May Douglas saw Betty again. Often he had said that he would like her to meet his mother, and Betty had responded that she had met too many people's mothers and had no desire for further boredom. Douglas insisted that his would prove different. Now he simply invited Betty to meet him at Christ's Hospital where he would show her his school. She arrived to find Douglas had also invited his mother and her annoyance was dispelled by the discovery that his previous assurance was right. Bethell-Fox was also there, Douglas having threatened not to visit his mother unless he came with him, and together they had tea on the Robertses' lawn, David Roberts also meeting Mrs. Douglas for the first time. At tea Douglas met C. A. Humphrey of Lamb A, and as Edward Malins was back at the school, invalided home from the army in India, Douglas called on him. Malins found him 'a totally different person . . . prepared to discuss his poetry, his life, and his views in a civilized way, with none of his previous arrogance'.

Douglas snatched one more unofficial visit to Betty on 22 May and took her for a day in the country.[1] Having missed one train, the one in which they travelled was delayed. They arrived just in time to cross the line

[1] On that visit, or another, he brought her his painting of Yingcheng to look after for him.

and catch the train back to London. Writing to Mrs. Baber a few days later, however, Douglas was able to announce a new confidence in his relationship with Betty: not only did Betty 'intrigue' him, luckily he 'intrigued' her. He had planned to see his mother after their walk in the country, but the timing of their journey had made the meeting impossible.

April and May had been filled with conferences, maintenance, training in co-operation with infantry and artillery, and exercises with landing craft which had culminated in a mock-invasion of Hayling Island on 30 April. What free time Douglas had was spent making his personal arrangements for departure. To his mother he wrote of sea boots, American drill slacks, the payment of royalties, bank accounts, and the checking of proofs. To Jocelyn Baber he wrote of the coming need for eau de cologne, razor blades, and baby powder, and defended his war narrative against her criticisms. The book had passed a last fence with a note from Mrs. Kellett, which thanked Douglas for allowing her to read it, and raised no objections; and now it was with the publisher, being checked for breaches of national security, the Official Secrets Act, military law, libel, and defamation.[1] Undeterred by the problems of publication, Douglas wrote on 28 May to Jocelyn Baber: 'I hope a second book (and bags more loot) will emerge from these events. Well, fair stands the wind for——?'

Having been sealed into transit camps in the Romsey area on 1 June, the Sherwood Rangers departed for Southampton Docks the next day. The sun was shining, and whenever they stopped, civilians appeared with tea and buns, seeming fully aware of the import of events which security precautions had for months tried to conceal. On the 3rd, accompanied by their tanks, they were in their landing craft, moored ten deep along the quayside.

During his two busy months at Sway Douglas had found difficulty in thinking about their forthcoming action. Fixed 'in the stomach of a war', his mind was 'too full of odd things' most of the time. But his fellow-officers were not only disturbed by his unofficial visits to London, they were troubled by his indifference. On a trivial level, Christopherson noticed that during exercises Douglas's map board was covered with even more drawings than previously. On a more serious level, Semken saw no reason to doubt Douglas's candour when he stated that he was played out as a soldier. Douglas, sharing a room with Bethell-Fox and talking more personally with him than with anyone else in the regiment, explained his lack of interest by saying that he would not survive. He had left the same impression with Malins at Christ's Hospital.

On a final visit to Oxford from Chippenham, after a meal at the Taj Mahal restaurant, Douglas had given Joan Appleton his watch, saying that

---

[1] Too late for Douglas to receive it before his departure, a full list of alterations to be made on these counts was forwarded to him.

KD's vision of the Normandy landings

he would not need it again, and he had asked her to get his poetry known, if he was not there to do it himself. He had said this simply, without sentiment: but the 'gloom' for which, in his letter to Betty, he had expected her to bawl him out had been talk of his lack of a future. Often he had spoken calmly to Betty of his conviction that he would not survive, and his very seriousness had led her to dismiss such talk as stupid.

The Sunday before the regiment's departure from Sway, their padre, Leslie Skinner, set up his altar beside Douglas's tank as the most convenient place in the squadron's line. Douglas, after directing his crew to tidy up the area and fold blankets to be used as kneelers, stayed to communion, and that evening, to Skinner's surprise, he joined the civilian congregation for evensong in the small village church, the only soldier there. After the service, Douglas came up to speak to the padre, and they walked in the New Forest, talking of Douglas's conviction that he would not return from Europe. 'He was not morbid about it,' Skinner recalls. 'He could talk of and even make plans for the days when the war was over, and having done so come back again to this feeling that it was unlikely he would survive. . . .

We walked and talked together, only separating as dawn was breaking.'

At Chippenham, Douglas had embarked on a speculative poem which first described his feelings on return from Egypt, then announced that 'Next month' was a window; after splitting its glass, the poet would find on the

Self-portrait in a steel shaving mirror, England 1944

other side, 'woman or the ominous skull of time / stretch out lips or the bone of death to kiss'. There was another possibility.

> All this is the curtain. Who would say
> beyond are islands, clouds, rivers and people
> the eyes and limbs, real to the touch
> of the legendary people, whose bones are
> hollow like bird's bones, whose fluting voices
> from time immemorial have resembled the swallow
> the women with fine Lethean violet eyes . . .

England

By the close of his draft there were three possibilities:

> Tomorrow I set out across Europe to find
> these islands, this land beyond the mountains
> these are the things which may happen to me
> to find them suddenly at the end of years
> to continue to death like the Jew
> to trip suddenly and fall in the earth, disintegrating.

When Douglas was ready to make fair copies of this, the last poem he completed before his departure, his speculations had narrowed. The islands and land beyond the mountains had disappeared, leaving the ambiguities of metaphor to hold all the suggestions he desired to offer. After the disturbances which had run through his previous work and enforced its development, his poem presented a triumphant return to lyricism. But here, for the first time in his work, the affirmation of a poetic quest was wholly retrospective.

ON A RETURN FROM EGYPT

To stand here in the wings of Europe
disheartened, I have come away
from the sick land where in the sun lay
the gentle sloe-eyed murderers
of themselves, exquisites under a curse;
here to exercise my depleted fury.

For the heart is a coal, growing colder
when jewelled cerulean seas change
into grey rocks, grey water-fringe,
sea and sky altering like a cloth
till colours and sheen are gone both:
cold is an opiate of the soldier.

And all my endeavours are unlucky explorers
come back, abandoning the expedition;
the specimens, the lilies of ambition
still spring in their climate, still unpicked:
but time, time is all I lacked
to find them, as the great collectors before me.

The next month, then, is a window
and with a crash I'll split the glass.
Behind it stands one I must kiss,
person of love or death
a person or a wraith,
I fear what I shall find.

10

France

June 1944

> . . . I move towards my end
> as a mosquito moves towards her shadow.
> (Undated fragment)

At midnight on 5 June the invasion fleet sailed. The bad weather which had delayed their departure persisted, and six-foot waves washed over the sides of the landing craft, which had no cover for the men. There was little room on board, many of the craft carrying six tanks, and by the time the Sherwood Rangers approached the coast of France most of them were sea-sick. Their entry, 'at the height of the din', however, remained as spectacular and frightening as they had anticipated: the sea covered with warships and landing craft, the sky full of planes, the ships, bombers, and rocket-carrying aircraft preparing their path with a massive bombardment. Because of the weather conditions the D.D. tanks of B and C Squadrons had to be taken closer inshore by their landing craft before setting out on their own, and five from C Squadron and three from B were submerged before reaching the shore. Their crews clambered out only to come under fire in the water as shore batteries opened up and hit several of the landing craft.

By the time Douglas arrived with A Squadron, ninety minutes later, the whole beach was congested with vehicles, some hit, their crews under cover beside them, others trying to manœuvre into some kind of fighting order. As Douglas drove out of the water he spotted the padre, stranded without a vehicle, and, Skinner recalls, hauled him on to his tank for safer passage through the minefield. As they followed radio directions and tried to move up the beach, two 88s opened fire, and rapidly destroyed four more of the regiment's Shermans. Gradually, however, they pushed forward, past the mined obstacles and wire of the beach and through the defence works which lay behind it. At Buhot they assembled according to plan and then moved on to Le Hamel, still occupied by the enemy despite the bombardment which had preceded their landing. Colonel Anderson, climbing from his tank and examining the situation on foot, was wounded twice by sniper fire. Evacuated at once, he was not to return to the regiment. Sweeney Todd took over.

Meeting pockets of stubborn defence rather than the counter-stroke which they had feared, the Sherwood Rangers' progress was more severely impeded by the congestion of traffic on the roads than by the enemy. By evening it was clear that they would be unable to reach the point at which they were supposed to leaguer for the night with the infantry of the Essex Regiment. So Christopherson, in charge of the move, commandeered a police horse which he found, conveniently saddled, at the roadside, and with tin hat and overalls rode two miles to make their rendezvous. Riding back to the regiment, he was able to inform them that they were to forget the infantry and spend the night where they were, just short of Bayeux.

Douglas had arrived late for leaguer. Outside Buhot, Jack Holman's tank had been hit, his driver severely wounded. Holman got the driver out and dragged him to cover in a ditch where they immediately came under sniper fire. Douglas, moving up the same road a little later, saw them huddled there. Spraying the area with his machine-gun, he climbed from his tank, ran to the ditch, and helped Holman and driver on to the back of their tank, still under fire, and returned with them to the regiment which was already settling down for the night.[1]

The following day the regiment entered Bayeux, the first Allied troops to do so. One machine-gun post offered brief resistance, but in the town's streets they found local people cheering in crowds and offering jugs of cider, despite the presence of snipers. By now all the first wave of the landing forces had successfully come ashore and the Sherwood Rangers were to move to the support of the Fifty-ninth Brigade, which, in turn, was following the Fiftieth Division. The next day, advancing as a brigade, they met occasional opposition from anti-tank units, but by nightfall they had reached their objective near Point 103, a piece of high ground dominating the villages of St. Pierre and Fontenay Le Pesnel.

That night Bethell-Fox went on a foot patrol to see whether there were Germans in the village of St. Pierre. He found the inhabitants cowering in cellars and unwilling to talk, but one of them said there were twenty Germans in the village. Bethell-Fox went into the street to explore, and as he turned a corner met a German patrol of one officer and eight men. Neither side waited but turned and ran.

The next morning, 9 June, the regiment turned out early with a thin drizzle making visibility poor and soaking everything. Having reached the top of a slope which was boxed in with hedges they came under intense

---

[1] 'This was the sort of work that Keith really enjoyed,' recalled Holman. 'He was so furious with the snipers and 20 mm. that were holding us up that he knocked the whole bloody lot out, otherwise we would never have got out unscathed.'

anti-tank fire, so they lined their Shermans along the edges of a square to hinder enemy observation. Waiting under this fire, they could hear the sound of tanks in the distance, on the enemy's side of them, and as they were uncertain to which army the tanks belonged, Bethell-Fox was once more asked to investigate. As he was being briefed, Douglas appeared and insisted that he too should go; Bethell-Fox was astonished.

The course of their patrol Bethell-Fox later described in a narrative of his war experience.

We trundled down the slope, and smashed our way into this orchard, driving along the parallel line of trees. I pulled off another piece of aerial going through this orchard. Eventually we reached the end of the orchard and there, in front of us, was the river. Another fifty yards on was a small church, and a road with vehicles churning up and down. We both got out of our tanks, took a few grenades and a German sub-machine gun: Keith had collected that somewhere, and crawled out of the orchard to the river.

Having waded across the river, they started crawling towards the church, when a machine-gun opened fire on them after they had made only a few yards. They turned and raced back to the cover of the river bank.

Douglas had been grazed by one of the bullets, and for a moment crouched under the bank, unwilling to move. Bethell-Fox was perplexed by this momentary failure of nerve, for Douglas, though often unconventional in action, had been well known for his courage; hardly had he noticed it before Douglas quite normally suggested they should swim a hundred yards up stream so as to appear where the enemy were not expecting them. The plan succeeded, and within seconds of reaching the orchard, they had swung themselves into their tanks and, followed by tracer fire, set off towards the squadron. Their patrol had found the desired information. The enemy were in the village but their tanks would be unable to reach the regiment's position because of the steep banks of the river.

Having safely reached the crest of the slope, they drove into the square of tanks, Bethell-Fox to report to Sweeney Todd, and Douglas to Christopherson. As Bethell-Fox got out of his tank, which he had placed alongside Sweeney Todd's, to his right two tanks, for some reason outside the hedge, were immediately hit. Heavy mortar fire now began falling inside their square and as Bethell-Fox reported what they had seen in the village, his own tank was hit, wounding two of his crew.

Douglas had climbed from his tank to make his report, when the mortar fire started. As he ran along the ditch one of the shells exploded in a tree above him. He must have been hit by a tiny fragment, for although no mark was found on his body, he was instantly killed.

Select Bibliography

Notes

Index

Select Bibliography

A full bibliography of Douglas's work and relevant criticism is given in my thesis, 'A Critical Study of the Writings of Keith Douglas, 1920-1944', Leeds University, 1969. A full description of the MSS. in the British Library (Keith Douglas Papers) is in preparation, and will be published in a *Catalogue of the National Manuscripts Collection of Modern Writers 1963-1972*, by Jenny Stratford (Turret Books for the Arts Council of Great Britain, 1974). All works listed below published in London unless otherwise stated.

I BY KEITH DOUGLAS

Books

> *Augury: An Oxford Miscellany of Verse and Prose*, ed. K. C. Douglas and A. M. Hardie (Oxford: Basil Blackwell, 1940)
>
> *Selected Poems*, Keith Douglas, J. C. Hall and Norman Nicholson, Modern Reading Library No. 3 (John Bale & Staples, 1943)
>
> *Alamein to Zem Zem* [with poems and drawings], Editions Poetry London (Nicholson and Watson, 1946)
>
> *Collected Poems*, ed. John Waller and G. S. Fraser, Editions Poetry London (Nicholson and Watson, 1951)
>
> *Selected Poems*, ed. Ted Hughes (Faber and Faber, 1964)
>
> *Collected Poems* [with drawings], ed. John Waller, G. S. Fraser and J. C. Hall (London: Faber and Faber; New York: Chilmark Press, 1966)
>
> *Alamein to Zem Zem* [with drawings], ed. John Waller, G. S. Fraser and J. C. Hall (London: Faber and Faber; New York: Chilmark Press, 1966); reissued with corrections, Penguin Modern Classics (1969)

Uncollected poems in periodicals

> *The Outlook* (Christ's Hospital, Horsham): 'Pan', Dec. 1934, p. 8; '*Ave Atque Vale*', Dec. 1934, p. 13; '*Xaipe*', April 1935, p. 5; 'Poem: The rabbits are out', July 1935, p. 14; 'The Alchymist', Dec. 1935, p. 4; 'Song of the Fisherman', Dec. 1935, p. 14; 'Countryside', April 1936, p. 4; 'Triton', March 1937, p. 12; 'For E.B.', July 1938, p. 11.
>
> *The Sussex County Magazine* (Eastbourne): 'Pan in Sussex' ('Song: You asked me for a song to sing'), Jan. 1937, p. 38.
>
> *The Cherwell* (Oxford): 'To a Lady on the Death of her First Love', 27 April 1940, p. 8.

Uncollected prose

> 'Death of a Horse' (story), *Lilliput*, July 1944, pp. 51-2
>
> 'Butterflies: *The Yellow Book*' (essay), *Citadel* (Cairo), March 1943, pp. 32-4
>
> 'The Little Red Mouth' (story), *Stand* (Newcastle upon Tyne), vol. XI, no. 2 (1970), pp. 9-11
>
> 'Poets in This War' (essay), *Times Literary Supplement*, 23 April 1971, p. 478

Select Bibliography

II   ON KEITH DOUGLAS

R. N. Currey, 'Poets of the 1939-45 War', *Writers and their Work*, No. 127 (1960), pp. 26-9

G. S. Fraser, 'Keith Douglas: A Poet of the Second World War', Chatterton Lecture on an English Poet, in *Proceedings of the British Academy*, vol. XLII (1956), pp. 88-108

D. Grant, 'War and the Writer', *Penguin Parade*, 2nd series, no. 3 (1948), pp. 57-68

M. Hamburger, *The Truth of Poetry* (Penguin ed., 1969), pp. 193-8.

I. Hamilton, 'Poetry: The Forties, I', *London Magazine*, April 1964, pp. 83-9

G. Hill, ' "I in Another Place": Homage to Keith Douglas', *Stand* (Newcastle upon Tyne), vol. VI, no. 4, n.d. [1964/5], pp. 6-13

T. Hughes, 'The Poetry of Keith Douglas', *The Listener*, 21 June 1962, pp. 1069-71

——'The Poetry of Keith Douglas', *Critical Quarterly*, Spring 1963, pp. 43-8

N. L. Ilett, 'Keith Douglas', in *The Christ's Hospital Book*, published for a Committee of Old Blues (1953), pp. 292-4

O. Manning, 'Poets in Exile', *Horizon*, Oct. 1944, p. 278

D. S. Roberts, 'Obituary: Captain K. C. Douglas', *The Blue* (Horsham), Nov.-Dec. 1944, pp. 22-3

A. Ross, 'The Poetry of Keith Douglas' (Personal Preference), *Times Literary Supplement*, 6 Aug. 1954, p. xxii

R. J. Sapsford, 'Edmund Blunden and Keith Douglas: Two Christ's Hospital Poets of the Two World Wars', *The Blue* (Horsham), Jan. 1966, pp. 62-8; correspondence, Sept. 1966, pp. 249-50; Jan. 1967, pp. 45-6

B. Spencer, 'Keith Douglas: an Obituary Note', *Personal Landscape* (Cairo), vol. II, no. 4 (1945), p. 20

M. J. Tambimuttu, 'Tenth Letter: In Memory of Keith Douglas', *Poetry* (*London*), n.d. [Dec. 1944], unnumbered pages (first article in issue)

C. Tomlinson, 'Poetry Today', in *Pelican Guide to English Literature*, vol. VII (1961), pp. 469-71.

J. Waller, 'Oxford Poetry and Disillusion, II', *Poetry Review*, May-June 1940, pp. 211-15

——'The Poetry of Keith Douglas', *Accent* (Urbana, Ill.), 8 (1948), pp. 226-35

Notes

In the following notes, for the sake of brevity, I have referred to Keith Douglas as KD, and have also used initials for the following: Mrs. Marie J. Douglas (MJD); Joan and Betty Appleton (JA, BA); Major John Bethell-Fox (JB-F); Lt.-Col. S. D. Christopherson (SDC); J. C. Hall (JCH); Alec Hardie (AH); Betty Jesse (BJ); Norman L. Ilett (NLI); Margaret Stanley-Wrench (MS-W); M. J. Tambimuttu (MJT); Jean Turner (JT); John Waller (JW). KD's friends and correspondents are referred to here by the names under which they figure in the book (e.g. Antoinette, Kristin, Milena, Olga, Yingcheng). The full names of many others interviewed or quoted, cited here by their surnames only, are given in the list of acknowledgements at p. xi. Other abbreviations and short forms used are given below.

PRINCIPAL SOURCES CITED OR QUOTED

I BY KEITH DOUGLAS   *Cited as*

Published work

> *Collected Poems*, ed. John Waller, G. S. Fraser and J. C. Hall, with
> an Introduction by Edmund Blunden (London: Faber and
> Faber, 1966)   *CP*
>> All poems quoted or referred to are from this volume, and
>> follow its text, unless otherwise noted.
>
> *Alamein to Zem Zem*, ed. John Waller, G. S. Fraser and J. C. Hall,
> with an Introduction by Lawrence Durrell (London: Faber and
> Faber, 1966)   *Alamein*
>
> In periodicals: *The Outlook* (Christ's Hospital, Horsham), 1933-8;
> *The Cherwell* (Oxford), 1940-1; *Citadel* (Cairo), 1942-3; *Personal
> Landscape* (Cairo), 1944-5; *Poetry (London)*, 1942-9

Unpublished material

> (i) Keith Douglas Papers, The British Library   BL
> Add. MSS. 53773-6 and 56355-60, with some uncatalogued
> items, comprising virtually all the MSS. and papers in MJD's
> possession after her son's death: 53773, poems and a few prose
> pieces; 53774, MS. of *Alamein*; 53775-6, paintings and draw-
> ings; 56355, letters from KD, 1926-44; 56356, letters to KD
> and MJD, 1937-65; 56357, poems and stories supplementing
> 53773; 56358, school and Oxford notes and essays; 56359,
> school exercise books; 56360, diary recording reading 1937-9;
> uncatalogued, letters and postcards to Margaret Stanley-
> Wrench.
>> Except for material in private hands (as detailed below), or

where otherwise indicated, all letters and unpublished writings cited or quoted are in this collection.

(ii) The Brotherton Collection, Brotherton Library, The University of Leeds

　　MSS. of nine poems sent to Mary Benson

(iii) In private hands

　　Two letters to MJD, two letters to Olga, the MS. of an unpublished story, miscellaneous documents, drawings and paintings, and KD's books, in the possession of MJD

　　Letters to Antoinette, Betty Jesse, Milena, Jean Turner, Yingcheng, and others in the possession of their recipients: Mrs. John Baber, Mrs. M. Gattegno, Mrs. Allan Guest, J. C. Hall, Alec Hardie, Mrs. A. G. Haysom, Mrs. M. Johnson, Mrs. J. F. O'Neill, Sir John Waller

　　MS. poems in the possession of Mrs. Guest, Alec Hardie, Mrs. Haysom, Mrs. O'Neill, Mrs. Phyllis Thayer, Sir John Waller, and author

　　Two school exercise books, the gift of H. R. Hornsby, titled by KD 'Poems 1934-6' and 'Poems 1936-7', in the possession of the author

　　Drawings and paintings in the possession of Lt.-Col. S. D. Christopherson, Mrs. Gattegno, Mrs. Douglas Grant, Mrs. Haysom, Mrs. David Roberts, and Mrs. Thayer

II OTHER SOURCES

Published

The Christ's Hospital Book, published for a Committee of Old Blues (London: Hamish Hamilton, 1953)

T. M. Lindsay, *Sherwood Rangers* (London: Burrup Mathieson & Co., 1952)

B. H. Liddell Hart, *History of the Second World War* (London: Cassell, 1970)

Other published sources are cited in the notes below, or listed in the Select Bibliography at p. 259.

Unpublished

　　Service records of KD and his father, Captain K. S. Douglas, consulted at the Ministry of Defence

　　Personal war diary of Lt.-Col. S. D. Christopherson

　　Extracts from personal diaries of David Hicks and Roger Lancelyn Green

　　Extracts from letters of Margaret Stanley-Wrench to her mother

KD rarely dated his letters, which are cited throughout the notes by the names of their recipients. All works mentioned are by, and letters cited from, KD unless otherwise indicated.

CHAPTER I

Early childhood and family background: childhood story [? 1932], and story with epigraph 'O spires O streams' [1937]; letters to MJD, his father, maternal grand-parents, and Olwen (BL 56355); MJD letter to Maurice Wollman, quoted *CP*, pp. 13–15; MJD recollections. Captain K. S. Douglas's military career: service record, Ministry of Defence. Edgeborough: *Edgeborough School Magazine*, 1926–30, and KD's school reports 1926–31. Holidays with the Rudds: Rudd. Drawings and paintings: in MJD's possession.

page

1   'As a child he was . . . ' / childhood story (MS. in MJD's possession), which MJD recalls finding when KD returned to Christ's Hospital after a holiday, *c.* 1932.

2   'shot by a measly old Turk' / ibid.

3n.   'the Napoleon of the City' / cf. Andrew J. Murray, *Home from the Hill: a biography of Frederick Huth, Napoleon of the City* (1970).

5   drew pictures with anything / MJD to Wollman, quoted *CP*, p. 13.

7   'Even the rain was interesting . . . ' / 'O spires O streams' story, BL 56359.

8–10 ' "My father", said Billy . . . ' / 'Keir waited two minutes . . . ' / '. . . Keir was woken . . . ' / childhood story.

12   made an early mark by entering / MJD.

13   First XV 'characters' . . . / *Edgeborough School Magazine*.
     'splendid beginning' / and subsequent quotes, school reports in MJD's possession.

15   'Waterloo' / BL 56355; another MS. is in 56357.
     History of the Boer War / MJD; mentioned *CP*, p. 13.
     a drama of mystery / details in letter to MJD, BL 56355.
     At sixteen, it was battles . . . / cf. 'November', *Outlook*, Dec. 1936.
     Alongside Sapper . . . / books and tastes from letters, BL 56355.

16   full-scale series of illustrations / in MJD's possession.

CHAPTER 2

Christ's Hospital: *Christ's Hospital Book*, *The Blue* (Christ's Hospital, Horsham), 1931–8, and recollections as below. Letters to MJD and Kristin; letters to KD and MJD (BL 56356 and MJD). KD at Christ's Hospital: NLI on KD in *Christ's Hospital Book*, pp. 292–4; *The Blue*, Nov.–Dec. 1944 (Roberts), Jan. 1966 (R. J. Sapsford), Sept. 1966 and Jan. 1967 (correspondence); recollections of Buck, Hornsby, Humphrey, Macklin, Macnutt, Malins, Newberry (con-temporary masters); Adams, Arsenault, Burdett, Cunningham, Dromgoole, Hatten, NLI, Nash, Stockwell (contemporary pupils); and MJD, Clarke, Mrs. Roberts, Rudd. Chronology of KD's career: dates and forms, NLI; one school report preserved by MJD. (School records on KD contain no details.) Early poetry and prose: uncollected, *The Outlook* 1933–8; unpublished, BL 56357, 56358, 56359, 56360, *1934–6*, *1936–7;* chronology of school poems derived from *1934–6* and publication dates. Pseudonyms: Billy, Flip, Raps, and initial K, verified through collation and recollections of school contemporaries and MJD.

page
22   'persons distinguished . . . ' / *The Public and Preparatory School Year Book 1959.*
     'Everybody here makes . . . ' / letter to MJD.
23   a miniature replica / MJD.
     'simple and unchanging . . . Rising early . . . ' / essay, BL 56359.
     the role of Theseus / *The Blue*, July 1934.
24   'Song' / *Outlook*, Dec. 1935; later published as 'Pan in Sussex', *The Sussex County Magazine.* Jan. 1937. (*Outlook* text used.)
     Fingal / in 'Fingal', *1934-6.*
     '*Xaipe*' / *Outlook*, Dec. 1935.
     'so as not to use the same word' / MJD.
     as a tap dancer / NLI and others.
25   Mr. Kennedy / he appears in 'Love and Gorizia', cited below; details from there.
     Sir Reginald Spence / MJD.
26   'November' / *Outlook*, Dec. 1936.
26n. Captain Douglas wrote / MJD.
27   'intensity and swiftness . . . ' / essay 'On Luxury', BL 56358.
     'hand' for 'ecstasy' / the fair copy is in *1934-6.*
27-8 'The Alchymist': *Outlook*, Dec. 1935.
28   Edith Sitwell's *Façade* / MJD recalls that KD enjoyed and imitated Edith Sitwell at fifteen; at Oxford, AH recalls, Walton's *Façade* was a favourite record of KD's.
     Hornsby used the set / NLI.
     Hatten later wrote / to author.
29   'Rabbits' / text from *1934-6*; published in *Outlook* as 'Poem: The rabbits are out', July 1935.
     'with no great effort . . . ' / this and subsequent quotes from masters, to the author.
30   'The Siren' / BL 56357.
     Mr. Dandy / a composite figure, according to NLI, made up of at least two masters.
     probably as fictional / NLI.
     a brief spell / KD's stay in Gorizia from recollections of MJD and poems.
30-1 'Out of proportion . . . new tang' / 'Creed for Lovers' / (see below).
32   'Forgotten the Red Leaves' / MS. (BL 56357, f. 19) later than source for *CP*, p. 43, has title 'Pleasures'; an earlier title was 'Exotic' (MS. in Antoinette's possession).
     'Creed for Lovers' / *1934-6.*
32-3 'Love and Gorizia' / *1934-6* (another MS. BL 53773, f. 1). KD later made a TS. of the first stanza as 'Bexhill' (*CP*, p. 32); the text followed here is the MS. version.
33   'Over and over . . . ' / 'Villanelle of Gorizia'.
     'beyond the ring fence' / a Housey term (NLI).
     Once outside the gates / MJD.

page

48 poetry lacked 'depth of feeling' . . . Douglas responded . . . / Roberts to MJD.

49 'against the government' . . . another 'safety-valve' / Hornsby.

51 a lively performance / leading his No. 5 Platoon / *The Blue*, June 1937. later recorded by Roberts / letter to MJD.
but for Roberts's encouragement / MJD.

51n. in a notebook / BL 56360; see below.

52 Sandhurst . . . to his mother / letter in BL 56355.
Two books . . . lent or recommended / NLI. Helen Waddell's *Medieval Latin Lyrics* (1929, rep. 1943) is among KD's books, also Merejkowski's *December the Fourteenth* (Travellers' Library, 1930), inscribed 'Merton 1939'.
'Leisure' / BL 56358.
'Notes and Ideas for Poems' / 'Book Diary', BL 56360, which also records reading, including a life of Dostoevsky, Strachey's essays in *Books and Characters*, Eliot on the Metaphysical poets.
'Triton' / *Outlook*, March 1937.
Michael Roberts's *Poems* / copy in MJD's possession.

52–3 'Commission' / perhaps Douglas took the title from Pound's 'Commission' (*Lustra*), which also outlines the poet's role.

53 *Art Debunked* / in MJD's possession.
'over the painted stage . . . ' / BL 56359.

53–4 'I am writing . . . ' / 'The composition . . . ' / letter to Kristin.

54 extensive notes on early French painting / BL 56360.
won his rugby colours / *The Blue*, March 1938.
a book about the school / G. A. T. Allan, Clerk of Christ's Hospital, *Christ's Hospital* (1937).
everything he submitted . . . was published / Hatten (editor that year).

56 collaborated on a dramatization / NLI.
a story he wrote in an exercise book / with epigraph 'O spires O streams', BL 56359.

56n. Ilett later defined / to author.

58 'His thoughts wandered . . . ' . . . notebook fragment / BL 56360.

60 'This season like a child . . . ' / *CP*, p. 36, dates the poem 1937; Kristin's dating of their meeting (to author) and KD's [January 1938] letter suggest 1938 as date.

62 in December had gone up to Merton / Harris recalls sharing a room with KD, talking little but listening a lot to the wireless.
with an option to read English / NLI.
a final scandal / Adams and MJD.

63 an essay on Sussex / recalled by Macklin; the essay has not survived.
'the most brilliant . . . ' / Roberts in letter to MJD (1944).
one of the most difficult / Hornsby to author.

64 'Douglas has gone . . . ' / *The Blue*, Dec. 1938.
a bundle of old exercise books / given to author in 1969; now BL 56359, *1934–6*, and *1936–7*.

CHAPTER 3

Oxford: *Augury: An Oxford Miscellany* of *Verse and Prose*, ed. KD and AH (1940); *The Cherwell, The Oxford Magazine*; *Merton College Register, 1900–1964* (1965); JW, 'Oxford Poetry and Disillusion II' *Poetry Review*, May–June 1940, pp. 211–15; Douglas Grant, *The Fuel of the Fire* (1951); and recollections as below. Letters 1938–9 to MS-W, JW, Yingcheng; 1939–40 to Antoinette, MJD, JT, Yingcheng; letters to KD and MJD (BL 56356). KD at Oxford: Blunden, Introduction to *CP*, pp. 17–20; MS-W letters to her mother; Lancelyn Green diary; recollections of MJD, Antoinette, BA, JA, Beaty, Blunden, Brown, JCH, AH, Hatten, Hearst, Hornsby, NLI, Lancelyn Green, Latimer, Matthews, Mellor, Meyer, Aye Moung, Oswin, Payton-Smith, Pennock, Porter, Sassoon, Stanley-Smith, MS-W, JW, Yingcheng, Young. Essays and notes, BL 56358 and 56360; unpublished poems, BL 56357, Antoinette.

Page
65 his 'masterpiece' / JA.
66 'captivated' by *Beowulf* / Latimer.
    'greater grasp of word-music' / BL 56358.
    no distaste for a course / Latimer, and Blunden in *CP*.
    'did not care about . . . ' / Blunden, *CP*, p. 17.
67 read her poems and said / MS-W to her mother.
    Bolero / 'Kristin', 'Poem from a Sequence' ('Forgotten the Red Leaves'),
        Winter 1938; 'Poem: Old man and young man' ('Point of View'),
        'Sonnet: Curtaining this country', Spring 1939. *Kingdom Come* /
        'Haydn—Clock Symphony', Dec. 1939-Jan. 1940; 'Russians', Spring
        1940; 'Search for a God', Summer 1940. *Fords and Bridges* / 'Poor
        Mary', 'Spring Sailor', May 1939.
68 a Merton acquaintance / Payton-Smith.
69 grants which left him / KD explained his finances in a letter to JT.
70 Harold Skimpole / KD was without Skimpole's vagueness.
    'lovat weskit' / letter to MS-W.
    'indescribably untidy . . . ' / Hornsby to author.
    Kristin also came once / MJD.
71 To Douglas she was / letters to Antoinette, below.
    Hornsby . . . well remembering / Hornsby to MJD.
    impressed his friends / Mellor.
    Three time Douglas painted / two of the portraits are in MJD's possession;
        one in Mrs. Roberts's.
    in little doubt of . . . rivals / evident from his letters to Yingcheng.
    '*To his lady* . . . ' / MS. in Yingcheng's possession.
72 Shakespeare's last plays / *The Tempest* referred to in BL 56359 and 56360,
        where KD defends Caliban as imaginative.
74 travelling to France / Sassoon.
    heard Daladier announce / postcard to MJD.
75 'old wine with a new tang' / 'Creed for Lovers', *1934–6*.
    'like black birds . . . ' / 'Invaders'.

75–6 in May he sent her . . . 'To a Lady on the Death . . . ' / MS. in the author's
   possession, envelope dated at the time by Yingcheng. This uncollected
   poem in *Cherwell*, 27 Apr. 1940; title from *Cherwell*, which has slight
   variants from MS. text followed here.
   78 a trip to Paris / Yingcheng; cf. KD letters to Antoinette, below.
   They got on well / Yingcheng and MJD.
   had found no difficulty / MJD.
   Douglas insisting on / Yingcheng.
   For two months Douglas hoped / letter to JT, and recalled MJD.
   In July he read in / letter to Yingcheng.
   Douglas felt that . . . 'how many handsome' / letter to JT.
   a winter semester in Munich / cf. Blunden letter to KD.
   79 Asking the girl there / KD refers to the occasion in a letter to Yingcheng;
   Hatten remembers meeting a man at the garage.
   'Cavalry of the Line' / enlistment document in MJD's possession.
   an Oxford already changed / preface to *Augury*.
   81 'incredibly rich . . . someone in art circles' / letter to JT.
   'strong Victorian upbringing' / Antoinette.
   'I think Antoinette and I' / letter to MJD in her possession.
   82 Conscious of the scepticism / cf. letters to Antoinette.
   84 One visitor recalls / JA.
   84n. Deirdre Newstubb / untraced; recalled NLI and others.
   85 *The Cabinet of Doctor Caligari* / *Alamein*, p. 28. *Fantasia* / Milena recalls
   KD's pleasure at seeing the film in the Middle East. *Ninotchka* / re-
   viewed by KD in *Cherwell*.
   meetings, generally over tea / recorded in Lancelyn Green diary.
   By design, the miscellany was / from preface to *Augury*, and recalled AH
   and Lancelyn Green.
   86 'Stars' / dedicated 'For Antoinette'. A letter to Antoinette (n.d., [Nov./Dec.
   1939]) refers to 'Stars' ' composition, coming after that of 'Haydn—
   Military Symphony' and before that of 'Haydn—Clock Symphony.'
   And he included / KD also published 'Head of a Faun', one of three
   translations of Rimbaud, probably made at Oxford; the other two '*Le
   Dormeur du Val*' and '*Au Cabaret Vert*'.
   burlesque of high-minded tragedy . . . paean to common sense / from
   programme notes.
   made papiermâché masks / Blunden, *CP*, p. 18.
   'a pacifist in a Sam Browne' / JA.
   87 offer of twenty pounds / letter to JT.
   88 his 'moods' / letter to Antoinette.
   88–9 'a most Scottish and cheerful . . . ' / letter to Yingcheng.
   89 driving the Hardies' car / letter to Antoinette.
   'I read 47 pages . . . ' / this and following details, to Antoinette.
   wrote to Antoinette's parents / letter, and accompanying poems, in Antoinette's possession.

90   'a totally seething state' / and subsequent quotes, to Antoinette.

     a Latin translation / letter to Antoinette.

     truculent, showing little of the vitality / Antoinette.

91   said to Betty on several occasions / BA.

     made linocuts as illustrations / used later in *Cherwell*.

     At Hill Crest Douglas worked / details in letter to Antoinette.

     'Do not look up' / MS. in Antoinette's possession.

     the collection Douglas made / red TSS. in BL 56357 (with further poems added the following year) could be from this collection; that the collection 'revealed work in a different vein' is inferred from KD's poetry dating from Oxford.

92   'A Round Number' / *Cherwell*, 25 May 1940.

     'Despair' / BL 56357.

     had taken her to the Cheltenham Gold Cup meeting / letter to Antoinette.

     in January his letter / to Yingcheng.

     In *The Cherwell*, beside his love poem / 9 March 1940.

93   'Leukothea' / a later MS. (AH) bears the title 'A Speech for an Actor', with 'Leukothea' cancelled by KD; among other variants from *CP* it closes:

> O hell and fury then, my trust's betrayed
> What are these bones, bones, bones so disarrayed?

94   'Sanctuary' / *Cherwell*, 3 Feb. 1940.

     from an incident reported / note on MS., BL 53773 (*CP*, p. 151).

96   'The Deceased' / *Cherwell*, 15 June 1940.

97   'The Happy Fatalist' / *Cherwell*, 1 June 1940.

98   'A pacifist stole' / Grant, *Fuel of the Fire*, p. 21.

     'The Undergraduate Fallen From His High Estate' / *Cherwell*, 2 March 1940; number on 'The Decline of Oxford'.

     'Here the follies . . . ' / *Cherwell*, 27 Apr. 1940.

     'The job of producing . . . ' / ibid.

99   a special poetry number / 9 March 1940. *CP* attributes two further poems in this number, 'Gender Rhyme' and 'Villanelle of Sunlight', signed 'Tancred Paul', to KD. As the pseudonym was used by other Oxford writers, and no MSS. survive, the poems may not be by KD.

     Shotaro Oshima / several other authors have been suggested; the poems under this name bear little resemblance to KD's work.

100 Nichols was ragged . . . responded with an attack / *Cherwell*, 1 June 1940 and 8 June 1940.

     his first *Cherwell* editorial / 27 Apr. 1940.

     Publishing few of his cynical poems / for *Cherwell* publication KD relied heavily on school poems: 'Caravan', 'Sonnet: Curtaining this country', 'Famous Men', 'Japanese Song' ('Encounter with a God'), 'Images', and 'Dejection' helped establish his prominence as Oxford poet through the writing of a schoolboy. Up to the end of May 1940 he had published only six Oxford poems; in June he published four more.

page
101 'Drunk' / TS. dated from school, BL 56357.
     'John Anderson with stubborn mind' / drafts BL 53773, ff. 17–20.
102 'Apt epitaph or pun' / the italics in this extract, from KD's instruction on
     sending the poem to AH [April 1941]: ' "John Anderson" . . . inci-
     dentally will appear much more effective in print, and with the stuff
     in inverted commas in italics, than it does in my writing.' KD omitted
     to mark where the italics should end. MS. in AH's possession has
     dashes not brackets (ll. 5–6) and capitals for 'Gods and Men' (l. 14)
103 his more recent and impressive work . . . yet to be published / Oxford work
     not published at University: 'Leukothea', 'Absence', 'The Poets',
     'Soissons 1940', 'Extension to Francis Thompson', 'Reproach',
     'John Anderson', 'A Ballet', 'An Exercise Against Impatience', 'An
     Oration'; also uncollected poems: 'Despair', in two sections, one
     published as 'A Round Number'; 'A God is Buried', in four sections
     (BL 56357), one published as 'Search for a God'.
    Douglas deposited the whole collection / clear from subsequent letters to
     JT, and Blunden to KD.
    visited the Robertses / cf. letters from Roberts and his wife to KD.
    staying with the Brodies / letter to Yingcheng.
    stated his preference / on enlistment document (MJD).

CHAPTER 4

Training from Redford to Sandhurst: KD's military service record, Ministry of
Defence, including reports (fullest for this period); letters to MJD and JT;
letters to KD and MJD (BL 56356); recollections of Chadburn, Lockie, Malins,
Morgan. KD and Second Derbyshire Yeomanry: A. J. Jones, *The Second
Derbyshire Yeomanry* (Bristol, 1949); letters to MJD, AH, and JT; recollections
of Crichton, Macnaghten, Parkhouse, Wrey. Other recollections: MJD, JA,
NLI, Litvin, Pennock, Sassoon, Thayer, JT. KD movements after May 1941:
Karrier Motors course in service record; other details from letters to MJD and
JT and recalled MJD. Final visit to Oxford, and Diana: recollections of MJD,
NLI, Pennock.

page
104 'boned' his boots / details, Morgan.
104n. Not all of them / Morgan.
105n. Mr. Appleton was so impressed / JA.
106 Several members of the training regiment / letter to MJD.
    debate the relative merits / Malins.
    'painfully moral romance' / letter to JT.
    Riding instruction in the Mounted Section / Morgan and Sassoon.
    'rather an awful horseman' / Malins.
    one member of the Oxford group / Morgan.
107 sketch of a huge mare / Lockie.

page

107–8 to make a short story / 'Death of a Horse', *Lilliput*, July 1944; previously published in *Citadel*, July 1942. Date of composition inferred from subject: dissection was part of the Weedon training (Morgan).

108 they would grow to love their tanks / Lockie.

Studying the theory / details, letter to JT; reports, service record.

109 stable guard / Morgan.

109n. From Sandhurst Douglas also paid / Hornsby letter to MJD.

110 'the filthiest scruffy hole . . . ' / letter to JT.

110n. had acquired . . . 'East Coker' / copy, dated by KD, in MJD's possession.

111 troop . . . had gained the highest marks / Malins.

'beautiful orgy of sentimentality' / 'above the Noted Snack Bar' / letters to JT; the second lists people KD wished to invite.

opinion of his squadron leader / service record.

revised list of preferences / service record.

112 Colonel Barnes, who always carried / Jones, *Second Derbyshire Yeomanry*.

112n. a member of the West Hertfordshire Yeomanry / Capt. K. S. Douglas's service record, Ministry of Defence.

113 'marvellous . . . Why do I always pick . . .' / letter to JT.

114 an unloved establishment / recalled by shopkeepers in Wickwar; the inn is now a private house.

one of the more senior Derbyshire Yeomen / Parkhouse.

'aggressive poverty' / Wrey, affirmed by Macnaghten.

115 'Am I going to sleep . . . ' / JA.

beautifully made Valentine card / Litvin; the card is lost.

Margaret Robinson / later mentioned in a letter to JT as someone who wrote to him in the Middle East, without detail. Crichton suggested possible identification.

Bunny Agarwala / letter to JT; untraced: detail of father from JA.

a bomb had hit his block at Sandhurst / MJD; Lockie recalls the raid.

115n. passing reference . . . in a letter / to MJD, in MJD's possession.

115–16 Now he watched from a distance / 'all this British heroism' / 'which stank . . . hung in a tree . . . ' / letters to JT.

116 'The Weapon' / unpublished; BL 56357.

decorated his manuscript / BL 53773, f. 29. The poem may have been written at Oxford.

116n. 'Extension to Francis Thompson' / *Cherwell*, 30 Jan. 1941; 'The Marvel', *Cherwell*, 19 June 1941.

117 'Sandhurst' / in the possession of AH; another MS. with title first 'The Critic' then 'The Officer Cadet', in the possession of JT.

'Coo! I had a letter' / letter to JT.

118 to send Eliot four new poems / MSS. in BL 53773, with Eliot's comments (see below).

'the beautiful stranger, the princess' / 'The House'.

120 'So Time has used . . . ' / one word indecipherable in third line.

121 In May . . . 'The Marvel' / *CP* dating followed (source not located); one

MS. on Merton letter-head (BL 53773, f. 37, another sent to Eliot [May 1941] with KD's address at foot 'White Horse Inn Wickwar' (BL 53773, f. 38).

121   in a mood antithetical to / letter to JT.

'Extension to Francis Thompson' / cf. Yeats's 'The Long-Legged Fly'.

123   On one of his earlier visits / inferred from MS. (BL 53773, f. 33) on the same paper as 'Time Eating' (f. 34).

Douglas told Diana he would marry her / letter to JT. (Diana untraced.) went to the Registry Office / NLI.

124   a cynical letter eight months later / to JT.

By 25 June Douglas was on board ship / letter to MJD, postmarked 'London 17 July', refers to being only about sixteen miles from his car, presumably in port. Service record gives 25 June as embarkation date.

125   had written a final poem / dating of 'Simplify Me . . .' uncertain: one MS. on verso of TS. of 'An Oration', another on paper KD used at Wickwar (BL 53773, ff. 41–2), another among pre-Middle East TSS. (BL 56357, f. 52). As it was not sent to Eliot in May, I have inferred that it was written after the Wickwar/Linney Head poems.

CHAPTER 5

The voyage: letters to MJD, JT; recollections of Benson, JB-F. Convalescent depot in Palestine: letters to MJD, JT. On camouflage course: Morpurgo letter to *The Blue*, Jan. 1967, pp. 45–6; letters to MJD, MS-W, JT. Staff officer in Palestine and visits to Cairo: Hicks diary and recollections; letters to MJD, Olga, JT, JW. (KD's letters to Olga sent to MJD after his death; Olga's present whereabouts unknown.) KD and Cairo writers: Durrell, Introduction to *Alamein*, pp. 11–13; Fedden, *Personal Landscape* (1966); Fraser, 'Keith Douglas: A Poet of the Second World War' (Chatterton Lecture, 1956); O. Manning, 'Poets in Exile', *Horizon*, Oct. 1944; B. Spencer on KD in *Personal Landscape*, vol. II, no. 4 (1945); *Citadel, Personal Landscape; Personal Landscape: An Anthology of Exile*, comp. Fedden et al. (1945); *Salamander: A Poetry Miscellany*, ed. K. Bullen and J. Cromer (1947); letters to MJD, Olga, JT, JW; recollections of Abercrombie, Fedden, Fraser, Hicks, Smith, Speirs, Tiller, JW. *Selected Poems*: letters to JCH; letters from JCH to MJD (BL 56356); recollections of JCH. KD in Alexandria: recollections of Arsenault, NLI, Milena; *Alamein*. Details on Sherwood Rangers, their campaigns before KD joined, their movements, conditions, and equipment: *SR*. KD's views of regiment's officers: largely from *Alamein*. Character of regiment and KD's activities with it: *Alamein; SR;* letters to MJD, MS-W, JT; recollections of JB-F, SDC, Holman, McCraith, Nelson, Nelthorpe, Ringrose, Semken, Warwick. Events of war beyond Sherwood Rangers: *SR* and Liddell Hart.

128   at all like 'being at war' / the cabin he shared / 'almost luxury liner' / letter to MJD.

page
129 'what a bloody town' / letter to JT.
  this poem of 12 September / 'Song: Do I venture away too far' MS. dated
    '12.9.41' (BL 53773, f. 43b); *CP* incorrectly gives '1942'.
  'Negative Information' / MS. dated 16.10.41 (BL 53773, f. 43b); *CP*
    incorrectly gives 'November'.
  as a child of four / MJD.
130 *otitis media* / MJD; his ear infection described in a letter to JT.
  'bandaged and riddled . . . ' / letter to JT.
  a novel to be set in Oxford / letters to Antoinette [1940] mention an earlier
    project to write a novel.
  Douglas felt a fraud / letter to JT.
130n. 'not in the least poetic' / letter to JT.
131 'three rather unoriginal poems' / 'The Hand' dated *CP* and MS. (BL 53773,
    f. 44); 'The Sea Bird' and 'Adams' dated 1942 by *CP*, evidently in
    error (MSS. missing).
  Douglas wrote to Hall from hospital / (BL 53773).
133–4 'The Sea Bird' and 'Adams' / the extent of KD's description of the bird
    suggests that 'Adams' is the later poem; details on the bird in 'Adams'
    stanza 10 ('The Sea Bird', stanza 6) are more likely drawn from a
    finished poem than conceived for 'Adams'.
135 sold three of his most valuable hunters / Semken and SDC.
136 stepped from the pages of Saki / *Alamein*, p. 96.
137 had at first been put off by / *Alamein*, pp. 44–5.
  a charm which Douglas saw as feudal / *Alamein*, p. 96.
  later described with sufficient venom / *Alamein*, pp. 79–80; this portrait
    is the most heavily revised part of *Alamein* (see MS., BL 53774).
  Kellett might simply have passed / Kellett's views recalled by fellow-
    officers.
138 one fellow-officer thought / Semken.
139 Eliot had taken up points of detail / MSS. with comments, BL 53773,
    ff. 31–2, 36, 38, 40. Cf. A. Coleman, 'T. S. Eliot and Keith Douglas',
    T.L.S., 2 July 1970, p. 731, discussing correspondence largely from
    Eliot's view, and this author's letter, ibid., 21 Aug. 1970.
  these were generally routine / e.g. 'Time Eating' (f. 36), l.6 'to mansize
    from the smallness of a stone': Eliot, 'but stones can be quite big'; 'The
    Marvel' (f. 38), l.4 'the sharp enquiring blade': Eliot, 'the *surgeon's*
    blade is "enquiring" but I'm not sure about this one'; l.6 'dim water':
    Eliot, 'was this water dimmer than most sea water?'; l.16 'who rotted
    into ghosts': Eliot, 'they might be ghosts before they rotted'.
  when he revised these poems / 'Time Eating', BL 53773, f. 35b, 'The
    Marvel', f. 35v (with variants from texts in *CP*), using paper and ink
    of MS. of 'Russians', BL 53773, f. 10, bearing road directions to East
    Grinstead on verso (KD first stayed there with MJD in Dec. 1943),
    are probably the latest versions, making no use of Eliot's comments.
    However, Eliot's note on 'The Marvel', '*v.* Marianne Moore on fishes,

etc. (Neater)', may have prompted KD's acquisition of Miss Moore's *Selected Poems*, at Port Said in 1943.

139 December trip to Syria / described in letters to MJD and to JT.
identified his fate / letters to MJD and to JT.
'Haifa and Tel Aviv . . . ' / letter to JT.

140n. Published . . . as 'Syria' II' / the only surviving MS. of 'Syria' [I] (BL 53773, f. 45) has on the verso a list of poems written up to mid-1943; it is unlikely that KD composed 'Syria II' after this date. Moreover, although *CP*, p. 152, suggests that ' "Syria II" is probably the later revision', it is improbable that KD would have changed the intense discoveries of 'Syria I' to the the leisurely, literary manner of 'Syria II'.

141 'Godforsaken spot . . . ' / and following quotes, letter to MJD; KD also described the accident in a letter to MS-W.

142 the Manis / not traced; letters to MJD, to Olga, and to JT.
'The atmosphere of gloom' / letter to JT.
'a fantastical sort of' / letter to MS-W.
'very sweet . . . ' / letter to JT.
glad to be back / letter to MJD.

143 'isolated and sandy spot' / letter to MS-W.
Douglas wrote to Christopherson / letter to MJD; SDC's letter of 25 Feb. 1942, BL 56356.

144 'I'm trying to fix . . . ' / 'interviewed the General' / letters to MJD.
a batch of letters from England / letter to JT.

145 'We found ourselves . . . ' / Morpurgo, *The Blue*, Jan. 1967.
a square white house / letter to MJD; he adds: 'I've painted, drawn or scratched ballet-dancers all round the walls. Some are scratched away to white plaster with a nail file and filled in with pencil. One is black silhouettes with white lines scraped on them and a red pattern behind and two are watercolours with scratched highlights.' KD's photographs of these murals are in BL 53775-6.
to visit a Jewish communal settlement / letter to JT (cf. *Alamein*, p. 27).
'If I come to see *you*' / letter to Olga.

146 'I am the only subaltern . . . ' / letter to JT.

146n. copies of 'Search For a God' . . . / in BL 53773.

147 'he is luckier than I . . . ' / letter to MJD.

148 and the poem 'Syria' / *CP*'s 'Syria I'.

149 'lovely hands . . . ' / letter to Milena.
one day she simply received / Semken.
'The question of the Turkish Delight' / letter in MJD's possession.

151 'absurd accent' / *Alamein*, p. 76.

151–2 Out of these weeks . . . wrote two poems / dating of 'L'Autobus' and 'Egyptian Sentry . . . ' uncertain; both are set in Alexandria, and Milena recalls frequently passing the sentry, on walks with KD.

153 'delicate bones . . . ' / *Alamein*, pp. 76–7.

155 'The Regiment advanced . . . ' / *SR*, p. 32.

page
158 'I came back by accident . . . ' / letter in MJD's possession.
   a brief scene / NLI.
159-60 his first poem to Milena / MS. BL 53773, f. 46, undated; dated *CP* '18
   Oct. 1942' (source not known). Milena confirms that the poem is to her.
160 'Milena' / MS. bearing this title, BL 53773, f. 47.

CHAPTER 6

KD's return to Sherwood Rangers: *Alamein*, and letters to MJD, Olga, JT.
Events in action: *Alamein*, *SR*, SDC diary; Charles Potts, *Soldier in the Sand*
(1961); letters to MJD, Olga; recollections of JB-F, SDC, Holman, Nelson,
Semken, and others as for Sherwood Rangers in chapter 5. Visit to Alexandria:
Alamein, and recollections of Milena and Nelson.

161 'Ronsons' / Semken.
162 Three days earlier / *Alamein*, p. 24.
   'The whole scene' / *SR*, p. 38.
163 four days after hearing / *Alamein*, p. 17, says 'six days'—four fits the
   subsequent chronology.
   '"I like you, sir"' / *Alamein*, p.17.
   'little-boy' mentality / *Alamein*, p. 16.
   '"We're *most* glad"' / *Alamein*, p. 20.
164n. Both letters were lost / *Alamein*, p. 24.
166 'the other buggers' / *Alamein*, p. 46.
   their re-entry was less smooth / made clear in *SR*, pp. 44-6.
   'crumbling process' / *SR*, p. 47.
168 'a magnificent fighting reconnaissance' / *SR*, p. 45.
   This day, 3 November / 'control your squadron' / *SR*, p. 46.
169 That evening, with the regiment / Holman; rum issue and Major Warwick's
   wound described in both *Alamein*, p. 58, and *SR*, p. 46: that the
   shell fragment remained visible is in *SR*.
170 Galal station / battle described by Potts, *Soldier in the Sand*, who also
   refers (p. 57) to the hunting calls.
   'the glorious brantub of war' / letter to Baber (TS. of part of the letter,
   BL 56355).
172 'Mersa' / poem dated, in the absence of other evidence (fair copy, BL 53773,
   f. 49, being 1944), from KD's only visit to the town.
173 'It was strange . . . ' / this and next brief quote, *Alamein*, pp. 76-7.
   Titsa / not traced.
175 Fog had lingered / *SR*, p. 56.
   'sardine tins' / Semken.
176 a landscape sown with mines / *Alamein*, p. 93, echoing letters to MJD.
177 'even in defeat' / *SR*, p. 65.
   to get to know his squadron's officers / *Alamein*, ch. XV, describes fellow-
   officers at length.

178 three books had arrived / list of books from *Alamein*, p. 98; some mentioned in letter to Olga. *The Faber Book of Modern Verse* in MJD's
possession.
From Milena Douglas heard / letter to MJD; the same letter refers to
Kristin's marriage.
Tambimuttu . . . so impressed by / letter from MJT to JCH, BL 56356.
179 had written nothing since Mersa / for dating of war poems see below,
note on p. 184.
'final phase of the North African campaign' / *SR*, p. 61.
Douglas had set out / *Alamein*, p. 112. KD's detailed account of Zem Zem
action followed.
180 ' "Give the bugger hell" ' / *Alamein*, p. 119.
182 'Look out . . . ' / *Alamein*, p.129.
'After a time they stopped' / 'We had taken more punishment' / *SR*,
p. 62.
182n. horoscope / in MJD's possession.
183 In these two days' fighting / details and n., Liddell Hart, p. 398.

CHAPTER 7

El Ballah and Port Said: letters to MJD and Olga; *Alamein*. Visit to Tel Aviv:
letter to Olga. Visit to Alexandria: recollections of Milena. Narrative and KD's
relations with regiment: sources and recollections as for Sherwood Rangers,
chapters 5 and 6.

184 the first of the poems which resulted / That KD wrote his war poems away
from the battlefield is suggested by a letter to MJT (quoted, p. 217).
Many cannot be dated exactly, but a more precise chronology than is
suggested by their arrangement in *CP* can be established. (All MSS.
BL 53773 unless otherwise stated.) Palestine and Egypt: 'Dead Men'—
published in *Citadel*, March 1943. 'Cairo Jag'—MS. carries a note [to
Olga] referring to recent publication of 'Devils' in *T.L.S.* (23 Jan.
1943) and mentioning a possible meeting, presumably that with Olga
in April. 'Desert Flowers'—dated 'Egypt 1943' in *CP* (source unknown); sent with other El Ballah poems to MJT on 1 June 1943.
'Landscape with Figures'—*CP* (see Notes, pp. 155–6) gives 'R.A.C.
Base Depot', but this is taken from the letter-head of a fair copy sent
to *Personal Landscape* (Sotheby's Catalogue, Sale of 12 Dec. 1961,
Lot 239); MS. of part II, BL 53773, f. 51, signed 'Wadi Zem Zem
16.1.1943', but this probably refers to events of that day, not to the
date of composition; these MSS. were sent with other El Ballah poems
to MJT on 1 June 1943. 'Gallantry'—MS. sent 1 June dated 'El Ballah
General Hospital, 1943', but letter to Olga of 2 April referring to
writing this poem 'the other day' was from Port Said. 'The Trumpet'—

published in *T.L.S.*, 26 June 1943 (*CP* takes 'Middle East R.A.C. Base Depot' from letter-head). 'Snakeskin and Stone'—only surviving MS. undated; fragment on verso prefiguring 'How to Kill' suggests composition before June 1943. 'Words'—MS. dated 'El Ballah 1943' sent to MJT on 1 June 1943. 'Tel Aviv'—MSS. undated; its relation to Olga through reference to 'your news from Russia' and other internal evidence suggests that the poem comes from KD's visit to Tel Aviv in April 1943. 'I Watch with Interest'—paper of MSS. similar to that of first draft of 'Tel Aviv': see discussion of internal evidence, p. 195, suggesting April 1943 (*CP*'s 'London 1944' dating taken from *Poetry* (*London*) text, without MS. evidence). Tunisia: 'Enfidaville'—dated 'Tunisia 1943' in *CP* (source unknown): KD was stationed just outside the town in May 1943. 'Aristocrats'—MS. dated 'Enfidaville, Tunisia 1943'. *'Vergissmeinnicht'*—MS. dated 'Tunisia 1943'. *CP* gives 'Homs Tripolitania' (source unknown). 'How to Kill' —poem undated in airgraph of 12 Aug. 1943 to JCH; *CP* gives 'Tunisia—Cairo, 1943' (source unknown). Egypt: 'I Experiment'— *CP* gives 'Egypt, October 1943' (MSS. missing). 'Behaviour of Fish . . .'—MS. dated '3 October 1943' (presumably source for *CP*'s '8 October 1943').

185–6 'I love the dead' / see note on p. 43.

187 Marcelle / drawn from KD's acquaintance; see chapter 5, p. 149.

'you can imagine' / *CP* omits 'clothes' in l.2 of quote (in MS. BL 53773, f. 57).

188 'Rosenberg I only repeat . . .' / there is no copy of Rosenberg among KD's books, but his school prize, I. Parsons's *The Progress of Poetry* (1936), contains a good selection of the earlier poet's work.

189 'like a man, whom . . .' / *CP*, p. 148 (first published in *Augury*).

190 safely witnessed ballet dancers / in *'Pas de Trois'*.

191 as striking in what it did not attack / comparison with Sassoon's 'The General' (referred to, *Alamein*, p. 16) and 'They' makes clear KD's emphasis. (After May 1943 MJD sent KD Sassoon's *Poems: Newly Selected* (1940, 4th imp. 1942): copy in MJD's possession inscribed by KD 1944.)

'I was discussing' / BL 56357, f. 8, slight variants in poem: I follow *CP*, but correct l. 11, 'auspicious' for 'suspicious', from MS.

191–2 'The Trumpet' / the only war poem by KD published in England during his lifetime: as 'The Regimental Trumpeter Sounding in the Desert', *T.L.S.*, 26 June 1943. Among slight variants from *CP* text, l. 1 'often' for 'after'.

192 Early in May Douglas wrote an essay / 'Poets in This War' (*T.L.S.*, 23 April 1971, p. 478). Internal evidence for May dating (references to 'fourth year of this war', soldiers still fighting in Middle East, JCH's employment) supported by paper of MS. being same as MSS. of 'Enfidaville'.

page

193 'Snakeskin and Stone' / sole surviving MS. (BL 53773, f. 98) has pencil variants in KD's hand, ignored by *CP*, l. 2, 'and' for 'or'; l. 4, 'a' deleted; l. 5, 'the' inserted at start; l. 7, 'is' inserted after 'Complication'; l. 9, 'and' inserted at start; l. 25, cancelled and re-written 'The words are dying in heaps'; l. 26, 'they' inserted after 'papers'; l. 36, 'And' deleted at start (this change followed in quote). The rhyme scheme establishes that the poem is in six-line stanzas: the MS. is crammed on to one sheet, but with some space between stanzas.

194 sitting at a pavement table / from *Alamein*, p. 143; details on Kellett's death from *SR*, pp. 74–5.

195 'It was impossible . . . ' / *Alamein*, p. 143.
'Imposed like a face' / BL 53773, f. 105.

195–6 'Tel Aviv' / MSS. in BL 53773, (ff. 104–18) reveal that the final stanza given this poem in *CP* was drafted for 'Jerusalem'—printed in *CP* (p. 157) as truncated. Pencil corrections in KD's hand to MS. of 'Tel Aviv', ignored by *CP*, followed in quotes.

196 a letter from Christopherson / *Alamein*, p. 143.
'second Balaclava charge' / Semken.
'the most spectacular . . . ' / *SR*, p. 80.
Douglas felt little relish / KD's mood and news of Player's death, *Alamein*, pp. 143–4.

197 Viscount Cranley . . . reputation / *SR*, p. 90.
At Mareth / details from *SR*, p. 79.
sent, with a three-ton lorry / KD's travels recounted *Alamein*, pp. 144–50: an instance of correlation between *Alamein* and KD's letters (May 1943 to MJD).
The Ninetieth Light marched / *SR*, p. 91.

198 In search of loot / letter to MJD.
He also visited Enfidaville / clear from the poem 'Enfidaville'.
a poem which never became / BL 53773, ff. 119–25.
final attempt / *CP*, p. 142, prints this as the second of 'two versions': the MSS. reveal that 'II' is a later revision of the draft given as 'I'. *CP*'s 'further rendering' (p. 157) is a draft of eight lines followed by a new draft of three.

199 'a figure straight out of . . . ' / *Alamein*, p. 91.
'I was amazed to find' / *Alamein*, p. 143.
'noble lunatics' / draft of 'I Watch with Interest'.
'Lt.-Col. J. D. Player' / *CP*, pp. 154–5 (second initial incorrect there).
Several members of the Sherwood Rangers / JB-F, Semken, and author of *SR* who writes, 'Keith Douglas had written of him [Player], "with courage in his eye, clean in the bone" ' (p. 90).
the yeomen's radio code / entertainingly described in *Alamein*, ch. XVII.

201 'Aristocrats' / letter-head of 'Sportsmen' MS. (BL 53773, f. 60) used by KD for September 1943 letters (BL 56355 and to Milena) suggests it is later than 'Aristocrats' MS. (BL 53773, f. 61) in letter dated 11 July

page

to MJT (source for *CP* text). I have followed *CP*, preferring July text
to later variants, made without reference to it. *CP*'s l. 12, 'falling' for
'fading', is without MS. evidence (first observed by J. Lewis, *Poetry
in the Making* (1967)).

worked hard at this second stanza / two early drafts in BL 53773 (ff. 58–9).

as would supply the documentary evidence / cf. sharpened satirical tone of
Sassoon's 'Wirers':

> Young Hughes was badly hit; I heard him carried away,
> Moaning at every lurch; no doubt he'll die today.

202 in his school notebook / BL 56360.

the heroes Owen had in mind / cf. Owen's '*Apologia Pro Poemate Meo*'.

a desk diary / KD drafted the complete text of *Alamein* in this diary for
1943, bearing the bookplate 'Boileau and Caloghiris, Librairie Cen-
trale, Le Caire'. Unless the diary (BL 53774) was a gift, it was presumably purchased by KD early in May 1943, on his only visit to
Cairo between early October 1942 and September 1943. Collation with
his letters (to MJD, JCH, Milena, Olga, JW) suggests that the early
part was written in May 1943, but beyond this the evidence is
inconclusive. The narrative is not mentioned in letters until early
March 1944 and then as a finished work, in two copies (see below:
one just returned from the colonel, one submitted to Editions Poetry
London). JA remembers KD working at *Alamein* in Oxford in February 1944, and SDC recalls that KD had access to his diary (in
England) and could have had access to the regiment's official diary.
It is likely that this 1944 work was on the final stages of the TS. (lost)
submitted to the publishers.

could not decide upon a title / cf. letters from MJT to MJD.

'I look back . . . ' / BL 53774, f. i.

even when he could order / *Alamein*, p. 15.

202n. Blunden had commented / letter in BL 56356.

203 'Code Words: An Ode in Code' / BL 56357; perhaps written as regiment's
entertainment officer, May/June 1943. An untitled sketch satirizing
G.H.Q. (BL 56357) possibly written at the same time.

204 'he always seemed to me . . . ' / JB-F to MJD.

'In battle he was . . . ' / Nelson to author.

had brought the respect of Colonel Kellett / SDC.

205 'To see these tanks . . . ' / *Alamein*, p. 22.

'We shared out the plunder . . . ' / ibid., p. 66. The ease with which *SR*
assimilates quotes from *Alamein* confirms the extent to which KD's
response fitted that of his comrades.

from T. E. Hulme / 'The Embankment', in *Faber Book of Modern Verse*
(1936), p. 71.

'like a few other . . . ' / *Alamein*, p. 64.

206 'felt very embarrassed' / ibid., p. 39.

'new ethics . . . fresh virtues' / extended version of 'Cairo Jag', *CP*, p. 153.

page
206 'a poet or a painter or a doctor . . . ' / *Alamein*, p. 16.
206–7 'caught out . . . ' / and following brief quotations, ibid., *passim*.
207–8 'Up above in the . . . ' / 'I watched them . . . ' / 'The column of tanks' /
ibid., p. 27.
208 'as though with . . . ' / and following brief quotations, ibid., *passim*.
'The Little Red Mouth' / *Stand* (Newcastle upon Tyne), vol. XI, no. 2
(1970); third and latest MS. (BL 53773, ff. 157–9) dated 'Beni Yusef'
(i.e. Sept.–Nov. 1943). KD wrote another war story, 'Giuseppe', unpublished. *Lilliput*, to whom KD submitted these stories in 1944,
published 'Death of a Horse' (July 1944) with a biographical note
(presumably from KD): 'At Wadi Zem Zem he tripped over a mine;
and started writing short stories during subsequent convalescence . . . .'
209 'This picture . . . ' / *Alamein*, p. 51.
210 '"Capture," I thought . . . ' / ibid., pp. 126–7.
211 'Silly Season' / ibid., p. 89.
His mother's criticisms / MJD.
'You want "selectivity" . . . ' / letter to Baber (TS. of main part, BL 56355).

CHAPTER 8

Regimental movements and conditions: as for above, chapters 5 and 6. Tunisia
and Tripolitania: letters to MJD; recollections of Sassoon and others as for above.
Stay in Palestine: letters to MJD and Milena. Relations with Cairo writers: as
for chapter 5. Last months in Cairo: letters to Milena, Olga, and JW. Correspondence with JCH: letters in the possession of JCH, one published in *CP*,
pp. 149–50; JCH letters to MJD (BL 56356).

212 'To write on the themes . . . ' / *CP*, p. 149.
'The country here is marvellous' / letter to MJD.
213 the Barbaras / letters from Mme Barbara to MJD.
'cutting remarks' / Of this exchange, JCH writes in a recent letter to this
author of his concern lest views he expressed in his early twenties should
be taken as his present judgement: 'I fully agree with the general
opinion that Douglas's most original and exciting achievement resides
in his Middle East poems.' See also 'A Villanelle for Keith Douglas'
in Hall's *A House of Voices* (1973).
213n. Wagner later wrote / 'The Poetry of J. C. Hall', *Poetry Quarterly*, Winter
1951/2, p. 177.
215 a couple of the reviewers / Sheila Shannon in *The Spectator*, 30 April
1943; Roland Gant, *Poetry Review*, May–June 1943.
'The Maturity of the Poet' / *New Statesman*, 17 April 1943.
217 On 1 June he had sent Tambimuttu / airgraphs in BL 53773.
had gained an unpromising impression / letter to MJD.
had found himself placed in / letter to JCH.
'As to including . . . ' / letter to MJT.

page
218 posted away from the regiment / letter to MJD.
218n. Blunden was also to express / letter to KD.
219 sent Hall another new poem / airgraph in BL 53773.
    had started it in Tunisia / inferred from *CP* dating; see above for dating of 'How to Kill'.
    'As a weightless mosquito who' / drafts of 'How to Kill' BL 53773, ff. 66–81; the version sent to JCH (see p. 220 n.), with variants from *CP*, f. 81.
222n. a gift from Eve / letter to MJD; Ruth Speirs's translation, dated by KD, in author's possession.
223 from Tunisia he had indulged / from Palestine he had written / letter to MJD.
    'innumerable' women / letter to Milena.
    'sink . . . the king is the biggest shit' / 'As Titsa and I knew' / letter to MJD.
    'cushy job' / letter to MJD.
224 Douglas joined them / inferred from address on a letter to Milena: Base Depot letter-head crossed out, name of regiment added.
    a course on the 'Observation . . . ' / service record, Ministry of Defence: the only entry for this period.
225 Durrell was later to write / Introduction to *Alamein*.
    'his talk was all . . . ' / letter in BL 56356.
    he saw no reason why / inferred from letter to JW.
    Douglas left copies / after publishing 'Desert Flowers', *Personal Landscape* published '*Vergissmeinnicht*', 'Enfidaville', and 'Cairo Jag' (vol. II, no. 2, [Summer?] 1944) and 'Behaviour of Fish' (vol. II, no. 4, [Summer?] 1945). 'Landscape with Figures' and 'The Trumpet' were also submitted (*CP*, Notes, pp. 155–6).
225n. said to have modelled / Fraser, *Lawrence Durrell: A Study* (1968).
228 On 5 November, assuring Olga . . . sent her this poem / letter to Olga, BL 56355; poem torn from sheet, BL 53773, f. 82.

CHAPTER 9

Regimental movements and activities: *SR*. KD with the regiment: recollections of JB-F, SDC, Holman, Semken, Skinner, and others as for chapter 5; letters to MJD, Baber, BJ, JT. On leave: recollections of MJD, BA, JA, Baber, BJ. Meetings with BJ: letters to BJ and her recollections. Dealings with publishers: MJT, 'Tenth Letter: In Memory of Keith Douglas', *Poetry* (*London*), no. x, n.d. [Dec. 1944]; contracts (BL 56356); letters to BJ; letters from BJ and MJT to KD and MJD (BL 56356); recollections of MJD, JB-F, BJ, MJT. Visit to Christ's Hospital: letters from Humphrey and Roberts to MJD (BL 56356); recollections of MJD, JB-F, Humphrey, BJ, Malins, Mrs. Roberts.

231 a contract for . . . his poems / undated, BL 56356.

page

234   the same notepaper / BL 53773. The *'Bete Noire'* fragments are in *CP*, pp. 114–15 and 158–9; their order has been corrected here by collation of the MSS. with letters to BJ.

      'sitting down to try . . . ' / *CP*, p. 158.

237   'an excuse (to be used as a preface)' / ibid.

238   'not wholly terrible' / *Alamein*, p. 16.

      series of illustrations / BL 53775–6.

      a postcard reproduction / sent to BJ, saying it was from his wall (BL 56355).

240   a contract / referred to in BL 56356; a later, revised contract exists in BL 56356.

      drawing for its cover / BL 53775–6.

      returned as being too similar / letter from *Lilliput*, BL 56356; rejection letter from *Horizon* also in BL 56356.

      six successive drafts / BL 53773, ff. 126–8.

242   '[he] was too good . . . ' / letter to BJ.

      'He was appalled . . . ' / *SR*, p. 98.

      was said to have been / ibid.

      They did . . . agree to meet in Europe / Arsenault arrived at Point 103 (see chapter 10) late on 9 June 1944.

242-3 'not much wine . . . ' / 'I didn't dance once . . . ' / 'delighted . . . excellent in many ways' / letter to BJ.

244   the 'most formidable tanks . . . ' / H. C. B. Rogers, *Tanks in Battle* (Sphere Books ed., 1972), p. 199.

      their first test at Chippenham / *SR*, p. 98.

246   'flowers and sunshine . . . however oily' / letter to Baber.

247   Douglas and Bethell-Fox left the camp / details from letter to Baber.

249   Drafting his valediction / BL 53773, f. 126b: the revised version is on p. 242.

      tea on the Robertses' lawn / letter from Roberts to MJD.

      'a totally different person' / Malins to author.

250   defended his war narrative / TS. copy of part of his letter to Baber, BL 56355.

      a note from Mrs. Kellett / a copy of Douglas's reply is in BL 56355.

      'in the stomach of a war' / 'Actors Waiting . . . '

      'too full of odd things' / letter to Baber.

250n. A full list of alterations / BL 53773.

252   a speculative poem / 'On a Return from Egypt'; collation of MSS. (BL 53773, ff. 86–91) with letters to BJ suggests the date in *CP*, 'Egypt–England 1943–44', given on the MS. in the possession of JW, is merely descriptive, not referring to date of composition.

CHAPTER 10

The invasion and fighting in Normandy: *SR*; recollections of JB-F, SDC, Holman, Skinner. Patrol by KD and JB-F on 9 June: JB-F, *Green Beaches* (see below).

page
254   ' . . . I move towards my end / on verso of MS. of 'Snakeskin and Stone' (BL 53773, f. 98b); it probably precedes 'How to Kill' (1943), which re-explored the image.

      'at the height of the din' / 'Actors Waiting . . . '

255   commandeered a police horse / *SR*, p. 105.

      Douglas had arrived late / Holman.

      That night Bethell-Fox went in / in *SR*, p. 106, KD is included in this patrol; the correction is from JB-F.

256   Waiting under this fire / details and quotations from JB-F's unpublished war narrative *Green Beaches*, written in hospital after being wounded in Normandy. Only a fragment, quoted in *Poetry* (*London*) no. x, survives, the MS. submitted to Editions Poetry London having apparently been lost.

      report . . . to Christopherson / SDC, who commanded the regiment after Sweeney Todd was killed on 10 June, mentioned KD in dispatches for his part in this action.

      was killed / Skinner and JB-F made a temporary grave for him on the hillside; KD's body now lies in the War Cemetery, Tilly-sur-Seulles, plot 1, row B, grave no. 2.

ILLUSTRATIONS: NOTES AND SOURCES
(References are to page numbers in the text.)

7, 8: childhood drawings in the possession of MJD. 31: watercolour of Gorizia, MJD. 47: pencil sketch from a school notebook, MJD. 44: linocut reproduced from *The Outlook* (Christ's Hospital, Horsham), July 1936. 69: watercolour self-portrait in the possession of Antoinette. 70: from a snapshot lent by MS-W. 73: letter to Yingcheng in her possession. 77: photographs of Yingcheng lent by her; KD's watercolour portrait of Yingcheng in MJD's possession. 83: photographs lent by Antoinette; envelope in her possession. 107: photograph lent by BA. 122: letter in the possession of JT. 151 (right), 160: photograph lent by Milena; drawing of Milena in her possession. 167, 180, 194: photographs lent by SDC. 177: airgraph to JT in her possession. 233, 234: photograph lent by BJ; drawing from the envelope of a letter in her possession. All photographs, drawings, and documents not otherwise acknowledged, in the possession of MJD.

     127, 200, 221, 236: MSS. of poems in BL 53773—'Simplify Me When I'm Dead', f. 41; 'Aristocrats', ff. 58, 58b.; 'How to Kill', f. 77; '*Bête Noire*', f. 130. 226: airgraph to MJT with MS. of 'Behaviour of Fish . . . ', BL 53773, f. 85.

     93, 119, 132, 157, 185: drawings for poems, all done in England in 1944, in

BL 53775–6. 209, 239: drawings done in England, 1944, for the war narrative published as *Alamein*, in BL 53775–6. 241: rejected sketch for the cover of *Bête Noire*, England 1944, BL 53775–6; cf. KD's 'Note' (*CP*, p. 158): 'The beast, which I have drawn as black care sitting behind the horseman, is indefinable . . . My failure is that I know so little about him, beyond his existence and the infinite patience and extent of his malignity.'

Index

Index

KD = Keith Douglas. Bold-face references are to pages on which illustrations appear.